I0021379

ENGINEERING
DOCUMENT CONTROL,
CORRESPONDENCE
—————— AND ——————
INFORMATION
MANAGEMENT
(Includes Software Selection Guide)
FOR ALL

ENGINEERING
DOCUMENT CONTROL,
CORRESPONDENCE
AND
INFORMATION
MANAGEMENT
(Includes Software Selection Guide)
FOR ALL

HUW R GROSSMITH

Copyright © 2023 by Huw R Grossmith.

ISBN: Softcover   978-1-7960-0897-5
             eBook   978-1-7960-0896-8

All rights reserved. No part of this book may be reproduced or transmitted in any form or by any means, electronic or mechanical, including photocopying, recording, or by any information storage and retrieval system, without permission in writing from the copyright owner.

Any people depicted in stock imagery provided by Getty Images are models, and such images are being used for illustrative purposes only.
Certain stock imagery © Getty Images.

Print information available on the last page.

Rev. date: 01/25/2023

To order additional copies of this book, contact:
Xlibris
AU TFN: 1 800 844 927 (Toll Free inside Australia)
AU Local: (02) 8310 8187 (+61 2 8310 8187 from outside Australia)
www.Xlibris.com.au
Orders@Xlibris.com.au
805914

CONTENTS

DEDICATION

This book is for Noi, Nui, Nine, Nam and last but most certainly not least the youngest (at the moment, 2014) Grosso – Neave. I love you all. Love too to every member of my very extended "family".

CHARITY

For years I have tried to help a lot of people especially in support of orphaned, abandoned and disadvantaged children. In fact I have sent myself bankrupt via my efforts and have accumulated a mountain of debt and other than dealing with the stress of paying the debt I'd still do it all again but maybe with a bit more help and the wisdom gained in hindsight.

2.5% of the Royalty of this book will be donated directly to FANAR in Doha, Qatar to manage as they see fit. This is called Zakat. I've seen just a small part of the wonderful work the Islamic based charities do in many African nations including in Senegal where they look after Orphaned and Abandoned children fully not just propagating the religion.

2.5% of the Royalty of this book will be donated directly to Buddhists in Thailand. Again they do wonderful work in South East Asia with orphaned and abandoned children.

2.5% will go to a charity in Australia who do great work in Nepal and Kenya – World Youth International

2.5% will go to SOS Children's Villages.

5.0% to my daughter Honey in the US who will earn it acting as my agent.

The rest will be used to pay down debt and invested for the future of ALL my children.

Copyright Information

This book is the sole copyright of Huw Robert Grossmith (copyright © 2014, 2015, 2016, 2017). The work within is entirely the Author's own work.

Any course manuals and other material I may derive from this work are also my sole copyright and are for my use alone unless my express permission is otherwise granted.

Images:

The majority of the images are screen shots from Drawcon10 (copyright Kevin Rollo / Rollosoftware) and I have his permission to use the application, screenshots of it and distribute the MDE file with 3 month licences for free. DrawCon will be made available either via a website built around this book or on a service such as mediafire.

All other images were found on a number of different websites. If I have infringed any copyright I apologise and humbly beg your immediate pardon.

In Appendix 11 there is a list of White Papers and Case studies by others. I have collected these over a number of years and a majority of the Copyright holders gave me permission to use them others did not reply to my request and I have therefore accepted no reply as tacit approval to continue. Due to the volume of the information the material will be made available either via a website built around this book or on a service such as mediafire.

Drawings. Appendix 4 contains some drawings. I asked permission to use them. In some cases I received an Ok others failed to respond and I have therefore accepted no reply as tacit approval to continue. ★★

★★Please note I never knowingly take drawings or documents from any company I have worked for, even those I may have contributed to in part or full, as they are not my Intellectual Property. I actively discourage others from doing anything similar. The material I do have that may belong to others I have by accident and not by design.

Any and all opinions made in this work are those of the author and the author alone and in no way reflect the opinions of others.

Reproduction or distribution/redistribution of this work in any way without the written consent of the Author/Copyright holder is forbidden and will be met with appropriate action.

FOREWORD

By Kevin Rollo (Programmer, Project Controls Manager)

Since the late 1980's, the introduction of computers has typically pushed the production of engineering documents from drafting board paper copies to electronic CAD system files. Document Control has also evolved from processing large volumes of paper to controlling many electronic files. Thrown into the mix is the evolution of Document Control from a manual card system into quite sophisticated database or web-based systems. The introduction of new technology has given some great advantages in how we conduct business, but Document Control has a number of very basic fundamentals that shouldn't be ignored. The creation of documents, typically the project phase, is a about tracking the document through the approval stages and ensuring that it gets sent to all those who need copies. Maintenance of documents, typically the operations phase, is about the upkeep of controlled copies of latest revisions and control of the native files.

Over the last decade, Electronic Document Management Systems (EDMS) or Electronic Content Management (ECM) systems have become more prevalent in organisations and are aimed at the organisation, collaboration and retention of electronic files and records. Naturally these systems have also tried to encapsulate the engineering document files into this environment as well. What has not always been successful is the context of control around these documents; very few have managed to emulate the functions of document control system with things like transmittals, status and expediting reports.

Huw Grossmith has been transcended this change from paper to the electronic world and has witnessed firsthand some of the mistakes made as the industry and software developers have grappled with integrating document control into electronic enterprise systems. In this book, Huw will take you on a journey covering the fundamentals of document control, all of which have been well road-tested over the years and if followed will make your document control experience a successful enterprise. The tools provide by your organisation will influence <u>HOW</u> you will have to conduct your work, but the fundamentals of this book will give you the <u>WHY.</u>

From Huw

Engineering Document Control and Data Management is by its nature and due to meeting legal and Quality requirements very procedural. That, however, is no excuse for not stepping outside of your "box/ducky bubble" and taking a "third party" view of what you do and how you do it on a regular basis. Only by thinking outside the box can we find better ways of doing our work without impacting Quality outcomes or taking short-cuts (a short-cut is the longest distance between two points).

Take my word for it there is ALWAYS a Better, Faster, Safer, Cheaper, or more importantly Smarter, way of doing almost everything although, I have to admit, that Faster and Cheaper are not two words that readily work with Safer but that is not always true.

I have a terrible head for names and more often than not will manage to remember the name of someone who p'd me off more than those who may have taught me something directly or indirectly years ago. There are people to thank here:

> Both my Mother (still going) who I tend to crash in on
> and my father, deceased, (got almost everything except

hair and hands from him) and ALL my siblings and every member of my very extended family.

Kevin Rollo a Project Controls Manager and Ace Access Programmer

"Jock" sorry I forget your correct name at FD who taught me Pro-Active DC for Design (I sort of had it sussed for vendors)

John Hampson −rock music is his life onya man

John Richardson (deceased)

Adele

Tuula

Deb Court − never failed to make me laugh on a daily basis :-D

To the wonderful people at FANAR in Qatar and the many Qatari people who helped both myself and my family when all appeared to be lost for me. You have ALL renewed my faith in Allah (God), the Universe and Humanity. I can only hope to repay you in kind at some point in the future.

Louhan Del Rio who drew many of the images from photo stock I was unable to either track down or get permission to use.

Last but by no means least − Albert Causo for encouraging me to write the book in the first place and to all those who put in a huge effort to get it published.

I've worked with some fab teams and people over the years and appreciate it all. The team at OT, my team, you were the best – wonderful people, quick learners, worked smart. I just hope you got as much from me as I did from you.

There are a legion of others who have guided me over the years or who I have by accident or design learned something from – when the pupil is ready the teacher will arrive – we just do not always see them for who they are.

20/20 hindsight is either a wonderful or terrible disease. We all of us have done things we are far from proud of or regret. There are people out there who would re-hire me instantly. Yet others who would, if they have the power to do so, never work with me again or stop me from being hired - that I have some regret for however, to those who my passion for doing things right has upset – get over it J…. Please!

To those I have had to "bite" over the years and who are still sore about it – well if I bit you - you deserved it! You'll be pleased to know I try to do it less often these days, I learn too J, but I'm not called The Rottweiler for nothing.

This might offend some (I apologise or not :-D), I've worked in many places over the years and in some cases DC's have been regarded as something that just gets in the way of Engineering and Design (until those who think that, even say it out loud, send out the wrong thing or lose something and then duck) as you will learn DC is about managing risk. Document Controllers in some places I have been have seen used as nothing more than glorified photocopier jockeys. True, when a paper-based system is deployed (in most countries now that really need not happen), we do a lot of copying and will copy masters for those that need a copy too but we are not there to stab numbers in to a copier and hit the green button for those who won't do it for themselves (when they have the document to be copied that is)!

I also must admit that in the main meetings are pet dislikes. They always seem to breed when the workload hits peak and for some odd reason be on the other side of town or on a floor the lift to my floor does not service which means stairs or a trip to the lobby and another lift (architects take note in multi-lift buildings there should be one that stops on all floors at least have an overlap e.g. in a 30 floor building have a set that go 1 to 15 and another that go 15 to 30 (ie. 15 is serviced by both sets).

As a method of communication, I have no huge problem with them but meetings that lack an agenda, motions and minutes with responsibilities and priorities assigned are not proper and correct meetings. My aim as a Lead has always been to try to be absolutely clear about what KPI's have to be met – when we are informed or have the tools to know what's coming. When we meet them then a Friday meeting – i.e. a Sun downer is called for or, at the very least, pizza and cola for lunch on Friday that I am happy to pay for on behalf of my team. I also get people who do not attend sun downers or other, after hours, "company events" and believe me they should not suffer for not doing so but they do tend to be overlooked or ignored when promotions are available or possible career changes are on offer which is just not fair but does go on. Just remember a lot of these things happen on a Friday. Not so bad on a remote site where there may not be a drive home, even then we have to be careful of how much we consume with respect to being fit for duty the next day, but in the CBD when we drive or use public transport to get home …. Well ……

In the main I am loud, if I go quiet I am fatigued, new to the employer and getting my feet under the desk, super busy or boiling over, I'm also opinionated and truly passionate about my profession some of these attributes you will see in my writing sorry it is how I am.

A. SAFETY

You will note that in various places in this book there are references to safety. From a Document Control perspective absolutely ensuring the right documents reach the right people at the right revisions and at the right time can have an enormous impact on safe construction and/or operations. Here are two examples of what could go wrong:

Example 1 (Oil Refinery/Platform)

Let's say that a datasheet has gotten through to Revision 0 – IFC with an error on it and it shows a section of pipe having a maximum allowable pressure of 100 bar (atmospheres) when it should have been 10. Just prior to commissioning or hand-over to operations someone notices the error and creates Rev 1 with the correct pressure. Now for some reason the document does not make it in to or out, especially out of, of document control on time, which could be to do with when it came in to document control, and an operator ramps the pressure in that pipe up to 100 bar.

The resulting explosion could be utterly catastrophic, lives lost, people seriously injured, the entire plant or a huge section of it lost and subject to a complete rebuild, government inquiries, production of, say, 10,000 barrels of oil a day at $100 per barrel lost for minimum 6 months (180 days).

$180,000,000.00 potential lost income and double if that oil was "sold" on advance contracts and has to be obtained from other sources to fulfil the contracts - plus government fines, court cases, coroners hearings, plant rebuild, compensation to be paid to the families of the deceased and ongoing compensation and medical expenses etc. for survivors, could add at least another 20%, or more, to that.

These are not unreasonable numbers consider this - Nigeria produced an average of 2401.6 thousand barrels of crude oil per day in 2010, 2.94% of the world supply and a change of 16.2 % compared to 2009. To achieve this production divide 24,016,000 by 365 = 65,797 barrels a day (at, say, $100 per barrel – $6,579,700 a day gross income). Nigeria is currently said to be the 10th largest oil producer in the world, now 6th, just imagine the output in those nations that are larger!

Example 2

Not a document control problem but a commissioning engineer pre-commissioning a liquid cyanide plant (used in gold producing plants) misread the pressure in a work pack or on a datasheet and added a 0 and ramped up the system accordingly. Fortunately, the pre-commissioning was being done with water. Had this happened with liquid cyanide the outcome, depending on which way the wind was blowing for the surrounding industry and towns or the nearby ocean would have been catastrophic – these things do happen.

Always remember that EVERYONE wants to go home, or get there, in the same condition that they went to work in. Also always remember that most accidents, while not recorded as lost time injuries, happen in your own home!

To those of you who travel to work on public transport and then walk some distance including crossing roads and who listen to music on the bus or train with headphones or ear buds please, I beg you; take them off/out when you step off the train or bus. Having those things on, no matter how good the music (or whatever else) you might be enjoying does take away from you one of the most important senses when dealing with traffic (of any variety, bar Electric powered scooters, bicycles, motorcycle and cars) – your ability to hear something coming! More people have been hit and killed because of the fact that not only did they not look or see the vehicle that hit them (probably because they were focused on the music) they did not hear it either.

In the Document Control field we can take some steps to ensure our own wellbeing in other ways too. Paper cuts I am sad to say are an occupational hazard they happen but need not be. Having a finger jabbed by the end of a staple is another DC operational hazard but this too can be avoided. To those of you who love staples – get out of the habit – please. Use paper slides/clips or bulldog/fold back clips instead it makes our life a lot simpler especially when we have to copy stuff. Also remember that an unseen staple in a document can do a power of damage to a copier either to the document feeder or glass platen and/ or the original gets wrecked.

Absolutely ensure, where we have to file paper away, that anti-tip filing cabinets are used and test them before filling them – if you can open two drawers at the same time they are not anti-tip. Fill them from the bottom up – a hard habit to get used to and try to keep the really heavy stuff in the bottom drawer.

If using bookcases, although somewhat simpler to use, it is wise not to use those (metal systems, e.g. dexion, are somewhat better than wood) that have adjustable shelf heights – where the shelf rests on a knuckle that can easily pull out of or rip a chunk out of the side of the bookcase itself causing the shelf to fall. If a shelf is starting to buckle take the weight off of it. NEVER put the really heavy stuff up high especially boxes of copy paper.

Should you be using a compactus make sure there is a locking mechanism that keeps the section you might be standing in open and disallows someone that did not see you from trying to move the sections over (thereby crushing you) if there is no mechanism get a wedge to use and hang a sign too. Oh and this is a classic - before a compactus is even installed the floor has to be structurally tested. They are heavy and what goes in them more so – I have seen them buckle and the sections collapse back in to the middle when opened (if they could be opened).

If you file drawings in Plan Cabinets (tanks) make sure they are not overfull and do not pull too many drawings on to the front forks although most or all have feet that extend outward when you open them the things can still tip over – I have seen it happen.

Should you use stick files try to keep the sticks down to an easily manageable weight –paper of good quality (used in Inkjets where Ink bleed can be an issue) can weigh over 120 grams a square metre. An A1 is close to ½ a square metre – 60 grams (give or take for borders etc.). 50 in one stick and you have 3.0kg. An A0, not often seen these days but still used, is almost 1 square metre i.e. one sheet 120gms – 50 sheets – 6kg. Also make sure there is plenty of free space in the rack to allow free movement of sticks in and out of the rack itself. They can and do fall – hopefully not on your feet – if they do fall get your feet out of the way and do not try to catch them.

TIP if you do use stick files it is wise to use a blank sheet at the top and bottom to protect the drawings in the stick it is always those that are damaged easiest. Some of the older plan printers used cut sheet paper, especially B sizes, these came in packs with cardboard at the top and bottom – if you receive paper like this keep the cardboard for use at the top and bottom of your file sticks.

Personally, although they cost considerably more and filing takes a little longer to do, I'd not use stick files – plan cabinets are much better for the drawings.

Better still, where it is permissible in law and corporate systems, scan all the paper, quality check the scans, save them to a well backed up network drive or EEDMS/EDMS then off the paper – shred and recycle it.

If you work at a desk make sure it is cluttered up as little as possible, this is not always possible in our trade, most employers have a clear desk policy now – often means a lot of stuff chucked in a bottom drawer or filing cabinet overnight. Make sure that the pathway to your chair is clear, taking into consideration you may have to move quickly if a fire breaks out, and that there is sufficient movement to turn through 360 degrees in your chair and you can move it at the very least 500mm clear of the desk while sat on it. Not always possible but try not to stack boxes of manuals and MDR's in walkways. For that matter, this drives me nuts, do not stand and chat in walkways – if you want to talk go to a kitchen area or use a meeting room.

Ensure any cables that touch the floor for any reason, where they are on the floor for more than (say) 300mm either have a mat over them, the mat should also lay flat at all times and not have edges sticking up, or that the cables are taped down with high visibility tape. Better yet where you are able to do so tape them to a wall or partition or ask IT to put bind them with cable ties. In the modern day this is still a problem even with networks being connected on WiFi.

If for any reason you have to plug something in to or remove a plug from a power point or board make sure the equipment itself is off and the switch on the power point/board is off too. To be frank I really dislike power points that have no switch – common in Thailand. I really do like a cross between the American system where the power switch to all power points in the room is on the wall in the room and the Australian/British one I am used to where the power point has a switch – turn off one or both and you know the power is dead. If you are not 100% certain you are not going to risk an electric shock go and find someone who can isolate all the power in your part of the building and have that done.

Most employers have an ergonomics person or contractor on-board – make sure you use their services. The computer age has brought on an increasing number of postural problems and RSI/OOUS were common place but are, thankfully, becoming less so. If you are uncomfortable at your desk get some help to fix the problem.

Stress is a common factor in all our lives and try as one might it is not always possible to leave home stress at home and work stress at work. Living to work or using work to escape other negative facets of your life is not the answer. Work to live and make sure you do so.

During the life of projects there are periods of peak load. You should be told or know how to find out when these will be and be relaxed and ready for them.

Find what some people call Freudian release mechanisms – get the stress out of your system. The gym (hit the heavy boxing bag until you can hit it no longer for example), walk/cycle home, if you use public transport read a book and/or listen to music – do not drive angry, do not go to bed angry. In the short term if someone has gotten you angry write them a stinker of an email then save not send it, let yourself cool down, then re-write or delete it (Abraham Lincoln did this with letters to his generals – found in his desk after his death). In the short term if you are at work and need to de-stress tell someone you are taking a break, go to a break-out room or leave the building and go for a walk.

It is wise to find a place of sanctuary – somewhere that helps you to calm down and where noise etc. may be at a minimum. This might be a church (you need not be religious to go sit in a church and some of the really old cathedrals have some sort of resonance that is calming), a park, somewhere you can just tune out the day.

Also, it is wise to learn to meditate and/or do yoga.

Weekend sports when you are starting to reach max stress by Wednesday are no good and if you go out to basically, legally, maul someone (rugby for example) you may come off second best and not be in good shape for work Monday.

We live in a litigious world and while there are an ever-increasing number of laws regarding safety in the work place the truth is that YOUR SAFETY IS YOUR RESPONSIBILITY. Your employer has a responsibility for providing the best possible safe working environment it is down to you to make sure it stays that way.

If you see an unsafe act, even if you are not qualified on what work may be being undertaken, stop it and report it immediately. If you see something you think is unsafe, cables across a floor area where there is a lot of traffic that are not taped down or "matted" – report it immediately.

This is meant to be funny but I know people who think it is not. Just think about when, if this were happening in front of you, you might have stepped up and put a stop to it.

https://www.youtube.com/watch?v=oc1iIRKZE9w

If you witness an accident or are in one, it is not your first responsibility to call a lawyer. Call the emergency services and where it is SAFE to do so render assistance to injured parties. NEVER walk/run/drive away.

TIP – this works by the way – if you witness or are in an accident and need assistance DO NOT yell HELP – people tend to disappear. Yell FIRE, someone will always, no matter where you are (as a kid we tried it on a beach) come and poke their nose in and when they have you have them where you need them.

Get home unharmed and turn up to work unharmed and unimpaired.

B. OBJECTIVES

There is absolutely no substitute for experience. Anyone entering the field of Engineering Document Control should try hard to take an interest in how the material they are asked to manage is produced and all other aspects of Project and Operational life. Take an interest in the big picture and ask lots of questions – the only stupid question is the one you never asked!

As far as that goes I am often referred to as a Subject Matter Expert. Expert is a term I dislike. Regardless of how much training, experience and reading one might do it is not possible to ever know everything there is to know about your subject matter – I certainly don't and others should be prepared to admit it too.

Ex   -   is a non sequitur it means no, nothing or non

Spurt -   is a drip under pressure

DO NOT take this a reason for ignoring others who have something to say on your subject matter – you might learn from them even if you think they may be wrong – shut-up, listen and get out of your box/ducky bubble and view the situation from their perspective. You may, if they are in a bit of a bad mood, have to cool them off first (coffee, joke of the day etc.) – i.e. if you feel you are being cornered or spoken down to do not come out swinging or go on the attack/defensive. Then head for a meeting room with a whiteboard and mind-map or flowchart the entire process/problem area and look for solutions. Hint any diamond in a flowchart that is not a decision being made by DC (except for

Document Review Status Codes – see Quality Audits sometimes we can check the box next to the code where quality/title etc. are a cause for concern but we still get the Lead/Package Engineer to sign off) it is wise to eliminate.

If it does not mean changing employers or roles too often it is wise to gain as much exposure as possible to Operations and Projects both in CBD offices and onsite.

A good Lead Document Controller (LDC), Document Control Manager (DCM), Information Management Coordinator (IMC) or Project Controls Manager (PCM) will take the steps necessary to move each member of the DC team around to give them best possible exposure to all elements and a far better understanding of the big picture. It is also wise to let DC's also work with or learn from others in the Project Controls field such as Cost Controllers (I more or less became a bookkeeper after my RAAF stint), Planners/Schedulers and others including IT people, Engineers, Draughts-people, Procurement/Contracts Administrators, HSE people, and QA/QM. Not everyone will want to make a career of DC and these are natural progressions. From the perspective of working smarter getting to know the Engineers and Draughts-people makes sense especially those who may also be system administrators for the CAD tools in use – obtaining a .csv file for, say, 10000 piping isometrics dumped on your desk may save a lot of pain doing data entry/updates in the DC tool. Understanding what others have to do and how they do it is only to the benefit of the DC taking the time to learn it all adds to the big picture.

Another great example of getting to know others and taking an interest in how they do what they do is to take an interest in CAD drawings. Knowing how to make a plot or PDF rendition from a native is pretty much a must these days. Looking at a CAD file you may have been given to manage and knowing it may be missing elements because what are called X-Refs are not bound on can be a critical factor. This is NOT uncommon as DC's may not have the same rights to the network or EDMS paths as the originators hence when they open a CAD file it might not be complete – most CAD/Viewer applications will tell you this during the process of opening the file but not all will. Being able to tell a Mechanical from a Piping from a Structural drawing and an Electrical from an Instrument drawing is also a serious benefit. Experience counts here but learning from others instead of the hard way is working smarter.

A good leader will always encourage out of the box thinking and take those ideas on-board and give those that had them credit for them too.

Take an interest in Engineering/Construction and the IT side of your field and those of others, the pace of change and new technology in both Engineering and in Document Control fantastic and that is what keeps me in – plus the people I meet and the places I go. Just think many people when I started in DC were still using Index cards… (I was lucky but have had to use them on the odd occasion but in the main have always used a computer and some form of software although I admit some of the software I have used was awful but miles better than index cards or spread-sheets – still think that – some of these tools have aged badly, especially with respect to technology, or lacked development and others were terrible out of the box or just being used for entirely the wrong purpose such as a collaboration tool as a DC tool……).

The progression for those people who started out before or at the same time as me was something like Index Cards, Lotus 123 (single dimension) on to Lotus 123, Excel, PlanPerfect or Lucid-3D 3D spread-sheets to some form of multi-relational database application in Access, Q&A, DBIII or VFP to trying to make an EDMS work and the really lucky ones got a full blown EEDMS if they are still in the trade/ profession that is.

I also got lucky in that I got to help develop a DC tool early in my career and quite often added fields to tables and forms, added queries and reports and then sent it back for hard coding. On other occasions I fired in, as I do with most DC tools I use, development ideas and more than once got told to get back in my box J a huge compliment.

My father was a building supervisor and I learned to read most drawings when I was growing up and took an interest in others when I entered the profession. You need not get to designer level but if you can look at a drawing that may have been, for example, numbered as mechanical when it is clearly structural (I've seen this done to conveyor box sections and pump skid frame drawings) then that will help you big time.

If, after a while, you do not love your job I suggest to find another (out of the trade/profession altogether or get out of operations for a busy project or vice versa).... One of my personal heroes is/was Steve Jobs – he gave a commencement speech at Stanford University it can be found here - http://news.stanford.edu/news/2005/june15/jobs-061505.html DON'T LOVE IT, LEAVE.... OR FIND SOMETHING YOU DO LOVE.

A change can be as good as a holiday but take it from personal experience when you are contemplating changing your position for whatever reason take a hard look at why you are doing it. Sure, we all like to make a buck but being mercenary will eventually cost you big time. If you must have a change but are not changing profession then is it a change you seek, promotion or some leave? Remember the original concept of a 20 day annual leave system, in Australia, was for employees to take 5 days every three months not to accrue them and hope for a big cheque (taxman whacks it hard) on the way out or a very long Christmas break. In some countries leave must be taken when 5 or 7 days is owing and is unlikely, unless workload planning etc. is woeful, to be accrued i.e. use it or lose it. That said I remember a political promise during one election in Australia that Sick Leave will be payable or transferable on termination/moving on - never happened another non-core promise! Those of us who rarely ever take sickies would appreciate having them paid out or transferable perhaps something similar to the Construction Industry Long Service Leave board for Sick days would be the way to go.

Most, not all, employers have a mentor system. If you have not been appointed a mentor ask for one. For Engineering DC/DM this need not be someone in the "trade" but should be someone that understands it such as a Project Controls Manager or a CAD system(s) Administrator.

It is also wise to develop a list of personal mentors who do not have to be in the industry at all but who inspire you to new ways of thinking about yourself, your work and others. I've already given one of mine and another is Eric Pepin.

The AIM of this book is to demystify what Document Controllers (we) do, why we do it and how we do it and provide DC's with the tools and skills necessary to do what we do properly. For most chapters there will be a practical and the appendices will contain written instructions on how to go about solving the problem set or an example solution.

The practical examples are mostly, not all, based on an EPCM designing and constructing an Iron Ore plant, Chapter 22B and 22C with Appendices 2B and 2C respectively are the practical material for an FPSO for Oil/Gas and for an Advanced Water Treatment Plant - civil.

I have to repeat experience counts for everything and never, ever, be afraid to ask questions or make mistakes – it's how, as human beings, we learn.

Questions – you will notice this gets repeated in one form or another throughout this book – There is NO such thing as a stupid question OR the only stupid question is the one you did not ask…..

Rule 1 of Document Control, life even, if in doubt ASK.

Mistakes – we are human we make mistakes it is how we learn best. A mistake that is not fixed and is allowed to go on (or worse perpetuate/ breed) can cost a lot of time, effort and money to fix.

Rule 2 of Document Control, life even, If you make a mistake – admit it STRAIGHT AWAY – fix it (or ask how) STRAIGHT AWAY, the world's least important word (in English) is I, even write down what you did, how you did it and what you did to fix it then publish it to others in the team so they learn from it.

Rule 3 of Document Control, life even, is KISS. Keep It Stupid Simple. Yes DC/DM can be complicated, Engineers (sorry guys) can make it that way, and there is no need for it to be. The simpler you can keep everything and still keep within the law/standards and quality required the easier it is for everyone to understand and comply with. As soon as something is in any way complicated there will be someone somewhere who will not understand it, won't or cannot comply with requirements.

Work Smart, Play Hard.

NEXT

Let's go…. Engineering and Engineering DC/DM is littered with Acronyms, Abbreviations and, what will appear to many of you to be, Techno-babble…. Let's call the whole lot Terminology.

C. ACRONYMS, ABBREVIATIONS AND TERMINOLOGY

Much of this information will be discussed in much greater detail in throughout this book but you should know what it all means.

Acronym/ Abbreviation	Description
PCM	Project Controls Manager
IMC	Information Management Coordinator
DCM	Document Control Manager
LDC	Lead Document Controller
SDC	Senior Document Controller
DC	Document Controller / Document Control
JDC	Junior Document Controller
1TA	Technical Assistant
ENG	Engineer
ENG'G	Engineering
IFC	Issued for Construction
IFU	Issued for Use
IFA	Issued for Approval
IFT	Issued for Tender
IFP	Issued for Purchase
IFR	Issued for Review
IFI	Issued for Information

	• Note in some cases the I can be A (Approved)
SC	Squad Check
DFO	Documents for Operations
OPS	Operations
MECH	Mechanical
ELEC	Electrical
INST / INSTRU	Instruments
PR	Process
CIV	Civil
STRUC	Structural
CP	Cathodic Protection
PIPE	Piping
	• Do not confuse with Discipline Codes
DocType	Document Type Code
SubType	Document SubType Code
• In some cases these are combined. Eg. BAC – B is buildings, AC is Archetectural	
DISC	Discipline
LME	Lead Mechanic Engineer
LPE	Lead Piping Engineer
LSE	Lead Structural Engineer
LIE	Lead Instrument Engineer
LEE	Lead Electrical Engineer
LFE	Lead Process Engineer
LCE	Lead Civil Engineer
LHE	Lead Marine/Hull Engineer
	• Drop the L for non-Lead,, in some cases add an S to the front for Senior
KISS	Keep it Stupid Simple / Keep it Simple Stupid
UW	Underwater or SubSea (DO NOT USE SS – that means something else)
INCSTAT	Incoming Status
DOCSTAT	Document or Review Status
DC/DM	Document Control/Data Management

DQ	Document/Data Quality
VDDRL	Vendor Drawing and Data Requirements List★
VDS	Vendor "Data" Schedule★
	• V can also be S (Supplier) can also be the same form i.e. designed to be completed internally then by the vendor see download material
DC Tool	Document Control Database Application – see Section 24
DMS	Document Management System (which can mean hard and soft)
EDMS	Electronic Document Management System – see Section 24
EEDMS	Engineering Electronic Document Management System – see Section 24
SaaS	Software as a Service (The Cloud)
IHOG	Information Hand-Over Guide
AIMS	Asset Information Management Standard/System
OIMS	Operations Information Management Standard/System
EPC	Engineering, Procurement and Construction Contractor★
EPCM	Engineering, Procurement, Construction and Project Management Contractor★
PMC	Project Management Company
EPIC	Engineering, Procurement, Installation and Commissioning Contractor (most often SubSea)
SCC	Specialised Commissioning Contractor
	★Often, not always, EPC/EPCM Contractors subcontract Construction to a Construction Contractor
CC	Construction Contractor

In this book:

Operator/Operations – A company that operates Assets from which they expect to make a profit. There is a definition of Asset below.

Project Management Company – often the end user/client will appoint a Project Management company which becomes, often, a go-between eg. Client > PMC > Primary Contractor or the other way around.

Contractor – A company (primary) providing to a client, often an Operator, EPC/EPCM/PMC/EPIC services for the design and construction of a new Asset (greenfield project) or upgrade/expansion of an existing Asset (brownfield project) or a CC specialist Commissioning Company contracted either by the Primary Contractor/PMC or Client to commission a completed Asset.

Vendor and/or Supplier – A company that provides materials and/or equipment (sometimes services) to a Client who could be another vendor – e.g. A pump vendor providing pumps to a pump skid provider; the pump skid manufacturer who provides pump skids either directly to an Operator or to an EPC/EPCM/PMC/EPIC contractor. Note often Operating Companies prefer to source equipment and materials from vendors directly and free issue them to the EPC/EPCM/PMC/EPIC or CC (Commissioning Spares). In this instance the responsibility for managing the Vendor Data may rest with the operator or be assigned to the EPC/EPCM/PMC/EPIC to manage.

Design Data – An EPC/EPCM/PMC/EPIC and sometimes CC provide as deliverables to the client design data such as Drawings and Documents and/or, for example, software/program files for Proprietary Line Controllers (PLC[s]) and Distributed Control Systems (DCS[s]) and may include the hand-over of the entire CAD system database too. Most often the client requires the Contractor to hand-over native files.

Vendor/Supplier Data – Vendors provide to the client or the clients' nominated recipient Drawings and Documents as per a PO or Contract Vendor (Supplier) Drawing and Data List. Often clients will ask for native files and most, not all, vendors will either ask for an exemption or not hand-over native files.

Native File – e.g. CAD files, Office Files

Rendition – a PDF made directly from the native file by using Save As or Print to PDF

Scan – a PDF, TIFF, JPEG or other image file made by scanning a printed copy of a document.

1.00 Terminology

Please also refer to the definitions document at Appendix 1. The most common terminology is shown here:

- **Asset** an item of value that is maintained by an operator for the purpose of producing income - such as, for example, (at the vendor level) a pump right through to (at the Operator level) an Oil/Gas Rig, mine plant, mineral/oil-gas refinery:

  - E.g. FEK, FEP, FED, FEG - 1st dimension

Looking at this image:

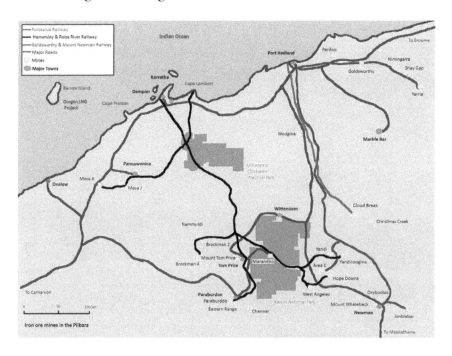

The Yellow squares are mines, each an individual asset, or potential mines (they are an asset).

The rail systems are generally regarding by the operating companies as one asset there are three separate systems on this map.

There are 4 separate port facilities – Dampier and Cape Lambert (Rio Tinto) and Port Hedland one each BHPB and FMG. Sometimes these are split in to two separate assets – the train unloading and stockpiling area and the port facility itself. They are assets.

Looking at the image on page 40.

For our purposes we will ignore the drilling rig – it is an asset but belongs to a third party who have been contracted to do the drilling.

The whole area or field is an asset but this is sometimes, due to complexity and cost etc., broken up. The seafloor and field itself and the Floating Production, Storage and Offtake (FPSO) vessel as a separate asset. Note that sometimes the FPSO can have a different ownership that is it:

1. Could be leased and operated by the Lessee
2. Could be leased and operated by the Lessor
3. Could be leased and operated by a contracted third party
4. Could be owned by the owner of the field and operated by them
5. Could be owned by the owner of the field and operated by a contracted third party.

Any one of these 5 options will have the FPSO recorded as an Asset.

> **NOTE:** The information above and below may also be referred to as Metadata and this is central to what we do and will also come up later in this book.

- **Plant or System Area Code** a logical breakdown of a large asset such as a mine plant in to correlated "chunks" or areas:

  - E.g. 001 – Mine, 100 - Administration Area, 200 - Workshops and Warehousing, 300 - Run of Mine Pad, 301 - Grizzly and 302 – Chute – 2nd dimension

Going back to the FPSO diagram the Wellheads and Pipelines on the sea floor are Plant/Systems belonging to the larger asset.

The FPSO will also be broken up in to Plant/System Areas see Appendix 2B.

- **Discipline** – an Engineering, sometimes business, activity such as, for example, Mechanical, Instrumentation or Scheduling/ Project Controls and HSE. E.g... A – Architectural, S – Structural, X – Subsea – Part of 3rd Dimension
- **Document Type** – groups documents in to particular correlated types e.g... DS or K -Datasheets, D or Drg- Drawings, CA – Calculations – 3rd Dimension
- **Document Sub Type** - (not recommended but often used) – A coding method that classifies specific document types in to subtypes where a discipline code may not provide enough data with the document type code for an accurate classification e.g.. MY - Noise Calculation, PI - P&ID, LO - Instrument Loop Diagram, IS -Piping Isometric.

★★Sometimes Document Types and SubTypes do not adequately define a document for Operations needs or they are coded incorrectly (along with Discipline) and operations will have their own coding system, which they either assign or audit against. These are often called either AIMS or OIMS Codes. (Asset Information Management Standard or Operations Information Management Standard). When that system is mature it is often a concatenation of a Document SubType and Document Type e.g... PID for P&ID, MYK (where MY is "Noise" and K denotes a Datasheet) or IYK (Instrument, Datasheet, Valve) or ISO – (Piping Isometric). – 3rd Dimension

- **Squad Check** - Documents issued either internally or from external contractors/vendors often require Review (IFR) the team that completes the review is a "squad" and the review is commonly called a Squad Check and may be done in a "War Room" – reviews are usually done on paper or electronically on a transmittal or workflow. Also known as an **Inter-discipline Review IDR even Inter-discipline Check IDC** – where the document(s) is to be reviewed by team members of more than one discipline. On rare occasions DC's may be responsible for creating transmittals or workflows for an **Intra-discipline**

review where the document(s) are to be reviewed by team members within one discipline only – generally this is done by the discipline lead and on a no revision document print and is rarely seen in DC.

- **Incoming Status** – The status of a document when it is received in DC (usually from an external party) e.g.. IFR - Issued for Review, IFA - Issued for Approval

- **Review Status** – The status of a document that was sent in for Review or Approval after review/squad check by a team or the lead/package/nominated Engineer e.g.. 2 - Proceed, Proceed except as Noted – Revise and Resubmit. 3 – Do Not Proceed – Revise and Resubmit

- **WBS - Work Breakdown Structure** – something DC's are becoming more commonly exposed to – WBS: A division of a project into tasks and subtasks. The tasks are numbered to indicate their relationship to each other. WBSs are indispensable for project planning – the schedule, particularly when estimating time and resource requirements. Some industries use established work breakdown structure systems for billing and reporting purposes. Note these structures are similar to but not always the same as those used to formulate controlled document numbers for DC purposes – the 4th dimension. In Oil/Gas this is sometimes called CTR – Cost/Time/Resource.

Others

Tag or Equipment Number – A reference number used for identifying individual pieces of equipment, instruments etc. in a plant. It is usually comprised of the plant area code (often numeric), an alpha code which is an abbreviation for the equipment type and a sequence number. E.g.. 301-GRZ-001 (301 being the plant area code for the Grizzly – GRZ being the alpha code for a Grizzly and 001 is the sequence number).

Piping/Pipe Line Number – Identifies pipe(s) running through each section of the plant or as a whole. The numbering methods vary but generally include:

- Line No – Generally just 1, 2, 3 and so on (there might be more than one for the same purpose)
- Material/Fluid – an abbreviation of the type of material being carried by the pipe. E.g.. PWA (Process Water)
- Area in Plant – Usually the Plant Area Code e.g.. 501 (Cyclones)
- Line Size – Internal Diameter (ID) of the pipe. E.g.. 300 (300mm)
- Material of Construction. The material the pipe itself is constructed from. E.g.. CS for Carbon Steel
- Insulation. Pipes are often insulated to prevent heat loss or gain. Usually H – Hot or C – Cold
- Phase. Usually S – Solids, L – Liquids, G – Gas
- Other. Sometimes used to denote Jacketing or Coating
- On a Piping Iso drawing all of the above and a sheet number E.g... -001, -002 and so on the title should show the number of sheets e.g. 1 of 10.

Instrument Number – Often an abbreviated form of a Tag Number shown above – due to the small nature of the symbols used and a lack of space on drawings these are often an alpha code for an instrument type and sequence number for that area of the plant with no dashes. E.g.. PSV001

Transmittal – A document that is used to "formally" send controlled documents to either Internal (Internal Transmittal) or External recipients in paper or electronic format.

Workflow – Some DC applications and collaboration tools have replaced transmittals with Workflows particularly for Internal recipients.

Both are described in much greater detail later on in and throughout this book and there will be practical work.

Distribution Matrices

- **Internal –** A list of recipients for specific types of documents usually discipline or package (Vendor P/O) based. E.g. Mechanical Documents requiring review Mechanical Engineer, Piping Engineer, Structural Engineer, Electrical Engineer, Instrument Engineer, Process Engineer back to Mechanical Engineer

- **External –** A list of recipients for specific types of documents, usually in "Packages" based on either a package of work to be carried out by a Vendor or Constructor. These usually evolve starting with a list of Tenderers. Once awarded the "losing tenderers" are "deactivated and others such as site DC and construction contractors (where a vendor package) are added.

Both are described in much greater detail later in throughout this book and there will be practical work.

Document "Profile" - The "form" or table view in our DC Application with the data that relates to the drawing or document we are querying or looking at.

Pre FEED, FEED, FID – *Pre Feed – usually a study.* Some form of exploration has found a resource that may be worth mining – more intensive exploration is now done with low level design and estimating of what the resource may cost to recover, process and what the income from sales might be – i.e. will the whole make a profit after all costs are taken in to account over the life of the resource. FEED – Front End Engineering Design – a more detailed study with more accurate resource analysis, cost to recover and income potential to take us in to FID – Final Investment Decision – Can we profitably recover, process and sell the resource we identified – do we have a project?

CAD – Computer Aided Design which includes such tools as, but not limited to, Calculation Packages, 3D design tools and other "intelligent" design tools e.g. SmartPlant, Autodesk - AutoCAD, Bentley - Microstation, Aveva.

Master, Controlled Copy, Superseded - *Master* – The Original, "Wet Signed" print of a document, *Controlled Copy* – a copy made for, usually remote locations which is replaced/updated by document control or a responsible person, *Superseded* – Out of Date Revision/ Version

CMS *or* ***CMMS –*** Computerised Maintenance (Management) System E.g. SAP, Agile.

QMS – Quality Management System

In most of our worked examples we will use most of these but NOT all. We will allow for WBS in our Project Set-up in our database but will not add any codes. We will collect some data that will ordinarily be fed in to a CMS but will not be populating one or extracting data for one.

2.00 Definitions/Classification – Level

2.01 Document Types and Responsibility for Managing/Controlling

For the purposes of this section of the book Document can mean Drawing, Letter, Email, Calculation etc.

ALL documents are classified by a Document Type code. E.g. CA – Calculation, DS – Datasheet, DR – Drawing. Some are then further classified by a Subtype and a combination of any/all Asset/Project, Plant/System Area and Discipline, which are not yet concerned with at this Level. The purpose of this unit is to understand that documents are classified initially by Type and there could be hundreds of different types.

Controlled Documents undergo revision, not version (although that is creeping in and discussed in later units), changes and go through a review/approvals process before being "used" in the field or elsewhere in the business. Any document that could be used for construction or operations that will cause problems e.g. re-work if it gets out at the incorrect revision/status MUST be controlled. From the operations perspective if an out of date (Superseded) document is being used for any purpose in the plant it could have disastrous effects or if they are, for example, standards sent to suppliers could result in materials being delivered to specification that are no longer fit for purpose and will need to be replaced.

Using the unworked Document Classification spread-sheet, Other\ Document Classification.xlsx, that is also available for download - "Classify" some document types with respect to who is responsible (position) for managing them once they have a Revision or Version (usually but not always printed) - we are not looking for authors - and add any document types that are not in this list that are important to you.

Note that this is a simple list. There are lists in existence that can go to 320 different document types - one will be provided in the downloadable material and see also Appendix 2.

Refer to Appendix 6 – The Worked Practicals available for download for a worked and unworked example.

ALL documents in the list which become the responsibility of DC's are CONTROLLED Documents. That is not to say that there is no control over the other types – there should be – but the controls are much less stringent.

Note that some organisations regard some documents such as Technical Queries, Requests for Information, Variations and Engineering Change Requests as correspondence. For the purposes of this book they are not they have to be responded to and this often requires the input of more than one member of the team. In some cases, especially where a Collaboration application is used – TeamBinder, InCite, Aconex among others, these types of Documents come as a pre-programmed form but it is still a document controller's responsibility to activate a workflow to ensure they are responded to and/or are disseminated to those that need to know.

3.00 Registers

3.01 Why must we have "Document Registers"

ALL types of Documents must have some form of "Control" register. These are sometimes built in Excel but this is not recommended. If you are not using an application such as, for example:

ANZO (http://www.cambridgesemantics.com/products/anzo-express); and Modern Project & Work Management Platform | Smartsheet spreadsheets cannot be shared among users so unless you already have a pre-described and highly disciplined method of adding document reference numbers that is unique to each spreadsheet for documents then the risk of reference number duplication is very high. More recently I've noticed spreadsheets being shared or used at the same time in Sharepoint. My experience with this is not good. Basically SP/Excel makes 2 or more copies of the same sheet and then Excel tried to merge all the changes to one file. The problem I experienced is that this does not always work and one or more people could lose their work.

For non "Controlled Documents" the best method is to have a simple Access database which is integrated to SharePoint, Sharepoint alone may well be enough depending on the requirements necessary in your document profile. The database manages document profile and other data relative to the document and SharePoint manages the file(s).

3.01.1 The benefits of having registers are:

Faster searches.

Basic profile data is recorded and is therefore easy to report on – who, what, when (in the EEDMS the why too)

A response date can be recorded and if a response is received the received date shown, where no response is recorded – we can expedite.

In excel hyperlink to the file.

In the DC Tool (EEDMS) load/save the file or "map" to the file in a windows directory/share.

3.02 Types of "Document" Registers

1. A Register for Controlled Documents ALL Controlled Documents must be managed by DC's. This is usually done in a tool built around a database application but it can, NOT recommended, done using spread-sheets or Index Cards.
2. Correspondence Register. Also define classifications and columns required – controlled by Admin.

   NOTE it is almost impossible to control emails without an integration to an EDMS application. However, most nations have an electronic transactions or digital signatures act and any commitment made by anyone on an email is legally binding. Therefore, it is important to have some form of control over emails. Where no EDMS is available the simplest method is to have a Subject Heading method that includes the project or asset number and for the email to be saved (dragged to) a windows explorer file share on the network. Similarly, it is wise to ensure that IT have set-up any system to store personal .PST files on the network not on a local hard disk. We need not worry about general chatter such as private emails or where engineers and others are discussing the resolution to a TQ we only need worry about the actual resolution itself.

3. Old project documents either in use in Operations or not. Do old projects stay in the "system" they are in or will they be Data Quality Audited and transferred across to a new register? ★Be careful with this ISO 15489 MUST be taken into consideration – see 17.02.02

3.03 Building a "Correspondence Register" Workshop with Excel

Let's identify the columns/fields we may need in a register and build together a basic register from scratch in Excel.

What "Fields" do we need?

3.03.1 Outwards Correspondence

DATE		
FROM/AUTHOR		Owner of the Document
TYPED/MANAGED BY		Who typed or manages it
ASSET		
SENT TO		
DOCTYPE		
SEQNO		
REFNO		Formula
DATE SENT		Date the Document Was Sent
TITLE/SUBJECT		
H/C FILE REF		Hard Copy File Reference
EFILE (LINK)		Hyperlink to Native or Scan
REPLY YES/NO?		Do we need a reply
REPLY DUE		When do we expect a reply
REPLY RECVD YES/NO?		Have we received a reply
REPLY REF		The Reply Reference No

3.03.2 Inwards Correspondence

DATE REC'D		
FROM		
SENDERS REF		
A REPLY Y/N		A REPLY TO ONE OF OUR LETTERS?
OUR REFNO		The reply is to our Ref No?
ASSET		
SENT TO		
DOCTYPE		
SEQNO		
REFNO		Formula
TITLE/SUBJECT		
H/C FILE		

EFILE (LINK)		
REPLY Y/N?		Is a reply required from us?
REPLY DUE		When is a reply due out?
REPLY SENT		When did we reply
REPLY REF		Our reply Ref No

Note that excel has been used for this purpose because it is easy to use and in the main correspondence registers are "flat" they have only one to one relationships (see 24.01.1) if no DMS exists then this is an OK method. The problem is that spread-sheets unless using something like ANZO cannot be shared and a strict methodology of ensuring no one makes copies of the register etc. has to be in place if spread-sheets are to be used. The author recommends a simple Access database linked to SharePoint for managing the files – the field names will remain the same as above.

When hard copy filing correspondence it is most common to have the document filed in two files – a copy of the upper most page in a chrono or day file which might be circulated the next day then emptied and the original filed in a correctly managed hard copy file system. The best hard copy (HC) file system I have seen was the one the RAAF used with a block numbering system for the files.

When a document is filed in its HC file it should be stamped on the top right with a stamp similar to:

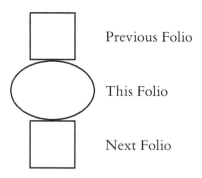

Previous Folio

This Folio

Next Folio

Each document in the file should have a folio number starting at 1 for the first document in the file and so on. The number to go in the oval shape is the folio number of this document in the file. If the new folio is related to an earlier document that folio number should go in the top box – previous folio. If another piece of correspondence goes out or comes in later that is also related its number should go in the next folio box. This makes navigating in the file a lot simpler to do.

In an entirely electronic system where all users have some form of access to correspondence then there should be absolutely no need for managed hard copy files – personal files can be kept but not managed by Admin or DC. Note too that it is the responsibility of the addressee in an electronic system to forward correspondence to others where they have not been To'd or CC'd by the sender.

3.03.3 Practical

Using the unworked example of your MS Excel Document Classification spread-sheet build an Inward and Outward Correspondence Register they can be on separate tabs (worksheets) in the same file – use formula to build the Full Document Number/Reference Number using Concatenate or e.g. $=+C2\&"-"\&D2\&"-"\&$_____ add at least 3 incoming and 3 outgoing documents at least one of which must be responded to and has been also hyperlink to any text based document or photo on your PC.

For those of you with database applications such as MS Access, OpenOffice (Free) you can build your correspondence register in that. HINT use one database with two tables and forms.

Other\Correspondence Register.xlsx

3.04 A "Controlled Documents" Document Register

For the purposes of practicals and to enhance your learning experience we will be using an MS Access/SQL based application called DrawCon. It can link to but not manage files and is not a collaboration tool nor does it have a correspondence system built-in but if necessary, correspondence can be registered in it – not actively encouraged.

The tool can be downloaded at the appendices website and is free for 30 days only.

Here is a screen shot of the document profile for a Controlled Documents Document Register:

NOTE this profile may be slightly different in a later version with some additional fields for Due Dates etc. added. ALL fields etc. in the Profile are discussed in much greater detail later in throughout this book.

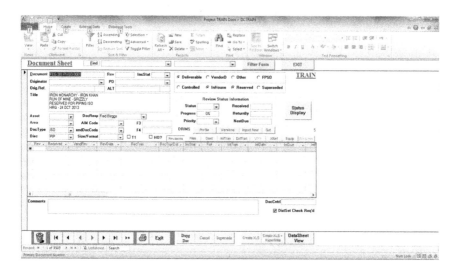

4.00 Dissemination of Up To Date Information

4.01 Distribution Matrices

NOTE we go into much greater detail regarding distribution matrices later and throughout this book. Also note that Matrices can be multi-dimensional (i.e. Who, What [format], Why and When) for this part of the book we will focus on the Who, Why and When.

4.01.1 Internal

Usually Review Teams (Squads) for Squad Checking/Review of Documents. E.g. A mechanical drawing – Mech Engineer (Eng), Piping Eng, Electrical Eng, Structural/Civil Eng, Instrument Eng, Process Eng back to Mech Eng

4.01.2 External

External Matrices evolve on the fly they typically start with a list, found in a PO given to you by procurement or Engineering, of Documents in the "Package" and vendors. On award the "losing" vendors are deactivated in the DC Tool but other people are added such as your own site DC and Constructor(s).

4.01.3 Workshop/Practical

Using our Document Classification spreadsheet define who will need to see that document type and why. R/A = Review and Approver, R = Review, I =Information Only (may choose to review), C = Copy Only

In Unit 1 you had a Document Classification spreadsheet. Open that sheet and click on the Matrix Internal and Matrix External tabs. If you need help with this ask us or speak to others at work. We will go into much greater detail on this later in throughout this book.

Internal

A purchase order has been placed for some Pump Skids – a mechanical package. The motors are electric motors.

Under "Drawings" insert a number of lines using the excel insert function. If necessary, use the Format Painter to keep to the same format.

Add the following to the new blank lines:

Drawings – Mechanical
Drawings – Structural
Drawings – Electrical
Drawings – Process (there will be at least one)
Drawings – Instruments
Drawings – Piping

Find DAS – Datasheet and use the Excel function to insert lines (at least 3) and add the following to the blank lines:

Datasheet – Mechanical
Datasheet – Electrical
Datasheet – Instruments

Then add to the columns to the right the appropriate reviewers for both the drawings and datasheets. (R/A = Reviewer/Approver, R = Reviewer, C = Copy [these people can choose to review or not] NO I = info only.

External

Before the Pump Skid Purchase Order was awarded it went to the following companies as Issued for Tender:

1. Pump Skids r Us
2. Jones's Pumps
3. Resource Gear
4. Wanna Pump Skid

It was eventually awarded to Pump Skids r Us.

This maybe repeated in this tome. Get to know your procurement people. Many companies tend to go with the cheapest supplier. You also know your vendors and those you've had to spend time on chasing overdue deliverables or those who send in material that gets regularly marked-up. Cheapest is NOT always the cheapest in the end. A good method to use when considering award is to sum the prices, divide by the number of prices received and go for the closest OR try to impress upon procurement that the vendors you have no issues with should be considered first.

Since award we have sent a DC to site who must get a copy of everything. Also, the vendor has asked that their onsite rep also get a copy of "reviewed" documents from us directly. The client, via their own DC, will not be involved in Reviews but wants a copy of all reviewed material sent to them for info. We now also have a third–party QA company and they must receive copies of all reviewed material. The Constructor is also to receive reviewed material (all for the time being) at both CBD and Site locations.

Note that ordinarily every Contract or Purchase Order would have its own matrix in this case set up your external matrix for this vendor only.

Add the same lines as for Internal above. We have done some basic design work and will send those drawings to the vendor to work from. Datasheets will be only partially completed by us and will be sent to the vendor for completion.

Then add to the columns to the right the appropriate recipients for both the drawings and datasheets.

X = IFT/IFC Document Issue, R1 = Reviewed Documents Only, C1 = Documents for Vendor to Complete and Return for Review/Approval.

4.02 Methods of Dissemination

Transmittals and Workflows, see below, are all built either manually (one offs) or using the matrices we have already discussed.

4.02.1 Transmittals / Workflows

Any controlled document that is "Issued" or otherwise sent to any internal party (usually for review or approval) or external party (for any reason) is sent either on a transmittal or workflow. ALL controlled documents issued Externally must be sent on Transmittals. Controlled documents issued Internally are issued on Workflows (where Workflows are not available, they are sent on Internal Transmittals). An example of both transmittal types appears in the appendices. NOTE that sometimes an external party, client or government appointed inspector etc., can be included on review workflows however, using a workflow to return status coded documents to external parties is NOT recommended.

EEDMS/EDMS and Collaboration Tool applications usually 100% audit trail workflows i.e. anytime anyone does something to the document(s) on a workflow the system records some kind of base level information E.g. Opened/Viewed, Marked-Up/Redlined, Saved/Closed, Who, Date/Time. These trails are unalterable.

EEDMS/EDMS and Collaboration transmittals are also tracked electronically − Delivered to recipients Mail Server, Read Receipt/Acknowledgement, Documents Downloaded/Accessed by Whom, Date/Time.

Transmittals sent via email from a DC Database tool can also be tracked, to a degree, electronically − turn on both Delivery (to recipient's mail server) and read receipt in Outlook.

External transmittals sent in printed form must be acknowledged by the recipient by returning (scan/email, fax or post) a signed copy (send one for them to keep and one to sign and send back). Transmittals not receipted within 5 working days must be queried and/or expedited we must know they got the material attached to it − evidentiary trail. Your DC tool must have a method of updating the transmittal system for acknowledgement of receipt and reports for expediting overdue acknowledgements.

Methods of Acknowledging Internal Transmittals vary. Single recipient transmittals (send 2 copies) can be acknowledged by returning a signed copy. Multiple recipient transmittals may need to either be tracked manually by DC or must pass through DC between recipients if on a Serial review – both are an excellent reason for using electronic methods or for a "war room" (also discussed in detail later in throughout this book). Parallel reviewers get a single transmittal and copy of the documents each attach 2 transmittals one for acknowledgement and return. We discuss Serial and Parallel in much greater detail later in the book.

4.03 Correspondence Delivery Methods

4.03.1 Courier, Hand Delivery, Email, Fax

It is most unusual to use transmittals for correspondence that is not managed by your EEDMS. Sometimes we require acknowledgement that the correspondence was received the simplest methods are:
Courier – Must be Signed for (at least by reception)

> Take it yourself (if nearby) and take with you a copy of the top page to be signed and dated by recipient

> Email – Turn on Delivery Receipt and Read Receipt. Note we can also drag and drop emails to our Windows Explorer share as an extra method of backing them up – remembering that often your personal PST file is on your own hard disk not on the network

> Fax – Turn on the send log and keep the print. Internet faxing has also become commonplace where the MFC's (Printers) no longer do faxes or if no other method of faxing exists. Get an email confirmation of the send and file it.

5.00 Engineering Document Control

5.01 The Who, What, How, Where, When and Why

5.01.1 Engineering Document Control – Some Definitions

Engineering Documents DO NOT become records until the design, construction and hand-over to Operations (where required) is complete.

Engineering Documents during Design and Construction have a lifecycle and are frozen, snapshots, at various revisions/statuses during that lifecycle.

Sometimes, not always, we are also required to collect data that relates to the documents for Operations purposes such as Document to Document relationships and Document to Tag Relationships.

We may also be required, if we have the tools to do so (sometimes without) manage the electronic files associated with the documents at those snapshot points in the lifecycle these can include native files (for complex CAD and other design tools these are often zipped), renditions (a pdf made from a native file) and scans.

Essentially what we deal with on a day-to-day basis is in 4 dimensions. Think of a 3D Rubik's cube and then add cost/time/resource limitations too.

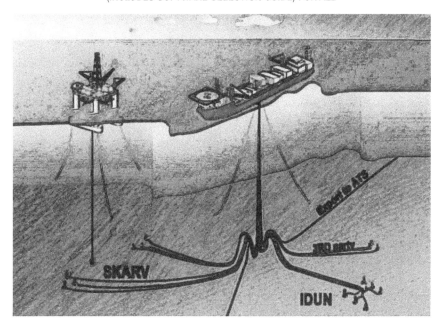

This shows two of the dimensions. Assets e.g. The Drilling Rig and the Floating Production, Storage and Offtake vessel (FPSO), the Well Heads, Pipelines and Risers are usually "Areas or Systems" as are individual parts of the FPSO but can sometimes be treated as a separate asset (i.e. FPSO 1 Asset, Seafloor (wellheads etc.) and Riser another asset with the Rig also a separate asset.

Then we have the Disciplines –

In this example there may be as separate disciplines SubSea, Piping/Pipelines, Marine, Structural, Mechanical and what we cannot see Electrical, Instrumentation/Controls, Process.

What we cannot also see are the document types, including Vendor Documents, associated with all the equipment – the third dimension.

This all had to be built and installed to a schedule and a budget, a controlled documents, and that dictates the fourth dimension being that of cost/time/resource.

5.02 Who

DOCUMENT CONTROL is a function or department which keeps track of all documentation, specifications, controlled documents and processes. The purpose is to ensure that everyone uses the correct and most current processes and specifications. Document Control is a profession, and it can take years to learn to do in the sense of different environments and methods.

Respect your document controllers please do not make schedule promises you do not convey to them early enough to be able to action without going in to full on panic mode and working late into a Friday night!

5.03 What

Simply everything that we determined was to be managed by Document Control on this list.

Document Classification.xlsx refer to your own work or the worked example.

Typically, but not limited to:

Drawings, Specifications, Datasheets, Calculations, TQ's, RFI's, Lists (Parts/Other), Manuals, Manufacturers Data Report/Records (MDR's), Standards, Scopes of Work, Design Criteria, Engineering Change Requests

Any non-correspondence, see definition below, document created during the lifecycle of a project or by operations during the asset management lifecycle which can include maintenance records where not managed by a Computerised Maintenance System (CMS) such as SAP.

Types of correspondence we do manage – those we DO NOT

Sometimes TQ's, RFI's and ECR's and other controlled items like Variations are lumped under correspondence they are NOT we manage them. Letters, emails and memos are not under our control (usually).

5.04 Why

Engineering Document Control is about managing risk.

We DO NOT want the wrong Revision of a Document going to the wrong recipient and/or at the wrong time.

SAFE ENGINEERING DESIGN AND CONSTRUCTION AND SAFE OPERATIONS IS A MASSIVELY IMPORTANT GOAL DOCUMENT CONTROLLERS CONTRIBUTE TO.

http://www.youtube.com/watch?v=0mF41eE1ekI This is manufacturing biased.

- Legal / Quality Requirements:
- ISO 9001:2008★ see updates at the end of this book.
- ISO 27001 Information Security Management Systems
- ISO 22301 Societal security -- Business continuity management systems --- Requirements
- ISO 15489 Records Management
- ISO 13567 International Computer-aided design (CAD) layer standard.
- ISO 15926 standard for data integration, sharing, exchange, and hand-over between computer systems.
- AS 4292 (In Part)

    "Changes to documents and data shall be reviewed and approved by the same functions/organizations that performed the original review and approval, unless specifically designated otherwise."

The law itself can be convoluted – in so far as those we must comply with but not necessarily how they are written. Do not be afraid to check the law – most is now written in plain English. Otherwise obtain permission and ask the company lawyer – who will almost always err on the side of caution and tell you to keep EVERYTHING…..

For example, in Australia a Gas Platform OR Well Heads may be in International Waters with its partners inside the 200km limit but outside the state's jurisdiction and another platform inside the 12 mile limit (state jurisdiction) with a processing plant on land (state and commonwealth jurisdiction may apply to land based assets).

This "whole" would then be affected by:

- Any law governing International Waters – it is likely that, for example, if the platform is registered in Australia that Australian law applies but if it is registered in, say, Panama then Panamanian law applies.
- Australian Government Law

  - Evidence Act 1995 (Best Evidence) – plus any published amendments and regulations
  - Electronic Transactions Act 1999 – plus any published amendments and regulations
  - To my knowledge there is no Commonwealth Mines Act but the Environment Act and Health and Safety Act could also have an outcome on how we manage deliverable documents and correspondence.

- Western Australian Law

  - Evidence Act (1906) (Best Evidence) and Evidence (Admissible Reproductions) Regulations 2003 [Note this is way out of date and to my knowledge has never been tested with a rendition/scan/print and audit trail from a DMS in lieu of an original document]
  - Electronic Transactions Act (2011) and Electronic Transactions Regulations 2012
  - Mining Act 1978 and Mining Regulations 1981
  - A number of the Petroleum Acts and Regulations - http://www.slp.wa.gov.au/legislation/statutes.nsf/main_actsif_p.html
  - Occupational Safety and Health Act 1984 and Occupational Safety and Health Regulations 1996
  - Environmental Protection Act 1986 and some of http://www.slp.wa.gov.au/legislation/statutes.nsf/main_mrtitle_304_subsidiary.html

The two most important laws we MUST comply with are any form of Evidence Act and Regulations [Best Evidence] and any form of Electronic Transactions or Digital Signatures Acts/Regulations. Others are important too but the Evidentiary Trail and whether or not documents can be electronically signed and used on the whole is sometimes referred to as Governance.

The simplest method of working is to find out which law or standard has the most stringent requirements and if by working to that it will satisfy the others.

We may also need, if granted permission, to approach any known regulator that we may need to deal with they may have interpretations of the law or other requirements we have to comply with. For example, in Mongolia ALL materials the regulator requires for what they call Red Books must be in Mongolian (dual languages are fine but Mongolian must be one of those languages).

Let's expand upon ISO 9001:2008 a little:

Documents required by the quality management system **shall** be controlled.

That "shall" word in there means you have to do it.

Here it is again:

"A documented procedure **shall** be established to define the controls needed"

This "shall" word makes this <u>one of the six procedures that you must document</u>.

So, what are the "controls needed"? Answer these questions in your documented procedure and you'll satisfy the requirements for ISO 9001 Document Control:

How do you approve documents for release?

How do you review, update and re-approve documents?

How do you identify the changes that have been made and how do you identify the revision status?

How do you provide access to the correct revision/ version where it's needed?

How do you find and control documents from external sources?

How do you prevent the use of superseded/cancelled documents?

5.05 Why is there so much resistance

A lot of "older" Engineers/Designers just think we get in their way (until they lose something) or have done things their way for the last 30 years and are not going to change now. Remember change scares people regardless of whether or not we believe that the change might benefit others or the "system" as a whole. Fear of the unknown (and the results of the change or the change itself may not be adequately explained and therefore is an "unknown") is not uncommon.

Also remember that IT trained people, IT does not stand for Instant Target, are trained on Records Management and the management of Documents that have become records. Their knowledge of Engineering Document Control and the life cycle of Engineering Documents is limited or none. This can apply to young Engineers and people in other positions such as Administration, Contracts Administration and Procurement.

You are welcome to "share" this material with people inside your organisation who might need a bit of enlightenment. Better still make sure they attend a training course!

Also see the Mind Map later in this book. It goes part of the way to explaining fear of change.

Remember too that sometimes procedures are not written in a KISS manner or have, due to changes in technology etc., become unworkable. If someone is not complying find out why it may be necessary to simplify the procedure or make an immediate change. Take it from me being a policeman and enforcing procedures does not work be open to the possibility that procedures need updating – i.e. think outside the box.

5.06 What can go wrong if there is limited, no or ignored DC

This is the West Atlas jack-up drilling rig the nearby Montara wellhead platform was also destroyed. A well leaked oil and gas into the ocean – the Commission of Inquiry stated that the fault lay with poor "cementing" which in and of itself meant, in my opinion, a lack of Quality Control over how that work was done. The platform and West Atlas rig then caught fire – luckily they had all people off both assets. A hugely expensive rebuild and loss of income from operations followed. This was NOT a DC problem but similar outcomes from the wrong document going out at the wrong time are possible.

More info/images http://www.nopsema.gov.au/resources/image-gallery/

Note "If it aint broke, don't fix it" when it comes to preventative maintenance IS NOT ACCEPTABLE lives were lost and others ruined in several rail accidents in the UK due to preventative maintenance issues/record keeping one of the earliest (after the selloff/privatisation of British Rail) was Paddington/Ladbroke Grove and there were quite a few more over the next 2 or 3 years.

If a drawing goes to a vendor or constructor at the wrong revision or updates are not sent who then builds from out-of-date information there could or will be a huge cost to it put right or it will force redesign (if it's not too late) of other systems. The wrong information going to an Operator who then uses that information to operate a plant from could result in people being killed and the plant being written off. IGNORING correct DC methods is just not worth it.

Missing or out of date drawings and documents in the package that goes to the "regulator" could/will result in the plant not being given the green light for commissioning or operation.

Any kind of delay or rework etc. . . . can and does cost millions.

NEVER assume that someone else has done something you may think they are responsible for or already knows something that you do. The third rule of Safety is to make 100% sure. Piper Alpha, not a DC mistake but related, 167 people of around 225 on-board died – why because practically everything that could be done wrong was –

http://engineeringfailures.org/files/Learning%20from%20the%20 Piper%20Alpha%20Accident.pdf

http://en.wikipedia.org/wiki/Piper_Alpha

This is a classic failure, of catastrophic proportions, to communicate and from there a mess of who assumed what and then just did not double check or pass on information correctly. Assume NOTHING. Check this out – if this is not a case of who/what thought thought I do not know what is - http://www.bbc.co.uk/news/uk-scotland-22840445 no one, person or company was ever charged (why is beyond my imagining) certainly smacks of Thatchernomic cost cutting to me let alone anything else such as bad design and poor permit to work systems etc.

In a recent interview the control room operator said something to the effect of "a lot of alarms went off and I was running around trying to turn them off when an explosion threw me across the control room".

In no way am I saying he or anyone else is at fault and his training may have been lacking. If an alarm goes off shut down the plant or that section of the plant where the alarm has gone off – hit the nearest available RED kill switch DO NOT turn off the alarm itself it went off for a reason that can be checked out later.

1st Rule of Safety – Take Personal Responsibility – Going home alive and unharmed is first and foremost your responsibility – In the event of an accident it is NOT your first job, or that of the injured party (if it is not you), to call a lawyer!

2nd Rule of Safety – If you see anything you think is unsafe or an unsafe act, regardless of what (even if you are NOT trained in that area) STOP it IMMEDIATELY and report it ★★

3rd Rule of Safety – Assume NOTHING make 100% sure

★★An excellent example of this comes from Western Australia. An LNG plant control room operator –granted he/she would have had excellent training – saw something weird happening in a/the flash drum(s) on the control system displays. He/she took a quick decision and shut the plant down entirely. Much later after all the enquiries and investigations when he was called to the office of someone much further up the food chain he thought the worst – that his job was over. He could not have been more wrong, on that point at least, he was given a good-sized reward cheque and a huge pat on the back – his action potentially saved the entire plant and all those working in/on it and nearby too.

The only stupid question is the one you did not ask that could cause loss of life, serious or other injury or some form of re-work or delay. i.e. **there is NO such thing as a stupid question.**

Similarly the only stupid action is the one you did not take to stop something you "felt" was wrong – trust your instinct if something "tells" you what you are doing or seeing is wrong, even if you are uncertain as to why it may be wrong, take immediate action to stop it and report it – even if that may mean a short or long term delay while your gut instinct is carefully checked by yourself and others.

IF IN DOUBT ASK

IF YOU THINK SOMETHING IS WRONG – TAKE ACTION TO STOP IT

5.07 How

This is a very basic swimming lane flow chart of how document control is done AusTrack in Australia. It is also for a Document Change process not the entire process but it is not hugely different from scratch to end.

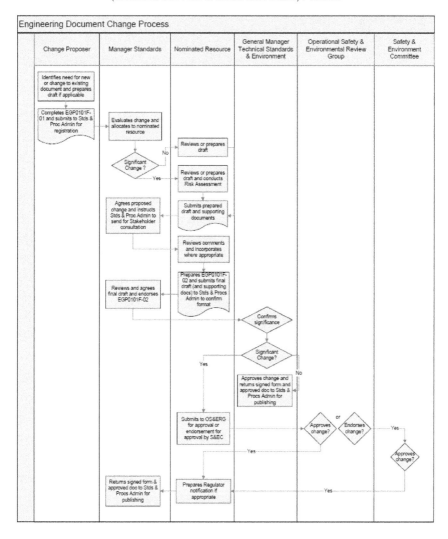

We will go in to much greater detail on the How further along in throughout this book.

Our own flowchart will not be a swimming lane flow-chart and it is a good idea to add to what you now have as we progress through throughout this book.

5.08 When and Where

When – 100% of the time – we MUST have control over all forms of controlled documents and some forms of "correspondence eg. TQ's" 100% of the time.

Where – Engineering Document Control is often done in a CBD office and onsite. "Swapping" i.e. CDB and Site, even for a short period (say 5 working days) is actively encouraged. As is swapping between document control roles in Projects, Construction, Operations etc. - this creates much better understanding of the big picture in its entirety. Also sending CBD DC's to site, for more than a day or two, helps them to understand what is being built, what the site conditions are and gets rid of the "us and them" attitude that can and does develop between those in the city and those in the bush.

If you do go to a site and can, even with an escort, go in to the construction or operations area (with all the PPE etc.) take with you a PFD (Process Flow Diagram and one or more P&ID's for the part of the plant you intend to visit and follow them from one end to the other – this will increase your understanding of what you deal with on a day to day basis and of how these things actually work.

City based people, regardless of profession, in the industry must know what some of these sites are like in terms of conditions and where they are.

In Western Australia for example most mine sites are often very remote and in areas where the ground is very very hard – there is little or no topsoil and what there is may just be a super fine red dust and that stuff gets into everything. Weather conditions can be extreme – seriously hot during the day and cold at night and Cyclones can be a real factor or the remnants of one i.e.. When it rains it really rains hard and the wind even from a remnant can be incredible – in some nations seismic activity can also be a factor. Insects, among other flora and fauna, can be a real issue too – blow and bush flies can be a serious nuisance and really distracting – repellent is fine but often it sweats straight off. In camps, because humans have come in and indirectly made food and water more readily available to, for example, mice their numbers increase and predator activity (snakes in the main) could be a problem in the camp area or, for that matter, lunchrooms around the site.

Remote sites might only be serviced by trucks and small aircraft the biggest likely to be a BAe 146 both of which might be stopped due to bad weather especially where dirt roads/airstrips are used or if tarmacked the road is in a low-lying area and/or is crossed by creeks and rivers and may be subject to flooding. During operations they may also be serviced by returning ore trains bringing in some freight, but this is often rare. A majority are nowhere near a sizeable town and in some cases where a town is nearby it may be a very small one and not have things like a stationery store available. Therefore, if someone onsite rings town and asks for a box of, say, A4 lever arch files, send them do not think they can draw petty cash or get a PO raised and go to the local store.

6.00 Document Control Setup and Closeout

6.01 Proactive v Reactive Document Control

6.01.1 Reactive -

We deal with what we get when we get it, no forward planning for manpower which can mean you will do shedloads of hours when the peak hits before they get help in - because unless they have bodies elsewhere they can bring in, fast, the whole recruitment process can take weeks. You could also end up with another Catch-22 situation – not many/any experienced people around and having to train the people you do get in taking time away from the task of processing documents quickly or causing you to have to work overtime and/or weekends to find quiet time and process documents through the system.

The other major drawback of this is that we can have dropped on our desks completely unexpectedly very late on a Friday afternoon a considerable number of documents that "must" go right now!

We have to update the database – potentially from scratch, prepare a transmittal and in the paper world make all the necessary copies – very time consuming. Be careful Engineers tend to make promises others have to keep e.g. Draughters and us without telling them and a Friday afternoon is usually the time the promise was made for. Often, we can use a bit of a work around. Couriers are not likely to pick-up after 4pm and the recipients are unlikely, if city based (not site), to work after 5pm Friday anyway. What we can do, especially in the paper world, is update the database and print the transmittal(s) and do all the copy work Monday morning or Saturday (if there is a lot of it to do and overtime is paid, or you are otherwise compensated e.g. time off in lieu). The other work-around is to have it in the procedure that documents due out by CoB on a Friday must be in DC by CoB Thursday (earlier if in large numbers) or they will be delayed and put a sign up to that effect too.

Remember the old Adage a Panic on your part does not constitute a panic on mine. We try to be helpful but there are limits that must be set and maintained.

Some, not all, collaboration tools (especially when not used with a DC Database tool) force the DC down the reactive path building a register ahead of need is difficult or impossible.

REACTIVE DOCUMENT CONTROL IS NOT, NOR SHOULD IT EVER BE, RECOMMENDED PRACTICE

6.01.2 Proactive -

the Lead or Document Control Manager sits down with, most often, the Engineering Lead and the Drafting Lead and works out what drawings and documents will be required and when they will first arrive in document control and date fields are populated in your application as the document numbers are reserved for use. Usually around 80% correct and allows forward planning for bodies etc. The real advantage of this is that we can expedite and will know what is due in DC and when and alleviate the Friday afternoon panic attacks by making sure documents are in by Thursday.

If you were to work for an operating company, let's say Iron Monarchy, who has awarded a contract to an Engineering firm, let's say Engineers r Us and they want to review and sign off on all documentation then the first thing you need from Engineers r Us is their intended document list and subsequently their Vendors intended document lists too. This also assumes you will manage giving out document numbers. These all go into a register, like DrawCon, so that you can either produce reports for expediters or managers to chase up late material or you chase the due and overdue stuff yourself - tends to vary - and to plan manning from.

Ditto if you were to work for Engineers r Us directly you still need the list to provide numbers for or obtain numbers for documents and put those in your register to expedite and plan against.

You could simply work for a vendor company who might provide, for example, pumps or a constructor/fabricator who does some limited design work, where the principal does not have the knowledge to do so (specialised plant – e.g. HVAC) or detailed fabrication drawings, shop detail drawings (shoppies), that the designer usually decides against doing. Again, you need to sit with the right people, or the Lead does, to build the document list, get it out to the principal, obtain the numbers needed (not always required for shoppies) and then add the lot to your register and as the documents are provided, update the register with revision/status etc. and send them, called transmitting, to the principal to review and sign off on.

The initial list does not need to be built in your actual register. Excel for this purpose is fine. Once the list is reasonably well honed then import it into your DC application as soon as you can. Again, remember that it may only ever be around 80% complete but 80% is a lot better than 0%. Don't let this drag out the sooner the list is in your DC application the better.

As far as the author is concerned PRO-ACTIVE ENGINEERING DOCUMENT CONTROL IS THE ONLY RIGHT METHOD. There are a number of ways to do Pro-Active DC.

6.01.3 Hybridised Proactive / Reactive –

some DC Tools allow the creation of a "semi" proactive register. I.e. we can add the details of the drawings and documents with a – in the revision or no revision number at all but no date fields exist – when documents are received at least we have a profile to update and some reporting functionality is available.

This is NOT the best way of doing DC but it's better than a purely reactive system.

6.02 Planning DC for the End Result

Ask if the client or operations (it will be their asset(s) after all and their needs must be met) have a hand-over guide or information management standard that we must hand over material to. This usually outlines how documents are numbered (including Asset, Plant Area, Discipline and Doc Type/SubType codes et al), how revisions are to work, often A, B, C pre-Issued for Construction then 0 IFC, 1 post IFC Revisions or As Built and so on. The standard might also specify what they require as/in native files for different types of documents. Then try to tailor that in to how the systems are set-up. As a junior DC this is not your problem but it helps to understand that the end point, operations, is key.

There will be certain documentation that the project itself has to have that the Operators will not need such as a Vendors Quality Plan but which could end up in what is called the Manufacturers Data Report (MDR, often also known as a Vendor Data Book, along with all sorts of other QA type documents - e.g. Heat Certificates for Steel or Concrete Slump Test Certificates - not always needed during the construct phase but should be in the MDR and might be needed, rare, at a later date if something goes wrong. Again, there will be a specific document for the package of work that tells the vendors what documents you want and usually some form of template they have to fill in to say what they will submit and when.

Try to find or obtain from any earlier engineering phase, say FEED, any Process Flow Diagrams and Piping and Instrumentation Diagrams. Note that sometimes although imported from an earlier phase the Document Number may have to be changed – in which case to preserve the history Supersede the existing document and state clearly in its profile the document number(s) it is being replaced by.

We also need from procurement, it will be rough, a list (with dates) of the packages (contracts and Purchase Orders) to be awarded.

All these things aid us in building a pro-active document control database – see exercise/practical in Section 22.

6.03 Manual and Electronic Document Control Comparison

Manual document control is basically done in all hard copy format with index cards kept for each document and matrices on a printed form with transmittals done in Word or Excel or on a printed form. ALL paper is filed – discussed later in the book. Manual document control DOES NOT entail managing electronic files of any description. NOT RECOMMENDED

Electronic document control is where we do everything electronically and involves an EEDMS application and we also manage electronic files – pdf renditions, scans and sometimes natives E.g. Word or CAD. THE BEST METHOD

Often a hybrid of the two is used. The law may require documents to be "wet signed" and kept in which case we have a hard copy file system and an electronic system. Typically, we would scan "wet signed" documents and add them to our system. The systems deployed vary which we will discuss in greater detail much later. NOT A BAD METHOD

6.04 The Differences

Different industries sometimes have different requirements for how Document Control is to be done and which records are to be kept.

6.04.1 Oil/Gas and/or Pharmaceuticals, Nuclear v Mining

6.04.1.1 Mining

is an inherently dangerous business however on simple mining plants such as Iron Ore there is not a lot, in the plant, that can explode or cause massive loss of life and injury or result in the entire plant being destroyed if it does. Therefore, sometimes a regulator will allow commissioning and operation if a document that is not critical to actual operations is missing. This does not apply to some mines where extraction of either an end mineral such as gold is carried out and/ or where hazardous chemicals are used to extract a concentrate that is sent to a refinery for further processing and it does not apply to mineral refining either. Another exclusion is where gas is either used in the process e.g. Hot Briquetted Iron production or where gas may be present as a result of the operation of the mine – some Thermal Coal (brown lignite) operations produce gas, as can the processing of Nickel ores.

6.04.1.2 Oil/Gas and Nuclear

Are ALL extremely dangerous and the risk of massive loss of life and/or the entire plant being lost if something explodes is very high e.g. Chernobyl. Any missing document that is required by the regulator, or those that the regulator identifies a problem with (e.g. language), will result in no commissioning or operations.

6.04.1.3 Pharmaceuticals

While there may be less chance of an explosion resulting in loss of life or plant (sill possible if the wrong chemicals were mixed together), if for example, there is a design flaw or the coating on a pipe possibly reacts with the chemicals it is carrying the chances of an impure and very dangerous drug hitting the market place is also very high (QA does not catch everything it perhaps should). Any missing document that is required by the regulator, or those that the regulator identifies a problem with (e.g. language), will result in no commissioning or operations.

When all is said and done it is best to treat every kind of plant the same way preferably Oil/Gas, Pharma or Nuclear. Also take in to account the law. If, for example, we have (Oil/Gas) an asset in International Waters with some wells in Commonwealth Water and a refinery on "State" land work to the law with the most stringent requirements then ALL law should be satisfied.

6.04.2 Project Managers v Operators

Project Managers and EPC/EPCM companies usually have to collect a lot of information during the life of the project some of which operations do not require – this is discussed in greater detail further on. Hand-over can be required where the Contractor's archive/retention systems do not meet an operator's requirements.

6.04.3 Designers v Constructors

Although a constructor should be involved in Document Reviews for design documents from a constructability perspective it is unlikely a Constructor, other than a shop fabricator, will create design documents. They will, and are required to keep, some controllable documents such as an ITP, Inspection or other test records e.g. Concrete Slump tests etc. but all of this material is likely to be handed to the Designer in a compiled MDR – Manufacturers Data Report/Record.

6.04.4 Contractors (Design) v Vendors v Shop Detailers/Fabricators

Design Contractors (EPC/EPCM or specialists such as Fire Systems and HVAC designers) draw/design high level drawings and while some are quite detailed they are not detailed enough for a fabricator to work with – particularly Structural Drawings – and are either sent to a fabricator who has an in-house Shop Detail application or specialist or to a Shop Detail specialist, in native file format, for Shop Detail drawings to be produced.

Quite often a PMC will contract out most or all design to one or more design houses. An EPC/EPCM may contract out some design for specialized equipment such as Fire Systems and HVAC to subcontractors but the documents and drawings they produce will be numbered in the same way as normal design drawings and may set aside a specific set of sequence numbers for that designer may be used e.g..

Sequence 001-499 Internal
Sequence 500-699 Fred Blogs HVAC
Sequence 700-799 Squeeze It Pressure Vessels
Sequence 800-999 Super Fire Systems

Vendors will produce drawings for the pieces of equipment, e.g. Pumps, they are contracted to provide. They rarely hand-over native files but may hand over an extract from a native for a design company to use in their main design drawings.

6.05 Technical Document Control

Engineering Documents DO NOT become records until the design, construction and (where required) hand-over is complete OR until the document is superseded by another document or later revision or otherwise cancelled.

Engineering Documents during Design and Construction have a lifecycle and are frozen at various revisions/statuses during that lifecycle.

These are commonly IFR, IFT and IFC or (Vendors) Certified Final, and As Built

Documents go through a review and subsequent approval process, although they try not to use the word approved these days (all sorts of negative legal connotations) and as design unfolds, construction issues (the fact that it is sometimes impossible to do stuff with steel, concrete, pipes etc. does not sometimes enter the heads of engineers and designers when using CAD applications until the constructor takes a look at the documents either in their office or, more often than not, onsite).

In operations as the plant ages, or needs to be changed to make maintenance simpler, or technology changes documents will go through a number of revisions all of which have some kind of review/ approval process - often preliminary design is done with "library" vendor information which could be out of date so the design, when real vendor data comes in, can be changed and re-reviewed.

Each of those has a status. Reviews can be called a number of things and you should remember some of these, in particular, Squad Check and War Room (although War Rooms are almost completely outmoded now but even in the electronic world still the quickest and best way of conducting a review). Each of these reviews either based on a Discipline such as, Structural, or on a package of work (usually discipline based) such as, Train Load-out Chutes, have a Review Team or Matrix of reviewers (the squad).

Once the review process is completed, usually with an electronic comments or mark-up system or a physical document covered in coloured ink (different disciplines have different colours) it is copied and/or electronically (note with paper it is recommended to make the best possible copy or high resolution scan and keep the copy and send the original mark-up) returned to the author or vendor and the next revision is usually Issued for Approval and goes to the Lead Discipline or Package Engineer who checks comments have been incorporated or exempted and signs off. Note the Package Engineer may then instruct DC that another full review is necessary – not recommended.

OR it could go to a client who may not have been in the earlier review process to check and sign off. If the client or engineer is not happy then the document is again marked up and sent back to the design team or vendor to revise.

Sign off then initiates the document going to Issued for Construction or Use (in the Vendor World – very confusingly - this is sometimes called Certified Final) and it attracts, usually, 4 signatures or sets of initials either "Wet" or "Electronic". After that it can be revised if problems occur during construction or go directly through to the As Built process.

IFC and later revisions are usually sent to constructors, your own site supervisors via a site DC, or vendors to work with in "packages" these are set-up in your system as External Distribution Matrices or in more modern systems are referred to as packages. The package engineer should advise what package which documents belong in or they will be listed in a document specific to the package of work such as an Engineering Requisition and/or Scope of Work. Workpacks can also be used. My approach to this is to make a distribution matrix or add to an existing one the workpack number so that when we do trnasmittals that pack is covered.

There are shedloads of "right" "Pro-Active" ways to do Engineering DC depending on the client's needs and local requirements, law etc. always start, or try to, from the end point. I repeat – Ask if the client or operations have a hand-over guide or information management standard that we must hand over material to.

Technical Document Control is responsible for managing the entire lifecycle (other than doing the actual drafting) of Controlled Documents from IFR to eventual hand-over. Depending on the size of the project being undertaken there could be one or more document controllers dedicated to managing Reference Material (brownfields)[rare to have a dedicated DC], Design Documents and Vendor Documents. They could also be split into teams based on Assets or a portion of an asset e.g. Platform Topsides, Platform Jacket, SubSea and Onshore plant. Upstream, downstream and facilities are other possible team designators. These teams might then be further broken down in to Design and Vendor. Some projects can be that big that one or more DC's may be responsible for managing a single contractor and/or vendor.

6.06 Corporate/Operations Document Control

Two levels of "Document Control" or "Management" occur at the corporate level.

Management of day to day low or no lifecycle documents such as general correspondence (rare) and Document Control at a basic level of Engineering Documents that have been handed over and have become a Record – for example changes driven by an MoC.

When documents are handed over to operations they are a record either As Built or Issued for Construction (with or without Engineering Change) and are frozen at that point in time. Change is rare unless something breaks down and is replaced with a newer model of the same type of equipment which sparks a Management of Change Request. Or if the plant is aging and is to be modernised or expanded in which case the documents are usually checked-out to a brown field project team and checked back in when handed back over.

Management of "Engineering" related corporate standards/ specifications and datasheets which have a life-cycle similar to Project Engineering Documents and are often issued to Projects and/or Contractors/Vendors to use on projects. An operations DC may also be required to manage maintenance records and even drilling logs.

There are "shedloads" of wrong ways to do Document Control and very few right ones will we be focusing on the best right one or at least in my opinion..

7.00 Document Control Tasks and Processes

7.01 Controlled Documents

Everything in our document classification list that we coded DC is the responsibility of Engineering Document Control to Manage. In Engineering Controlled Documents are generally as listed in your Document Types category in DrawCon Valid Codes. These include but are not limited to: Drawings, Specifications, Datasheets, Calculations, TQ's, RFI's, Lists (e.g., Parts), Manuals, MDR's, Standards, Scopes of Work, Design Criteria and (but not limited to) Engineering Change Requests.

There will be certain documentation that the project itself has to have that the Operators will not need such as a Vendors Quality Plan but which could end up in what is called the Manufacturers Data Report (MDR) along with all sorts of other QA type documents - e.g. Heat Certificates for Steel or Concrete Slump Test Certificates - not always needed during the construct phase but should be in the MDR and might be needed, rare, at a later date if something goes wrong.

The best way to manage a hand-over assuming no changes to the clients requirements (data cleansing/massaging) is to Set-Up a new DC database (in DrawCon FEG OPS) and export across all documents that have T1 (To be As Built) and T2 (To be Handed Over) Checked at the current revision only (drop the history in the new database – IF THE OLD DATABASE IS TO BE PRESERVED WHICH IT SHOULD BE – a client/operations should not require the entire history) then copy the respective files to a portable hard drive. There is freeware on the internet that allows a user to make a list of the files to be moved or copied, usually based on a .csv file, which can be done from DrawCon and will use the list to move/copy files from the specified locations to another. In an EDMS or EEDMS the entire application might be copied less the older, superseded (not required) information thereby negating the need to copy files at all.

7.02 Controlled Hardcopies

Quite often there are remote parts of your company or plant that need specific documents, usually drawings, kept in-situ. These are called controlled copies. The simplest method of doing these is to set them up as internal distribution matrices, raise a transmittal, make the prints and do the filing yourself use A3 document wallets and take a self-inking superseded stamp and stamp old revisions Superseded. Stamp the new Revision Controlled Copy. It is simpler not to use controlled copy numbers on the documents themselves. Where the site is remote transmit the documents to the site DC to update the necessary files from – note sometimes the site DC is the person who will do any necessary copying and transmittals too.

7.03 Document Classification, Numbering and Filing

Engineering, Controlled Documents, are classified in much greater detail than our original classification spreadsheet.

To make filing, electronically or in hard copy somewhat simpler we "classify" and have a numbering methodology for documents. There is a detailed document classification schema in Appendix 2A/B/C.

Controlled Document Numbers:

Usually look something like this (n's are numbers, a's are letters):

nnnn-nnn-a-aaa-nnnn

> nnnn- usually some kind of project identifier. If working for a client/operator they might be letters that identify a particular asset or site.
> -nnn- usually an identifier called an area/system code - this is done to break the plant or site into smaller manageable areas.
> -a- is a discipline code, can be 2 letters and sometimes even numbers
> -aaa- is a document type code - sometimes 2 letters but most commonly 3

- nnnn is a sequence number issued out of the document control database/system which can be preceded by a V or F for Vendor/Foreign documents

In our example (our Iron Ore Mine) an example would be:

FEG-301-ME-GAD-0001
> FEG - The Asset/Site – Iron Khan
> 301 - Grizzly
> ME - Mechanical Discipline
> GAD - General Arrangement Drawing
> 0001 - Sequence Number for the combination of all the above.

For electronic files we also have a file naming convention in this example the file name(s) are:

FEG-301-ME-CAD-001_A.PDF   and   FEG-301-ME-CAD-001_A.DWG
> the _A denotes the revision.

Sometimes the file name also includes the current status e.g.

FEG-301-ME-CAD-001_A_IFR.PDF
> IFR denotes Issued for Review or
FEG-301-ME-CAD-001_A_RSP-01.PDF
> RSP-01 denotes Review Status (Response) Code 01.

If we are dealing with vendor documents it is best done in a separate project database in our example FEG is internal design and FEGV could be vendors. The numbering method is slightly different (not always) too. Usually an F (Foreign) or V (Vendor) is placed in front of either the discipline code or sequence number to denote an externally (vendor) produced drawing or document e.g.

FEG-301-VME-GAD-0001 or FEG-301-ME-GAD-V0001

Electronic file naming would include the V or F in the appropriate place e.g.

FEG-301-VME-CAD-0001_A.PDF   or   FEG-301-ME-CAD-V0001_A.PDF

NOTE WELL Vendor Numbering methods that DO NOT include Discipline, Plant/System Area and the internal Document Type Code (as opposed to a vendor document type code from the VDDRL – where two codes are used [silly in the extreme]) are useless to both constructors and operations and MUST be actively discouraged. I've seen numerous variations of these and none of them are any good and on one project my team and I had to re-number (along with correcting a lot of other document profile data that was also incorrect) over 60,000 documents before they could be used in operations.

NOTE also that it is OK to use the vendor's document number and revisions for documents that will NOT be handed over but this does tend to get confusing and it is best to use one of your own numbers on everything.

A logical and sensible document numbering method[s] for controlled documents and correspondence is a critical factor to the successful outcome of projects and will cut search times dramatically. I have also seen numbering methods where the actual number applied varied between disciplines for example HSE and Design documents had a different way of being numbered instead of identifying the HSE document via a discipline code, document type or combination of both – DO NOT DO THIS. Have one methodology, KISS it, and only vary it by adding a V or F as outlined above to differentiate design from vendor documents.

There are exceptions to the document numbering method above the two most common are:

Piping Isometric Drawings the Piping Line Number-Sequence No is a unique ID we do not need to give them another unique ID. Loop Diagrams often also have a unique ID we do not need to give them another unique ID.

Also note that sometimes specific sets of sequence numbers are used e.g.

Sequence 001–499 Internal
Sequence 500–699 Fred Blogs HVAC
Sequence 700–799 Squeeze It Pressure Vessels
Sequence 800–999 Super Fire Systems

However, when we file, it is unlikely that we will actually file on this "order" as in the Document Number the most common will be:

Asset (FEG) then Discipline (ME), then Area (301) and Sequence No.

Drawings are filed together, usually in A3 binders in document wallets and documents are filed separately based on type either in A4 ring binders sometimes but not always in wallets. Filed by Revision and Status e.g.:

A   IFR (Lowest down in the file)
A   RSP-01 (2nd, from the bottom, Document in the file)
B   IFA (3rd, from the bottom, Document in the file)
B   RSP-05 (4TH, from the bottom, Document in the file)
0   IFC (Uppermost in the file)

<u>Old revisions should always be clearly stamped Superseded.</u>

NOTE some members of the larger team can get upset by this, why is beyond me, but I almost always put the Superseded stamp smack in the middle of or over the title block and (on a drawing) in the centre.

When filing A3 drawings keep them all in one wallet per drawing with the superseded drawings below the current one in Rev/Status order.

NOTE WELL Vendor or Foreign documents are filed in the same manner but in clearly marked Vendor or Foreign files not with our design documents.

If we have to file A2, A1 or A0 drawings the most common way is to have the current drawing stapled to the top of one or two old revisions e.g. B RSP-01 stapled to B IFR and A RSP-01, A IFR

This allows for quick back checking. Once we have too many revisions, in this example let's say Rev 0 IFC has come in we remove some of the Superseded revisions (A – RSP-01 and A-IFR) and file them away in the same sort of order but in a plan cabinet/tank or stick file marked Superseded.

Old revisions should always be clearly stamped Superseded.

For documents keep one back revision, in this example, B – RSP-01 with the current revision and file the older revisions in the same order but in a clearly marked Superseded file.

Old revisions should always be clearly stamped Superseded.

NOTE WELL we DO NOT use the word Obsolete. It can happen that a document is cancelled. That document should be added to the Superseded file or another file specifically for that purpose and be clearly stamped Cancelled. Also note that unless they were never issued to anyone to use or used in the first-place obsolete document numbers SHOULD NEVER be re-used. The DC database must always reflect this information.

Sometimes a document can be superseded by another. In which case the Superseded document must be shown as Superseded in the DC database and a note made either in a comment box or title field of which document has replaced it. The superseded document should be clearly stamped Superseded, and a note also made on the document of the document number which replaced it.

If your DC database allows Cross-Referencing to other documents, DrawCon does, cross reference the Superseded document to the current one and the current one to the Superseded one if that information does not automatically update itself also check if any other documents referenced to by the Superseded document now need revision.

Some Electronic Document Management Systems, those that manage files, will have a structure similar to the hard copy filing (except we do not split drawings and documents) e.g.

FEG – Iron Khan
    ME   - Mechanical
       301 -   Grizzly

Or

FEG – Iron Khan
    301   - Grizzly
       ME - Mechanical
       EE - Electrical

Where it is a requirement to split drawings and documents the structure may look something like this (it is simpler not to split the different document types by type/subtype)

FEG – Iron Khan
    ME   - Mechanical
       301 -   Grizzly
             -      Drawings
             -      Documents

Or

FEG – Iron Khan
    301 - Grizzly
       ME -   Mechanical
            -      Drawings
            -      Documents
       EE -   Electrical
            -      Drawings
            -      Documents

Sometimes native files and renditions/scans are kept separately so the schema could be e.g.

```
FEG – Iron Khan
      301    -   Grizzly
            ME  -        Mechanical
                              Natives
                              Non Natives
            EE  -        Electrical
                              Natives
                              Non Natives
```

It is also probable that the team will prefer to have only current files readily accessible and all superseded material filed in directories for that purpose (note most EDMS/EEDMS applications do this automatically) e.g.

```
FEG – Iron Khan
      301  -   Grizzly
            ME  -        Mechanical
                              Current
                                    Natives
                                    Non Natives
                              Superseded
                                    Natives
                                    Non Natives
            EE   -       Electrical
                              Current
                                    Natives
                                    Non Natives
                              Superseded
                                    Natives
                                    Non Natives
```

Often, in an EEDMS or EDMS application, these schemas are "virtual" only but the schema sometimes allows for faster searches or is just there because people are used to seeing a structure in Windows Explorer. See section 27 this is NOT entirely recommended or the "view" with the tree should be hidden.

There is an argument with document numbering where a full file management EEDMS/EDMS or DC tool/application is used that has all the necessary "mandatory" fields in the document profile that a document number itself is unnecessary. This is because, often hidden from view, the database element that you create the document profile in actually assigns a unique ID to the document and that if the Unique ID assigned makes some sort of sense e.g. A simple 8 digit sequence number, then that is all you really need. Often, not always, the Unique ID assigned by an EEDMS/EDMS is long and complicated and contains special characters such as % and makes no sense at all and we therefore must have a controlled number that does. In some cases the Unique ID field in the EEDMS is not hidden and where it is a straight sequence number a numbering mask can be deployed that uses that number as the sequence number for the document e.g. if the Seq No in the system is 10000001 then the document might be numbered FEG-301-ME-GAD-10000001 note that the sequence number is NOT unique to the balance of the document number itself i.e. the next document might be FEK-999-HS-LTR-10000002. Not recommended practice unless there is a simple way to batch/block reserve numbers for specific assets etc.

Refer to Appendix 2 for the Classification Codes we will be using in our workshops and practicals.

NOTE WELL for correspondence your electronic file structure should mirror your hard copy file structure.

7.04 Revisions and Versions

Engineering Documents during Design and Construction have a lifecycle and are frozen, snapshots, at various revisions/statuses during that lifecycle.

This is the ideal, rarely happens, there is often a 2nd review and, where the client/operations, are not in the review process, changes made after the IFA is issued so we can go all the way up to Rev D or

E before we get sign off. It also happens that when the constructor gets to site he finds a problem with the Rev 0 and makes mark-ups and fires it back in and changes are made again how the Revisions are handled varies some just go 1, 2, 3 and so on but others may go 0A, 0B etc. until sign off then to 1 and the As Built would then be Rev 2 or even later.

Revision	Status	Notes
A	Issued for Review* [IFR]	(In DrawCon the review teams are called Internal Maps but the reviews are done in print (they could be done electronically if everyone had Acrobat Standard or something similar or better such as Brava Viewer) – in newer DMS applications they are called Review Teams and Reviews are on a workflow which is "activated" by DC and the application includes a reviewing tool built-in.
B	Issued for Tender	Issued out to Tenderers
C	Issued for Approval	Issued to the Client for Approval (Usually after some back-drafting when Tender Drgs/Docs are in)
0 [Zero]	Issued for Construction or Issued for Use	Signed by all those that have too and sent externally to Vendors or Constructors usually identical to C.
1	As Built	Rev 0 is often marked-up on site by the constructors and commissioning team and then sent in for the CAD guys to amend the drawing to As Built

The most common system of Revisions (a revision is applied at a certain point in the life of a document e.g. IFR) followed is: A, B, C, D and so on with no I, J or O used for obvious reasons then IFC Rev 0 and post IFC revisions 1, 2, and so on.

There are lots of variations to this. One employer used P1, P2 and so on til Rev 0. Another, post IFC used 0A, 0B and so on until 1 – As Built (not recommended if drawings need not be As Built). This was somewhat, but not totally, similar to the Rev system recommended in BS1192 – which I consider to be necessary but awful – no DC input.

The method used is often dictated by the client. Some clients, because it is how (by default) most databases sort, like numeric then alpha so 1, 2, 3, (pre IFC) then A, B, C (IFC and Post IFC).

Some systems/companies now, use a Revision and a Version similar to the above 0A or something like A-1, 0-A, 0-1 – most often this is applied when a document has come in from a vendor or designer is stamped, reviewed and given a return status – i.e. the incoming Revision is A but after the review status is applied it may become A-1. NOT recommended practice – however some DC tools may only link or map to one file per document profile in which case, if we want both the unmarked and marked files, mapped we are stuck with it. Some DMS applications do this automatically but the Transmittals they generate do not show the Version just the revision.

Revision/ Version	Status	Notes
A	Issued for Review* [IFR]	(In DrawCon the review teams are called Internal Maps but the reviews are done in print (they could be done electronically if everyone had Acrobat Standard or something similar or better such as Brava Viewer) – in newer DMS applications they are called Review Teams and Reviews are on a workflow which is "activated" by DC and the application includes a reviewing tool built-in.
A-01	2	Reviewed as Noted, Revise and Resubmit Transmitted back to the Author/ Vendor

B	Issued for Tender	Issued out to Tenderers
C	Issued for Approval	Issued to the Client for Approval (Usually after some back-drafting when Tender Drgs/Docs are in)
0 [Zero]	Issued for Construction or Issued for Use and sometimes Issued for Purchase	Signed by all those that have too and sent externally to Vendors or Constructors usually identical to B.
0-A	IFR	ECR No 999 Changes and Noted by Diamonds – IFA
1	IFC	ECR No 999 Changes and Noted by Diamonds - IFC
1-A	As Constructed	Site mark-up of Rev 1 post Construction
1-B	As Pre-Commissioned	Site mark-up of Rev 1-A post pre-commissioning
1-C	As Commissioned	Site mark-up of Rev 1-A post commissioning
1-D	As Handed Over	Site mark-up of Rev 1-B post hand over to Operations for a trial run of the plant
1-E	Operations Post Commissioning Mark-ups	Mark ups made during the trial run of the plant of any changes that have been made during that period
2	As Built	All site mark-ups incorporated

There is NO such thing as a version on any document with two exceptions

1. Mark-ups especially for As Builts. Privately while they are undergoing an Intra-Discipline review i.e. NOT a Squad Check the designers may use "Versions" until they release a Revision.

2. Post IFC documents being changed as a result of an ECR or MOC may also be given versions at various stages in their life cycle while a review/approval process is undertaken to save using up too many Numeric revisions.

7.05 File Naming Convention

As outlined above under filing/file naming - electronic files should also carry the current revision of the document and, the file type – E.g.

– FEG-301-ME-MDR-001_A.pdf
– FEG-301-ME-MDR-001_A.doc

Sometimes an electronic file, especially if exported from the EEDMS may also show the "version" and Status E.g.

– FEG-301-ME-MDR-001_A1_IFR.pdf
– FEG-301-ME-MDR-001_A2_RSP-01.pdf

The same exemptions as for Document Numbering apply.

7.06 Title Convention

For Controlled Document Titles we will be insisting on the standard 4 line format - like:

Iron Monarchy – Iron Khan
Run of Mine
Chute
General Arrangement and Details

OR

Iron Monarchy – Iron Khan
Plate Feeder
Over-speed Detector – 400-OSD-0001

Datasheet

For Correspondence we should also insist on a Title Convention something like:

Iron Chinggis – Grizzly - Letter of Intent to Award.

Keep titles short and simple but meaningful – this aids searches.

8.00 Interface with contractors and subcontractors

In the main DC's only deal with vendors, contractors and sub-contractors when receiving and transmitting documents.

We do sometimes become expediters where there is no expeditor, or an engineer/contract admin/procurement person does not take or has been given this responsibility. Not wishing to denigrate engineers but if there is no expeditor, I prefer to do the expediting I do not see this as an engineers' role and it means that the process of managing vendor data becomes disjointed and not centralised.

The preferred method is telephone first*, and then email (usually some kind of multi-level expediting "letter"). *Telephone calls are deniable stick with email. Sometimes, if we are permitted, a visit to the vendor's premises really helps and the LDC or DCM should be at Kick-Off meetings and lay down the law and also make notes of any changes to the Vendor Drawing and Data Requirements List.

If you do have a 'phone conversation with anyone that results in say, a submission date change – make the change in your DC tool and add a comment "who you spoke to, date/time and agreement reached" this does assist if someone denies a "deal" was reached.

Your DCM or LDC must ensure that Engineering and Procurement use some form of Vendor and/or Contractor Drawing and Data Requirements List – similar to:

Download Material\Worked Examples\VDDRL-VDS Example 1.xlsx or VDDRL-VDS Example 2.xlsx Both included in the downloadable appendices.

Note that although the "description" shows, for example, General Arrangement drawing this is not an acceptable title from the Vendor they must adhere to the titling convention in 7.06. Remember we could be dealing with 100's of thousands of documents. If the title is just General Arrangement drawing try finding it in a hurry (GA of what......).

There should also be a Standard that clearly describes each of these Documents and how they are to be delivered and the content needed/required.

In terms of "data" a contractor usually must provide all "native" files in a specified format. It is not uncommon to ask Vendors for but they often will not provide "natives" due to the proprietary nature of the equipment.

An example of the multi-level expediting letter/email is:

> 3 days prior to due date – an email asking if the documents in the list will be submitted on the due date – just a friendly reminder.

> Due date an email asking if the documents on the list will be delivered today – just a friendly reminder.

> 3 days overdue a notice asking politely for immediate delivery of the overdue documents on the list signed by the Package Engineer citing that Liquidated Damages can be applied where delays are caused to schedule.

> 10 days overdue a notice, signed by the Package Engineer or Project Manager, this usually depends on the value of the contract/PO, stating the either Liquidated Damages are to be applied by the day until overdue documents are delivered or, more effective, all progress payments will be halted until overdue documents are delivered or a combination of both e.g. Progress payments will be delayed and have liquidated damages applied.

It does pay to read the provisions in each contract for Liquidated Damages for non-delivery of documentation. Unfortunately, sometimes there is no effective way of going after a vendor for overdue documents because provision for LD's etc. was not added to the contract/PO – a good reason for having a knowledgeable LDC review any Contract/PO before it goes out! Application of LD's can also cause head-aches! For example of enigineering forgot to ask for, say, spares/critical spares lists and we then ask for them they could be held to ransom or charged for due to the previous application of LD's. LD's can also result in terribly long, complicated and drawn out court cases.

9.00 Receiving Documents

First and foremost, you must do a number of things:

1. In a hard copy system or where hard copy documents are likely to be received keep a file called ACE (excuse the language) it means Arse Covering Exercise. Where documents may be received via email to your own (not recommended) or DC inbox start a sub-directory with the same name – ditto if you are using or receiving documents in a collaboration tool.

2. Create a Work Instruction/Request form (printed) – this should have fields for the name of the person who is giving you the instruction, a list of documents (and/or where they may be found), what is to be done with them (e.g. Issued for Review) and who they are to be sent to. If you chose not to have an ACE file staple the completed form to the back of any transmittal (or one of them) generated. Ask IT to create a similar form in Outlook for email requests. If you are using a collaboration tool it too should already have something similar i.e. a pre-built form – if not open an ACE folder and ask for a form to be developed.

3. Start three files for transmittals – Internal Transmittals (you raise to members of your project team), External Transmittals (you raise to Third Parties) and Transmittals from External Sources. Note that everything is done entirely electronically through a collaboration tool, EEDMS/EDMS then this becomes unnecessary.

4. Develop a form, which includes the Review Stamp and "get out" clause and that also shows the Document Number, Title, and Revision and provides space for comments. This form is to be used by Vendors and Contractors when they submit documents but NOT used for drawings. The cover page must be with EVERY document so it must go out with the "Award" package.

9.01 Documents from Internal Sources

Unless the documents are being sent from another project or from a central unit they are unlikely to be sent to you on a form of transmittal or workflow. In the main documents will be received from project team members either via email (with files attached or a link to them) or in print. Insist on an instruction form being completed – your memory might be fantastic but with a tray full of work and dealing with people all day it can be easy to forget who gave you what and why/what for. Some people will not fill out a form but write an email or provide instructions on scrap paper or post-it notes – provided those instructions are clear and concise and remain with the documents that is fine. When you have done the work staple the instruction to a form and either file that in the ACE file or staple it to a transmittal you raised as a result of the instruction.

9.02 Documents from External Sources

In the modern era most documents are sent from contractors and vendors to DC via a collaboration or other similar tool. If this is the case even though everything is tracked electronically there will be some form of transmittal. Print it. Use it to compare against the files received – **make 100% sure** you have everything listed, check document numbers, revision numbers and titles. By rights there should be no errors but people can and do, as do electronic systems, make mistakes they must be checked.

If all is well it is not entirely necessary to sign, scan and send it back – the system will have a record that you received and downloaded the documents. If there are errors, wrong files, missing files, incorrect revisions, etc., send an immediate email to the sender and explain the issue and ask them to correct it ASAP. Process the correct documents and await corrected documents on a new transmittal. DO NOT delay processing what can be done. The third-party transmittal must state why they are sending the documents – e.g. Status – IFR, IFA, IFC and so on. If IFI at the very least send them to the package engineer for his acknowledgement of the status or take other action at his request such as sending out on a full review – never ever just file IFI documents been there, done that, results are rarely good!

Some third parties may use email to send documents in. The files will either be attached or there will be a link and instructions on how to download them from an FTP site. There must be a transmittal. Print it. Use it to compare against the files received – **make 100% sure** you have everything listed, check document numbers, revision numbers and titles. If all is well sign, scan and send it back. If there are errors, wrong files, missing files etc., incorrect revisions, send an immediate email to the sender and explain the issue and ask them to correct it ASAP. Process the correct documents and await corrected documents on a new transmittal. DO NOT delay processing what can be done. The third-party transmittal must state why they are sending the documents – e.g. Status – IFR, IFA, IFC and so on. If IFI at the very least send them to the package engineer for his acknowledgement of the status or take other action at his request such as sending out on a full review – never ever just file IFI documents.

NOTE When you process documents you may have to apply a "Review Stamp" either manually or electronically. See status codes later in the book.

In our system we have a facility for recording the receipt of signed transmittals and we will have to use it although expediting tardy signatories on transmittals is often time consuming, we must have some proof they got the documents, a necessary evidentiary trail, a signed transmittal or email acknowledgement is just that.

Some third parties may send hard copy documents in the post or on a courier. There must be a transmittal. Use it to compare against the files received **make 100% sure** you have everything listed, check document numbers, revision numbers and titles. If all is well sign, scan and send it back via email, fax or a copy via post. If there are errors, wrong files, missing files, incorrect revisions, etc., send an immediate email to the sender and explain the issue and ask them to correct it ASAP. Process the correct documents and await corrected documents on a new transmittal. DO NOT delay processing what can be done. The third-party transmittal must state why they are sending the documents – e.g. Status – IFR, IFA, IFC and so on. If IFI at the very least send them to the package engineer for his acknowledgement of the status or take other action at his request such as sending out on a full review – never ever just file IFI documents.

Note that many DC tools may only allow a single line title and/or have limited characters available and the title might be abridged. Some vendors, in particular Electrical and Pipe Fittings, use titles only another Electrical or Piping person will understand. Put yourself on the review at 1, do an immediate review, mark-up the title and show the title that is expected under the convention and send it on to the rest of the review team. It should come back from the "Approver" coded 2. If it is coded 1, 4 or 5 ask the signer to re-code it.

Also note that some vendors and contractors will not necessarily follow your revision method or history. For example, a contractor may send in a document as IFA at Rev B or C but it's the first time we have seen it. We need to establish early on if we will register it with the same revision or if ours will be A and stick to that course through-out the project life. The other possible scenario is that the contractor or vendor uses an entirely different Revision system, if they use one at all, let's say that they use P1, P2 and so on to Rev 0 and we use A,B, C and so on to Rev 0 – show your own revision in the Rev field and the contractors revision in the field next to Orig Ref as per the example below Orig Ref is 8333-452 and the Vendor Rev is 1 (ignore the Actual Controlled Doc No used):

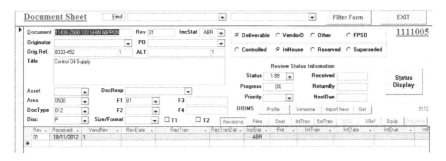

You will have put yourself on the review and show our revision number as a mark-up.

Some, not all, contractors and vendors tend to either be stubborn or do things in a "turnkey" manner and just do not show your document number anywhere on the document or cover page. Unless some form of agreement was reached to allow the use of their own numbers and not your own, which you should resist in the strongest possible way (means having to make a lot of changes at hand-over and someone even having to re-work the documents with the correct numbers), the practice is NOT to be tolerated.

The first action that must be taken is to find out if a number was reserved in the system for the document. You should have recorded any vendor/contractor document number when building your register from the Vendor Drawing and Data Requirements List/Schedule. If you can't find it do a search on a keyword or words in the title. If still no result create a new number(s) for the document(s). Put yourself on the review and show the new number on the document as close to their number as you can but in clean space. Where you did have a number reserved update your database and put yourself on the review and show the new number on the document as close to their number as you can but in clean space. Do this in **RED**.

When these documents come back to DC from the "Approver" they must at the very least be Coded 2 – Revise and Resubmit. If it is coded 1, 4 or 5 ask the "approver" to re-code it. Incorrect Titles, Document Numbers and Revision methods are NEVER to be tolerated.

Some DC tools, if a transmittal is sent in electronic format and in the right layout allow direct import of the data from the transmittal itself. Ours does – from the Main Menu choose 2 Quick Receipt and Export .xls Template. Where you have an electronic transmittal but in the wrong layout to allow direct import it is possible to use other worksheets to re-order the columns. Note that many systems do not import data from fields that have formulae in them so where you use formulae to re-order columns copy and paste special the results to another worksheet – then import that sheet. Rule of thumb here is if the transmittal has 10 or more documents on it an import can be quicker than data-bashing.

Regardless of whom sent in the documents or how - they must, within 24 hours, be processed through your controlled document register, DC Tool or EEDMS/EDMS. There is no good reason for any form of delay – delays ultimately cost money.

We've received documents and have checked the information on the transmittal or work instruction form – what next.....

10.00 Document Control – Data and Document Quality "Audits"

As we progress in our document control careers we will continue to learn about drawings and documents and some of the quality issues with the, in particular, drawings and quality of the actual data that relates to the document profile too.

Here are some examples:

Download Material\Drawings\qas-arch-l1-001_f_ifc.pdf

Download Material\Drawings\qas-arch-l1-002_a_ifi.pdf

Download Material\Drawings\qas-arch-l1-003_b_ifr.pdf

Download Material\Drawings\qas-fire-l3-001_c_ifc.pdf

These drawings are ALL incorrectly numbered.

QAS-ARCH-L1-001_F_IFC is not Architectural it is a Structural Shop Detail Drawing. It has no Revision History and it would have come from a third party there is no evidence of review/approval nor at Rev F can it be IFC.

QAS-ARCH-L1-002_A_IFI is not Architectural it is a Structural Shop Detail Drawing. It has no Revision History. Note the status is IFI – never accept anything as IFI unless the Package Engineer has indicated on a stamp that that fact is true.

QAS-ARCH-L1-003_B_IFR is not Architectural it is a Structural Shop Detail Drawing. It has no Revision History therefore the status is questionable unless we have a transmittal to that effect in which case we would put the document on review.

QAS-FIRE-L3-001_C_IFC is not Fire it is a Structural Shop Detail Drawing. It has no Revision History and it would have come from a third party there is no evidence of review/approval nor at Rev C can it be IFC.

Download Material\Drawings\version1.pdf and Download Material\Drawings\version2.pdf

Unless these drawings need us to provide a document number, which they should already have been given, the title blocks are incomplete – no Drawing No, Rev No/History, Title or E-Signatures etc.

Most, not all, drawing borders/title blocks contain a section for Cross References. I am sad to say that in the modern era this box is often not completed. True some drawings may not refer to others but that is very rare. On P&ID's we should check the Reference box and where shown on the drawing connectors (a rectangle with a pointy end either on the left or right side) the connectors should have drawing numbers in them – sometimes left blank. Note that it is not possible to reference a P&ID to every drawing that may reference to it, there are just too many, however, it should at least show other P&ID's (connectors) and in a 2D design system at the least a Mechanical GA, a Piping GA and an Instrument Layout.

We must also check the quality of the print and electronic copy what we are looking for in particular is legibility. Most of these examples are OK. However, it is not uncommon where a rendition has been made from a native CAD file that the settings were incorrect and some of the drawing is either not there at all or very faint and difficult to read. Generally, this is because the person doing the conversion did not set the print settings to monochrome and coloured lines and fonts do not then convert to black or grey (grey is also not recommended as a setting) – a give-away for this is feint or missing text which are often done in yellow in a CAD drawing.

Other issues are a conversion of a "busy" A2, A1 or A0 drawing to A3. These become difficult, if not impossible to read, because they are either too cluttered or the fonts etc. have become too small in the reduction process. Multifunction centres also do not do great scans and to keep file size down scans are done at low resolution and some data can disappear or become illegible. Often, especially after a paper review, scans are made from prints that may have been made from scans etc., and the resolution is set too low and the drawing becomes illegible. Prints from prints and scans from prints from scans can all affect drawing legibility.

In the main we do not delay the review or approval process of any drawing or document on which the quality is suspect. We mark-up a copy with our concerns and either take them by hand or raise a transmittal or workflow, to the relevant Engineer and let them decide on the status. Sometimes a DCM or LDC will have the right to mark-up and return low quality documents directly to the provider but it is not recommended Engineering may still be able to use some of the information received for their own purposes.

There are other quality issues with drawings and associated data we must check carefully.

Some Vendors will send in drawings that have multiple sheets as a single file. This is acceptable as a CAD native but NOT in 99% of document control systems – the actual individual sheets must be separated. Therefore, on receipt of the pdf rendition or scans we must split them in to their respective sheets and process each one individually and they must each have a unique number. On the odd occasion this may mean having to modify the pre-existing document no to add a sheet no. e.g. FEG-301-MM-GAR-001-01, -02 and so on (-01 being a sheet number). Worthy of note here is if you are building a proactive register and issuing out drawing numbers to use always built-in some float. If you are asked, for example, for 10 Mechanical GA drawing numbers give them 15 as it can save having to use sheet numbers at a later date.

Sheet numbering is a common and acceptable practice with Piping Isometrics and Loop Diagrams and some Shop Detail Drawings. Therefore, you will need Acrobat standard or some similar application like CutePDF to split the drawings. Also note that some vendors send as the last sheet of multi-sheet drawings a parts list. Unless it is an "exploded" drawing with a table of parts it is NOT a drawing it is a list and should be numbered and processed in that way. I have seen on a Vendors SDS a single line entry GA Drawing (of what) but when the drawings came in (in one file) there were 5 or more sheets the top one was a GA followed by a Single Line Diagram, a Connection Diagram, a Termination Diagram and a Parts List – these are ALL individual deliverables and have to be split and renumbered.

Some EPC's, this is becoming common but SHOULD be caught when processing the Vendors completed drawing and data requirements list/SDS, award a package as a discipline – let's say Mechanical and then process every document in the package as Mechanical. They are NOT. For example, a conveyor system is awarded. The conveyor system as a whole is mechanical but some individual elements of it are not there is likely to be a P&ID, Instrument Drawings, Motor Drawings, Electrical Cables and Controllers, box sections etc. these are NOT mechanical and MUST NOT be processed as such so check every drawing carefully to ensure the data in the profile is actually correct when processing – if it is incorrect renumber the drawing and provide the correct data and ask the lead engineer/package engineer to status code 2 (revise and resubmit) the incorrectly coded drawings.

Your "Specification or Standard" for drawings may dictate a language or languages that are acceptable – usually English - and sometimes one other, for example, Mongolian. Not all vendors comply. Therefore, at the very least the drawing should be review status 2. Again, if you see something of this nature put yourself on the review team, first, mark-up the drawing straight away and send it on.

The way drawings and documents are being superseded or cancelled is becoming an issue too. If a document has never been submitted to DC and is to be cancelled this is not a huge problem – tell DC. They will then record in their DC tool that the document has been cancelled and the number becomes available for re-use. However, if a document is cancelled that does have a revision history then it MUST be cancelled correctly:

> Take the Document up to the next Revision and in the Revision History the word Cancelled must be added. On documents the word cancelled must appear at 45 degrees across the entire top page and on drawings in across the entire drawing in very large, bold, letters. E.g. If the existing Revision is 0 the document MUST be revised to Rev 1 as Cancelled.

> Submit to DC, who will update their DC tool and send the document out on a transmittal or workflow to others who had already received it (except losing bidders). Under no circumstances can the document number ever be re-used where history exists.

Superseding documents correctly is also very important. The ONLY, in my opinion, correct method of doing this is to:

Take the Document up to the next Revision in the Revision History the word Superseded By and the New Document Number must be added e.g. Superseded by FEK-302-ME-GAD-0010. On drawings the word Superseded (IN CAPS) by and the new Document number MUST appear in big, bold, letters at 45 degrees across the entire drawing. On documents the word Superseded, and the New Document Number must be added and appear at 45 degrees across the entire top page in very large, bold, Capital letters.

It is arguable that the correct revision for the new document should either be A or 0, depending on where in the design the older one got to. However, it is now not uncommon and acceptable for the new document to begin its revision history at one revision higher than the last document. E.g. The last document was at Rev 1 and was taken to Rev 2 when superseded the new document would be Rev 3. Note that in the revision history the words Supersedes (Document No) must appear.

Submit to DC the correctly revised and superseded document and the new one. DC will update their DC tool by updating the revision, changing the status(s) to Superseded and adding ★★★Superseded by [Doc No]★★★ to the front of the document title or in a comments box. Where cross referencing to other documents is done the new document is cross referenced and vice versa. The new document is also to be added to the database and transmitted to anyone who had the old document (except losing bidders).

Additional steps for DC's:

Add the new document, with a reference in a comments box back to the Superseded document, to the DC database.

Supersede the old document, with a reference in the Title and comments box to the new document, in the DC database.

In Drawcon in the superseded document click on the Dset tab.

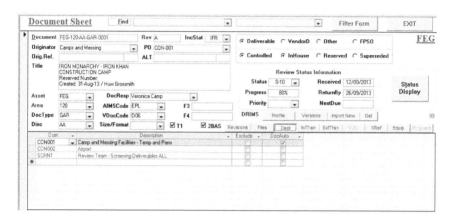

Place your cursor in the grey area to the left of the first DSet Number hold down CTRL and drag down so they are all highlighted then hit CTRL C.

Find the new document profile, select the DSet tab place the cursor on the grey area to the left of the first blank line hit CRTL V.

Raise a transmittal for BOTH documents to all active recipients in all DSets.

Go back to the document profile for the S/S document. Select the Dset Tab. Check off DocAuto and check Exclude for all DSets.

In other tools you may need to enter the Matrix system and apply a filter on the S/S Doc No obtain a list of matrices, add the new document then follow similar steps to those above.

Superseding or Cancelling existing documents just by stamping them and writing (in the case of S/S) across them what the new document number is IS NOT and NEVER has been acceptable practice.

Your "Specification or Standard" for drawings may dictate a measurement system to be used - most commonly metric. Not all vendors comply. In some cases, the use of Imperial is acceptable for example pipes/pipe fittings are still manufactured in Imperial sizes. Therefore, at the very least the drawing should be review status 2. Again, if you see something of this nature put yourself on the review team, first, mark-up the drawing straight away and send it on. Imperial is most common on Docs/Drgs from the USA and Canada but generally, oddly, not the UK.

I always also quickly check or get to know any Standard or Procedure that tells vendors or us how we/the client require Manuals and MDR's.

I'm sad to say I have seen two big issues recently with MDR's. One is common the other not so. An MDR should contain the fully signed off ITP. Further if you see an MDR that has no "quality issues" that were addressed such as Non-Conformances start asking questions. It is rare, does happen, that during the construction/manufacture process a mistake is not made that requires some form of corrective action – especially where there is a lot of welding done by humans or machines. Remember we are human mistakes are made and machines make them too. I have on more than one occasion seen faultless MDR's and the equipment delivered was faulty or had welds that failed further inspections.

11.00 The Controlled Document Register

11.01 Mandatory Document "Profile" Meta-data – What must we capture?

In Chapter 6 – pages 47 and 48 – we discussed the most Common document control methods. We will be required to maintain one of three different types of document control register they are:

Reactive – We add documents to the register only on receipt.

Proactive – We populate the register before design work or vendor data is due including due date fields

Hybridised – We populate the register before design work or vendor data is due but do not have due date fields (many do have date fields for "next due" once transmittals and workflows are raised to track the progress of the actual transmittal/workflow or the date when a re-submission is required.

It is wise, where the DC tools in use permit it, to keep 2 or 3 separate registers for each project:

- Design (In-house and subcontracted Deliverables)
- Vendor (for Vendor Data)
- Reference Material – drawings and documents either provided by "corporate" or the "client" that are unlikely to change as a result of the project design work.
- Shop Detail – this is not often done however, where bandwidth can be an issue across a network it is wise to keep a separate register for Shop Detail Drawings as they can number in the 100's of thousands.

Regardless of whether we use Reactive, Proactive or Hybridised methods or if the registers are split as above, we must collect certain information against every document.

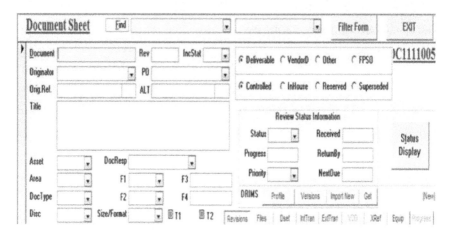

An example screen shot of a Reactive Document Control Database Document Profile

We MUST capture – Document No, Rev, IncStat, PO No (where a vendor) any Originators (third party) reference number or a client's document number [where we cannot use them as the Controlled Doc No for any reason] in the Alternate (ALT) document number field, Asset, Area, DocType, Disc, Title and later Review Status, Received, Return By and Next Due are mandatory but populated by the system from workflows or transmittals or when data (i.e. a new revision) is entered. Note a reserved revision – may not have a date recorded.

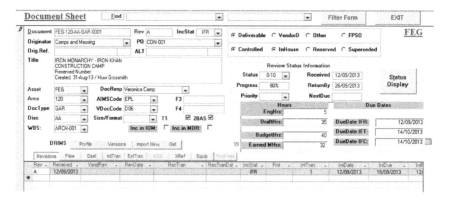

An example screen shot of a proactive document register document profile. Note that the revision history should show a – (no revision, Reserved Status) from when the information was first added. Sometimes, quite rare now, document controllers need to partly manage the budget hours against each drawing for Contracts department, Engineering and Drafting. Therefore, fields for these values must be present when this information has to be collected.

The mandatory fields for a Proactive document control register document profile are:

> Due Date IFR;
> Due Date IFT;
> Due Date IFC★
>
> ★These can then link out to early start and late finish date in Primavera/Scheduling tool,
>
> To Be Handed Over (2BHO shown here as T1); and
> To Be As Built (2BAS)
> We should also populate the check boxes In IOM and In MDR

Many of the other fields shown here are user options and may not be mandatory however any new system should allow the user, DC, to populatable drop downs (shown as F1, F2 and so on above) with names for the fields provided and in the actual configuration/library table a check box for Mandatory. ALL other fields are non-mandatory but in the main useful.

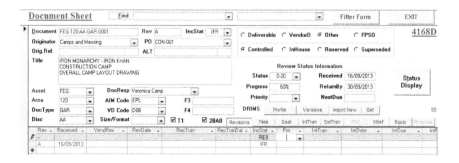

This is an example screenshot of an Hybridised Document Register – Document Profile (note I have not yet raised transmittals therefore they do not show in the Rev History subform). Also note the Rev History starting with – and the IncStat of Res. There is no received date as the document has not been received but this can be populated with the date the document number was reserved. There are no Due Date fields but once transmittals are raised date fields are populated by the system.

We must also be able to collect relationships to other files, especially Controlled Docs (one to many)

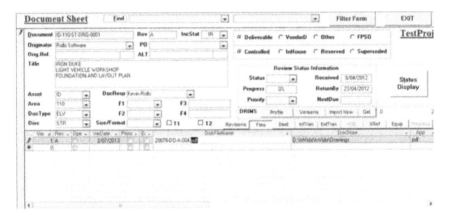

And

Relationships to Internal and External Distribution Matrices – NOTE this information should be recorded by your DC Tool when you set-up each Matrix

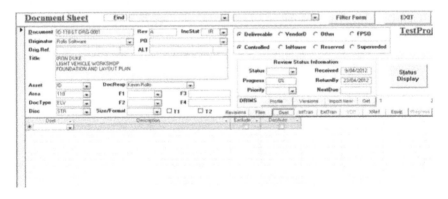

Having some function to be able to see Internal and External Transmittal Histories is also important it need not be in this format but must be easy to find (this information MUST be recorded by your DC tool when you raise transmittals or activate workflows):

External Example

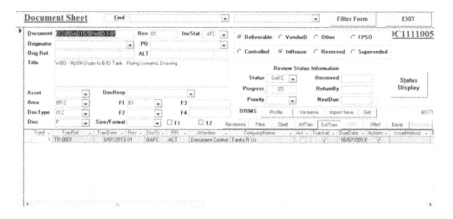

Internal Example

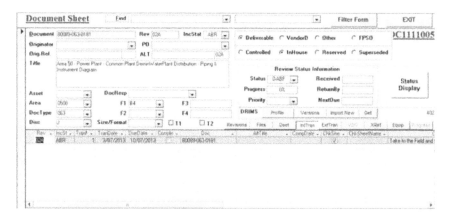

11.01.1 Populating a ProActive or Hybribidised Regsiter – Where do We Obtain the data

11.01.1.1 Design Register:

- A majority of projects would have undergone some form of Study (Pre-FEED) and FEED. There will be valuable data we can obtain from these at the very least PFD and P&ID drawings. The PFD's will be close to 100% correct. P&ID's will be around 60% complete. There may also be an overall and other model files we can obtain – all this information provides us with a clear idea of what we are going to design and build.

   PFD Drawings are very easy to read. The FEED P&ID's will not be too difficult to read.

- Where we are working for a "client" they should have required the submission of a Drawing and Data List – this will even provide us with some valuable dates
- Procurement – will have some form of Contracts and P/O's schedule (often in excel) this will also provide us with some valuable dates and provide a guide to what Engineering Requisitions, Specifications, Calculations, the List of our Documents to be sent out, the Vendor Drawing and Data Requirements List to be sent out and Datasheets will or may need to be done.

   In the main we would expect to have a majority of the documents to be sent out on a Tender to have been submitted to DC for IFR approximately, depending on how compressed the schedule is, 4 to 6 weeks before the tender package is due out. We would expect IFT documents in DC about 1 week prior to the issue of the Tender (longer if we have to chase signatures) and IFC documents in DC about 1 week prior to Award (longer if we have to chase signatures).

Note that there could be another review period between IFT and IFC often designers use information they have to hand which might not be 100% up to date and/or Tenderers will make suggestions relative to the design and this will be cause for some back-drafting. There may also be an IFA process where documents must be sent to a client or other third party, for example a government appointed "authority" who checks/approves design of, e.g. Pressure Vessels. Therefore, the time between the end of the Tender Evaluation period and Award might appear to be a bit extended.

○ Scheduler – the Project Schedule (early start and late finish) will also provide us with some valuable dates and the WBS from which we could derive our Work packs.

Nearly all Project Schedules will have entries for Design of various Plant or System Areas (by discipline) we would expect to start to see documents in DC around 4 to 6 weeks (depending on discipline and the complexity of the "system" being designed after the early start date shown on a schedule. The late finish date is often the IFC date – As Building is normally a separate schedule element.

We also need to find out from the Drawing Office and Engineering Managers what kind of design will be being done. If the project is going to be mostly or completely 3D we will need to find out if they intend to produce 2D drawings at all. Note Electrical and Instrumentation Drawings, piping under 5mm (and Piping Iso's – all diameter pipes) and most Civil drawings are done in 2D however, 3D design tools might also produce 2D structural, piping and mechanical drawings.

Purely 3D design, where 2D "cuts" are to be taken by the constructors etc, significantly reduce the number of 2D material we will deal with.

Any Hybrid or Pro-Active Design document register is only likely to be around 80% correct. 80% is far better than 0%. Amendments are made on the fly for unexpected documents or subject to TQ's/RFI's. MoC's and ECR's.

Working with the information we were able to obtain from others and in close conjunction with the Drawing Office and Engineering Managers we should be able to develop a list of deliverables and other documents to be produced. Often this is done in excel and then imported into the DC application. We will be using a Bulk Number generator in DrawCon but we could import, using queries, an excel spreadsheet.

Other information that we may need can be obtained, often on the fly from:

- o Equipment Lists
- o Valve Lists
- o Instrument Lists (May Be in Valve List where the Valve is controlled by an Instrument)
- o Piping Line Lists (Pipes) ★★
- o Cable Schedules (Cables) ★★

★★ This information will appear on drawings and in some documents but is rarely associated with Documents in the Document Register. My preference is to record these in the Equipment list in Drawcon but they can be one later as a catch-up when snowed under by the amount of material passing through DC.

11.01.1.2 Vendor Register:

- o During the IFT process the potential vendors should have been sent a Vendor Drawing and Data Requirements List (VDDRL). On award or shortly after a discussion related to this list at a Kick-Off meeting we can start to populate our Vendor Register.
- o Vendor registers are also built on the fly as not all contracts and PO's are awarded at the same time and often TQ's, RFI's and Variations from the vendors will bring about change to the register.
- o VDDRL's are often the first deliverable required from a vendor and re-named Vendor Document Schedule (VDS). These are often excel spread-sheets with deliverables due a set number of

days or weeks post award. We can calculate (if the spreadsheet does not) due dates from this data.

11.01.1.3 Shop Detail Drawing Register(s):

○ When PO's or Contracts are awarded to specialised Shop Detailers they will be able to provide us with a rough number of drawings they will produce and in what order on something similar to a VDDRL/VDS.

It is possible that Shop Drawings will be done in-house, and we will need to speak with the people doing this work, possibly via the Drawing Office Manager, regarding the approximate number of drawings they will produce broken down by Plant/System Area.

To my knowledge only some of the major 3D design applications can produce Shop Detail drawings in the same way they can produce Piping Isometrics – this might have changed. When I last worked on an all 3D project the specialist fabrication companies/detailers did not have a method of "feeding" the native 3D files in to a system that then produced the Shop Detail drawings, as many/most can for 2D natives, it was all done manually – again this may have changed.

○ Management of SD's varies – some EPC's add them to a DC tool but do not review them at all. Some review only the high level Marking Plans and only review the "lesser" drawings if an error is found. Yet others manage and review all SD's.

11.02 What "might" we need to capture for Op's Portals / CMS

It can be argued that it is NOT a DC responsibility to collect this information and some DC tools lack the functionality to do it. Some of the more integrated/intelligent CAD tools capture the data for internal design but for subcontracted or vendor design they cannot or have to be manually updated which, often, does not happen until hand-over (in a panic). When we have a lot of material to process it is simpler to process that material and get it out and then go back to capture this information.

As with document profile data, where internal design is concerned, we may be able to obtain a .CSV file from the CAD system administrator with a lot of this information.

> Document to Equip/Tag Relationships. Simplifies making an Operations Portal and DOES speed up searches during construction – site people in construction and operations tend to know their Tag/Equipment numbers very well and if that information is not in a document title (not unusual), or another field specifically for that purpose, it can make finding a document very difficult where no X-Ref exists in your database to work with. Sometimes, not always, equipment numbers may not carry a plant/system area code which could make our search for a non-referenced document even more difficult.

> Document to Document Relationships. Very handy to do – for example - if the P&ID in the Screenshot below were to be the subject of an ECR/MOC we can ask if the related P&ID's & other drawings listed might also change or need to be changed. If the relationships were a little more complete in this example, we may also be able to ask what GA drawings, piping isometrics and/or loop diagrams might need to change.

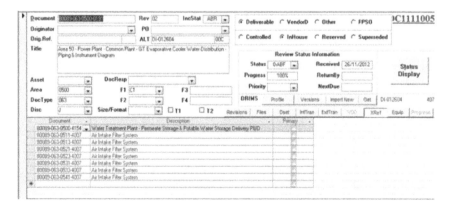

The system should also have some intelligence. This example only shows the cross references on the actual P&ID drawing itself however if a search were done it is likely we would find piping isometric drawings and loop diagrams that are also associated with the P&ID – these should automatically populate the P&ID cross reference metadata too so we see a full list. In an Access based system or one that uses, for example, Crystal Reports if you are familiar enough with the table structure it is quite simple to write a query structure for a report that will find all cross-referenced drawings/docs based on a filter using a drawing or document number.

11.03 Basic Education on How to Read a Drawing and "Mine" Drawings and Documents for Data

In the appendices are a number of drawings. Some are good and some bad. Refer Appendix 4.

Let's look at these:

> Download Material\Drawings\lf806-03rev0r14.pdf
> Download Material\Drawings\lf806-04rev0r14.pdf
> Download Material\Drawings\lf806-05rev0r14.pdf
> Download Material\Drawings\lf806-06rev1r14.pdf
> Download Material\Drawings\lf806-f-1rev0r14.pdf
> Download Material\Drawings\lf806-f-2rev0.pdf

We need to "Mine" them for data to add to our DC application, assuming we have not added them proactively and need to add the information reactively.

For each one we must find:

The Document No
The Project or Asset ID
The System/Plant Area Code
The Discipline

The Document Type
The Revision
The Tag/Equipment No(s)
The Title

For LF806-F-1 and F-2 also find Tag/Equipment numbers and valve numbers.

11.04 Practical Exercise

11.04.1 (Reactive Document Register Document Profile)

Follow the DrawCon installation instructions in Appendix 2.

NOTE WELL DrawCon is a Database with very limited exceptions it is not necessary to click Save each time data is entered.

From the Main Menu under Processes click C – Projects then

Click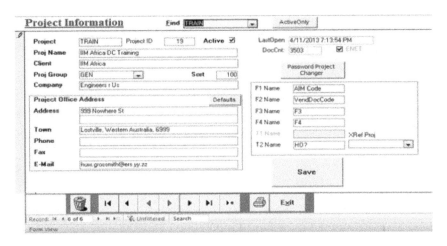

This opens a new form complete it as below

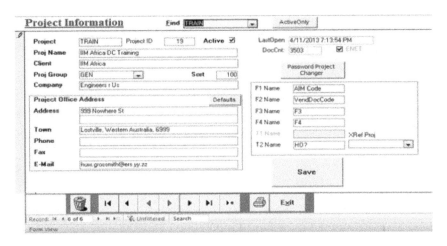

E-mail must be your own email address and a valid one for returning this assessment to.

Click Save to create a project – this is quick you may not see it happen. We will accept all the default values it imports for the time being.

Click exit.

Open the Document Form from the main menu. Enter the data for the six drawings you are mining data from. Note that the Asset, Area, Discipline and DocType drop down fields are not set to mandatory but MUST be completed.

Our Document Numbers will be:

FEK-750-ST-DTL-NNNN (you find the next available No) for …. M-03,

FEK-750-ME-DTL-NNNN (you find the next available No) for M-004, 5, 6; and

FEK-750-PR-PID-NNNN (you find the next available No) for F-001 and F002.

NOTE, in the "real world" these drawings may not be the first in each sequence.

The drawings themselves above the title block contain a list of reference drawings – add those too with a – as the revision number and Reserved as the Status Codes. F-002 has no list but there is a connector on the drawing showing a connection to F-001 add that to the database too.

Our Revision is A for the three drawings above and the IncStat / DocStat will be IFR / 0-20 respectively.

The Vendors Document Number must appear in the Orig. Ref. Field with their revision in the box to the right of that.

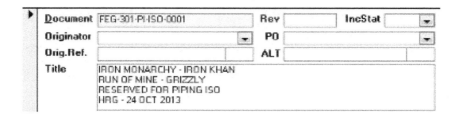

There is a Dupe Doc button that can be used to copy data from an existing entry to a new one, document numbers CAN NOT be repeated you will have to provide a new Sequence Number. Once done go into the document you just made and update any necessary information in the profile.

Set-up ALL Document/Document Relationships by selecting the XREF button – note by default the Revisions Button is depressed.

XRef

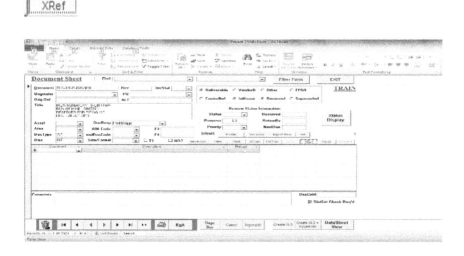

Select the Cross-Referenced drawings by using the arrow at the right side of the Documents field. The document you numbered 0001 must be the primary document.

Select the Files button and for each drawing

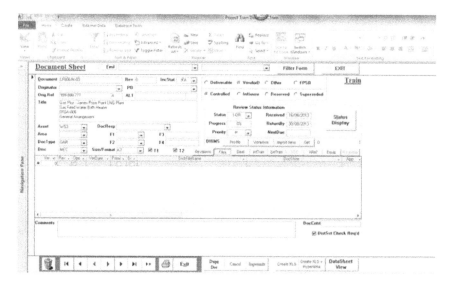

Drop your cursor in

DiskFileName

and double click then browse your way to where you downloaded or otherwise saved the file to. Normally this would be a network share or something like Sharepoint.

11.04.2 (Hybridised Document Register Document Profile)

Now add to your Training/Train Database the following Drawings (with appropriate 3 or 4 line titles):

1 x 3D Model – FEK-700-ST-D3D-nnnn

5 x Structural GA Drawings (uncommon in an all 3D project) – FEK-700-ST-GAR-nnnn (must be

sequentially numbered and the last line of the title must contain [at the end] Sheet n of n

Refer to Appendix 9 - How to Use the Block Number Generator in DrawCon Pages 273-279 (Steps 1 through 5) Only and add:

> 1000 Piping Isometric Drawings – FEK-700-PI-ISO-nnnn; and

> 1000 Shop Detail Drawings – FEK-700-ST-SHF-<u>V</u>nnnn (these drawings will come from a specialist vendor)

NOTES: 1. We usually use the Piping Isometric Drawing Number but in this case we are NOT. 2. The design for each of the load-out chutes is identical therefore the drawings all go in Area 700 instead of 701, 702, 703 and 704. In the "real world" it is likely that the first set of drawings IFR/IFA will all be done in Area 701 and once approved replicated at Rev 0 – IFC for Areas 702, 703 and 704.

11.04.3 (Proactive Document Register Document Profile)

At present the Due Date fields have been removed from the DrawCon document profile form (they do appear in the table(s) when updates are complete (with fields in the Block Number Generator for them) the Document Profile will look something like this:

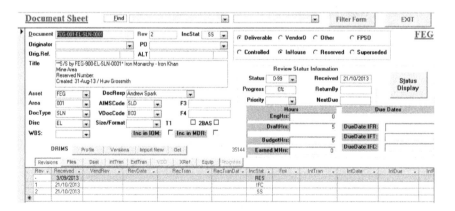

Because the fields exist in the relevant table we will populate them using a query. We will set the dates as follows:

Drawing	Due Date IFR	DueDate IFT	DueDate IFC
3D Model	Today plus 4 Weeks	Today plus 8 Weeks	Today plus 12 Weeks
GA	Today plus 6 Weeks	Today plus 10 Weeks	Today plus 14 Weeks
Iso's	Today plus 6 Weeks	Today plus 10 Weeks	Today plus 14 Weeks
Shop Drawings	Today plus 12 weeks	N/A	Today plus 16 Weeks

Open Drawcon and ensure your project file is the one that is open. Select Create from the Menu Ribbon

Select Query Wizard (X)
Select Simple Query Wizard

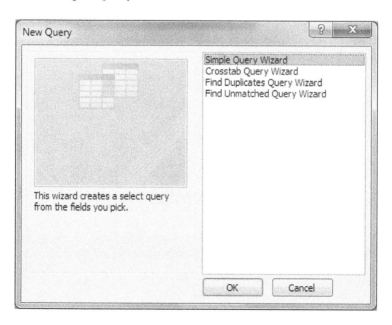

Select the Table tDoc

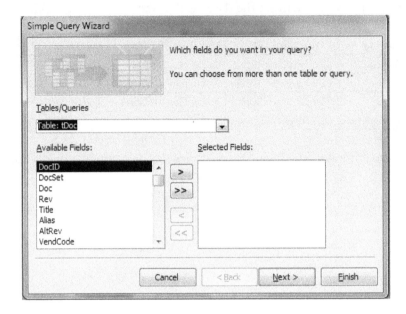

Select the fields as shown below:

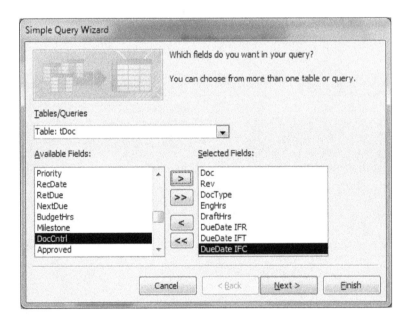

Note we are "assuming" [assumptions are dangerous] that we will be populating Budget Hour fields too.

Click Next

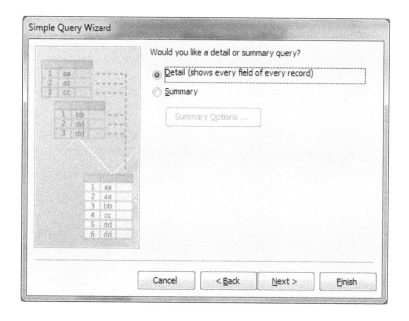

Click Next

Select modify the Query Design

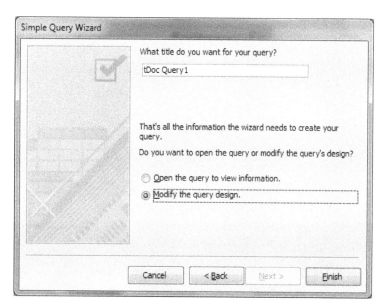

Click Finish

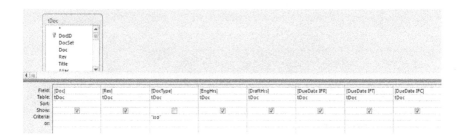

Check the Show check box off for DocType and add under Criteria – Iso
Click the Run Button

Run

Make sure you have 1000 entries. Shown in the grey ribbon at the
bottom left 1 of xxxx
Click the View (Design) button

View

Click the Update Button

Update

Open Excel (or another spreadsheet application)
In A1 add todays date (in the example 7/5/2014 – UK Date Format)

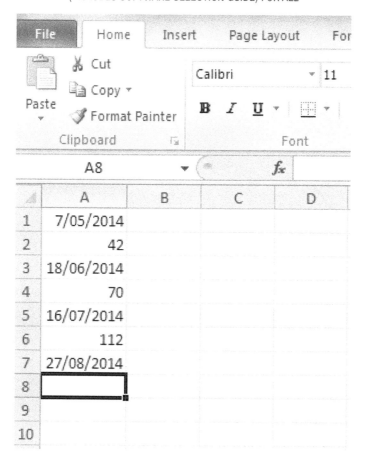

In A2 (for ISO's) add +6★7
In A3 the formula is +A1+A2
In A4 (for ISO's) add +10★7
In A5 the formula is +A1+A4
In A6 (for ISO's) add +16★7
In A7 the formula is +A1+A6

Add the dates and hours to the fields as shown below

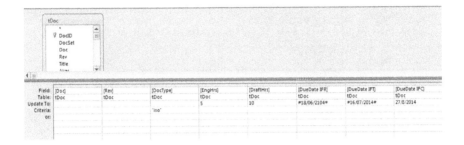

Field:	[Doc]	[Rev]	[DocType]	[EngHrs]	[DraftHrs]	[DueDate IFR]	[DueDate IFT]	[DueDate IFC]
Table:	tDoc	tDoc	tDoc	tDoc	tDoc	tDoc	tDoc	tDoc
Update To:				5	10	#18/06/2104#	#16/07/2014#	27/8/2014
Criteria:			"iso"					
or:								

Select Run

You should get a Pop-up message saying you are about to update 1000 rows.

Select Yes.

REPEAT the above with SHF in the Doctype field. There will be no budget hours for drafting ([drafthrs] but there will be 5 budget hours for Engineering [EngHrs] for the reviews.

ALSO note the dates must be changed to meet the criteria in the table on page 78.

Select Run and Yes (if 1000 records)

Close the query no need to save it.

If necessary, return to the Main Menu

Select the Database Tools Tab from the Menu Ribbon

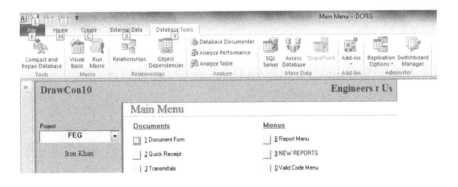

Select Compact and Repair Database (F)

The program will close and re-open. This reduces the file size and removes any deletions and repairs any other odd "lumps and bumps".

11.04.4 Document Register - Document Profile [ALL]

From the Main Menu select 3 Transmittals

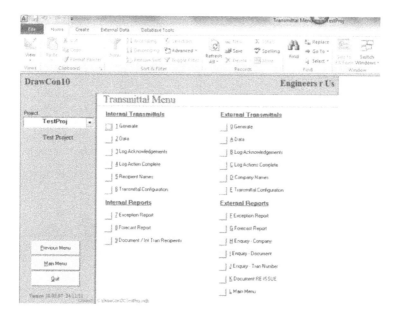

First select 5 Recipient Names – these are people who are on the "internal" project team and add some names/positions and details with made up email addresses.

This is just a simple table and you can use any code that makes sense to you.

When done click exit.

Then select D Company Names and add the names of two fictitious contractors, Topsides r Us and Jackets r Us, with made up email addresses

Attn. is DocCon@ and CC is QA@. Then Exit and select main menu. Note you must select >* to enter each new company the lines in the subform are for addressees at each individual company only.

NB After adding the first Company you must click the ▸▸ button for every new company to be added.

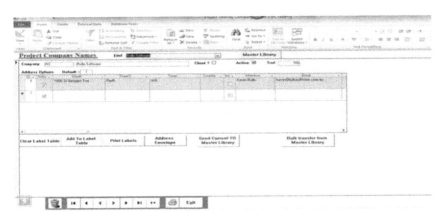

Open B Equipment Under data and add all the Tag/Equipment and Instrument Numbers from the P&ID (LF806-F-1 and 2) if you are unsure what they are make up a description.

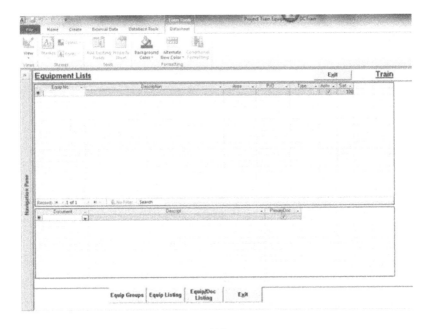

Select the drawing(s) from the drop down box.

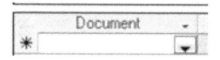

HINT

for the FEK-750-ST-DTL-NNNN (you find the next available No) for …. M-03; AND

FEK-750-ME-DTL-NNNN (you find the next available No) for M-004, 5, 6;

drawings we added the only Tag Number is 01-HX-06

For the P&ID's add the relevant drawing number against the Tag/Instrument numbers shown on the drawings.

Exit and Return to the Main Menu

NOTE This also can be done in "reverse" by exiting from the Equipment List and Opening the Document Form then selecting the Equip button and selecting the Tags/Instruments from the Drop Down list (one line each). This tends to be a little slower.

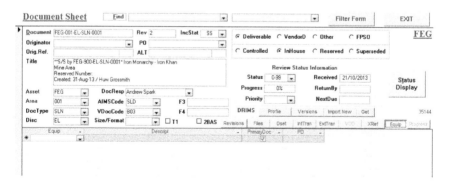

From the Main Menu under Data - Open A PO List

Order List			Vendors	Resp	Groups		Exit	
PONum	PoName		Vendor	Resp	Group	Vend-Data	Active	Sort	ID
▶			▼	▼	▼	☑	☑	100	(New)

This is a simple table one line per entry.

CON-001 is Design/Construct Platform Topsides and it has or will go to Topsides are Us the Responsible Person is the Lead Process Engineer

CON-002 is Design/Construct Platform Jacket and it has or will go to Jackets are Us the Responsible Person is the Lead Structural Engineer

Exit and return to the Main Menu

Select Document Form and against the 6 drawings you entered to the Reactive Database (11.04.01) and select CON-001 in the PO Drop down.

Next.......

12.00 Dissemination of Up-To-Date Information

We have received all of these documents and have entered them in to or updated our DC tool now what….. well we send them out!

12.01 Transmittals/Workflows

We've collected all this information what must we do with it – DUI - Dissemination of Up To Date Information. Some of this material is a repeat of material seen before:

Any document that is "Issued" or otherwise sent to any internal party (usually for review or approval) or external party (for any reason) is sent either on a transmittal or workflow.

Most commonly in an EEDMS internally issued documents are sent on a workflow and externally issued documents are sent on a transmittal.

Workflows and Transmittals, unless one offs, are managed in distribution matrices:

12.02 Distribution Matrices

12.02.1 Internal

Usually Review Teams (Squads) for Squad Checking/Review of Documents. E.g. A mechanical drawing – Mech Eng, Piping Eng, Electrical Eng, Structural/Civil Eng, Instrument Eng, Process Eng back to Mech Eng.

12.02.2 External

External Matrices evolve on the fly they typically start with a list, found in a PO given to you by procurement or Engineering, of Documents in the "Package" and vendors. On award the "losing" vendors are deactivated but other people are added such as your own site DC and Constructor(s)

Let's recap and go back to our Classification spread-sheet. We established the who against document types.

Document Classification.xlsx

UNLESS YOUR EMPLOYER USES AN EEDMS/ EDMS THAT HAS A CHECK-OUT FUNCTION NO DOCUMENT SHOULD EVER LEAVE DOCUMENT CONTROL UNLESS IT IS SHOWN ON A TRANSMITTAL OR WORKFLOW. COPIES, MADE BY DC PERSONNEL, MAY BE GIVEN TO INTERNAL PERSONNEL ONLY AND THEY ARE NOT TO GIVE THEM TO ANY THIRD PARTY BY THAT PERSON FOR ANY REASON. IT IS ALSO WISE TO STAMP COPIES MADE AS COPY. SOME EEDMS/EDMS APPLICATIONS DO THIS AUTMATICALLY WHEN PRINTS ARE MADE.

LETTER'S, EMAIL'S, FAXES ETC. UNDER NO CIRCUMSTANCES CONSTITUTE A FORMAL TRANSMITTAL HOWEVER MAY BE USED TO CONVEY A TRANSMITTAL AND CONTROLLED DOCUMENTS TO ANOTHER PARTY (USUALLY EXTERNAL)

12.03 Review and Approval

During their life cycle all Engineering Documents undergo some formal Review and Approval process – as we established in our matrices.

Documents coming into Document Control will have a Status the most common are (incoming status):

IFR - Issued for Review
IFT - Issued for Tender

IFA - Issued for Approval

IFC - Issued for Construction

After the Review/Approval process another status may be applied – the most common are (review status):

1 - Proceed

2 - Proceed as Noted, Revise and Resubmit

3 - Do Not Proceed, Revise and Resubmit

4 - Accepted as IFC/Certified Final

5 - Accepted as As Built/Delivered

6 - Information Only

NOTE WELL – we have not used the word Approved in any Status Code – Incoming or Review there have been legal problems associated with the use of the word Approved even where a "get-out" has been used on the "stamp".

Also note that if the company is reviewing documents from Third Parties it must have a "get out" clause on the review stamp/cover sheet similar to:

Review by The Principal does not absolve the contractor/vendor of the responsibility for ensuring that the goods/materials provided are fit for the purpose specified.

Internal reviews can be done in a number of different ways. The most common are:

Parallel – where the order is, for example:

Order	Position	Days
1	Lead Mech Eng	1
2	Lead Elec Eng	5
2	Lead Instr Eng	5
2	Lead Process Eng	5

2	Lead Structural Eng	5
2	Lead Civil Eng	5
2	Lead Piping Eng	5
2	Eng Mgr	5
3	Lead Mech Eng	2

In this example the Lead Mech Eng is the Reviewer/Approver and first in the order as a heads-up that the document(s) have been received. This is most common with External documents. If this review were being done on paper it does mean a lot of copies (often one each) and those at 2 cannot see each other's comments – which is not a problem in an electronic system where a viewer/collaboration tool is in use. In the main this is the best method.

NOTE It is smarter to use the position rather than the person's name a people tend to move around either within the company or outside of it. Using a name then means having to update the matrices each time someone moves on.

Serial – where the order is, for example:

Order	Position	Days
1	Lead Mech Eng	1
2	Lead Elec Eng	1
3	Lead Instr Eng	1
4	Lead Process Eng	1
5	Lead Structural Eng	1
6	Lead Civil Eng	1
7	Lead Piping Eng	1
8	Eng Mgr	1
9	Lead Mech Eng	1

A common approach but limiting – it only gives reviewers one day each and if this were being done on paper and DC had to track it through each reviewer that means it goes out and back in the snail mail each time. The advantage is that each person can see the others comments and are unlikely to repeat something. Where a viewer/collaboration tool is in use this still means managing an electronic method of out and back and expediting if the tool itself does not manage this process – collaboration tools do but a viewer/mark-up tool might not.

Where we have to use paper we usually for Internal Documents print the transmittal on to Pink paper – to make it easy to find when we have to expedite (we will have to) and for external documents the transmittal is blue. For that matter any two separate colours that stand out in in trays and on desks. Pink and Blue are most common. For drawings print the drawings and transmittal to Pink or Blue paper.

What can and does often happen is that a "War Room" is used. There are two methods of doing this.

1. DC taking the document to the designated room/workstation (if prints are used) and emailing the team to tell them the document is available with a copy of the transmittal. The DC then checks the room 2 or 3 days before the closing date and sends an expediting email to the late reviewers cc to the Reviewer/Approver.

   In the electronic world, where there is no collaboration tool in play, this may mean that the DC has to organise a meeting room, or keeping one block booked as a war room, that has a PC, with a viewer/mark-up tool installed and large format TV or large screen, min 21", monitor. Then sending an email with room no and link to the documents and the team can either use the room or mark-up from their own desktops.

2. The Reviewer/Approver contacting the reviewers and organising a meeting room and conducting the review in one go with all present or exempted. This can and does happen in the electronic world too.

Regardless of how they are set-up War Room reviews are by far the better way of getting reviews done. War room transmittals are usually parallel but either method is fine the order in which people attend in option 1 is up to them.

Most DC applications manage two status codes but it is none the less confusing. If the DC application has one status code and copies the "old" data to a "revision history" table when the status is changed then this is much less confusing and a simpler way of working.

Also note that until the responsible Engineer says so anything sent in as Information Only is NOT. This has been a cause of a number of problems in the past. Anything received as Information Only must be sent on "review" to the responsible engineer who can either sign off or ask for a full review.

Another rarity is document control being responsible for Intra-discipline checks. A document or document(s) to be reviewed only by the team members of the discipline that created the document.

12.04 Too many "Reviews"- what can go wrong

The ideal unless a previous review has identified an incorrect submission or a lot of errors is to allow only "one bite at the cherry" on a full review.

The issue becomes one of a reviewer finding something that was missed before and adding new comments.

Internally this causes delays and can push back the schedule.

Externally I have seen vendors who have had multiple mark-ups done on their documents, where previous comments were exempted or addressed, take one of three actions:

1. Take the job out of the workshop and put another client's, bigger, job in setting ours back some months
2. The vendor submits Variations for additional costs and possibly time
3. A combination of the above i.e. BOTH

For internal documents if the responsible engineer advises us to do a partial or complete re-review then we do what we are asked but we should keep a close watch.

For external documents sent in as Issued for Approval or second submission documents go to the responsible engineer only with access provided to the now superseded mark-up for checking. If the engineer needs a re-review in part of full comply but we should keep a close watch.

Also keep a watch on the use of Code 3 – Do Not Proceed, Revise and Resubmit some engineers tend to use it where a Code 2 – Proceed as Noted, Revise and Resubmit could be used.

NO matter what multiple reviews can cause delays and potential re-work. ALL DELAYS/RE-WORK COST MONEY

12.05 Expediting

Also refer to Proactive Document Control

All projects should have, regularly updated, a clear set of KPI's. These should not only be discussed at the "high" level meetings (because often that information is not well disseminated or suffers Chinese whisper syndrome) there should be large posters for one month ahead, a fortnight ahead and a week ahead, on notice boards through-out the project along with posters patting the team on the back for making previous KPI's. I've worked in many places and two are stand-outs in my mind with respect to this being done well and both had the same Manager – WMC and Alcan Gove G3. I have also had fantastic support from a number of CEO's, Project Control Managers and Project Managers too over the years and lacked support on other occasions making working life very frustrating indeed.

In DC if we have a proactive register, we can run Expediting reports on a daily or weekly basis and either take action or pass the report to those who have been tasked with taking action.

Late Vendor Drawings and Documents can impact final design and cause delays which ultimately cost money or force a speeding up of construction, to still meet schedule, which is NOT wise. Therefore, we must expedite.

We must also expedite internally too. We must chase internal design documents that are late or we know must be out by a certain date. We must also expedite the review team so we can send documents back to third parties without being late which also causes a lot of problems not the least of which is the possibility of your package being taken out of the workshop and someone else's going in and ours being held while that one is completed!

Internally it is wise, even if done manually, to have some form of reporting system with respect to expediting new material or tardy reviewers the ideal is a card system:

A "Yellow Card" (first strike) and "Red Card" (second strike) reporting/warning system. A Yellow Card is issued, via email or the EEDMS, at 5 working days overdue and the Engineering Manager will receive a copy, a Red Card is issued at 10 working days overdue, and the EM and Project Manager receive a copy.

While it is usually easier to take the gentle approach to expediting if DC's have been tasked with it then they must also be given some authority to expedite and where necessary to behave like a policeman in a bad mood. With no authority the attempts at expediting individuals or third parties will fail.

12.06 Practical

Open DrawCon
Then Select 0 Valid Code Menu
Select D Distribution Sets

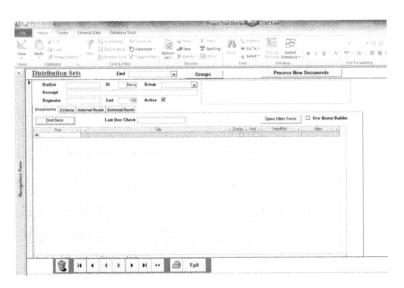

Add CON-001 in DistSet and add Topsides as the description to Descript and ignore Originator

Select the >* Button and Add CON-002 in DistSet and add Jacket as the description to Descript and ignore Originator

Click the Internal Route Tab

Internal Route

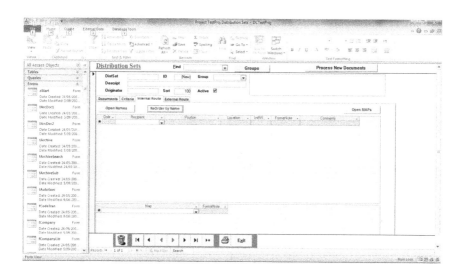

Use the Drop Down Box to select all the Internal recipients you set-up previously make Lead Mechanical Engineer First and Last

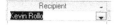

Click the External Route Tab

External Route

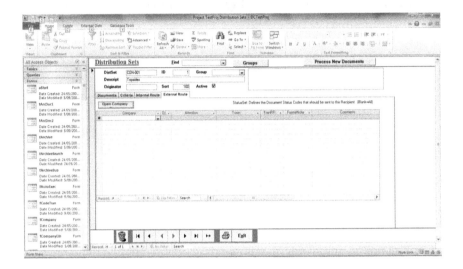

Add your two fake companies.
They are selectable from the drop down button

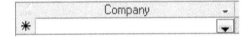

Do not select drawings and documents in these screens but you can.
Exit and return to the main menu.
Click 1 Document Form and then the DSet Tab

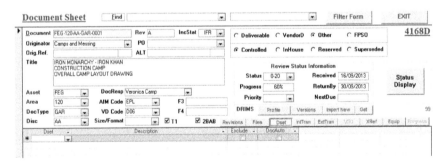

Select your matrices from the Drop Down

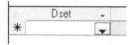

Check DocAuto

Do this for all your drawings. From now on when we add drawings we will select the DSet in this manner.

Exit

Select 3 Transmittals

Select 1 Generate under Internal Transmittals

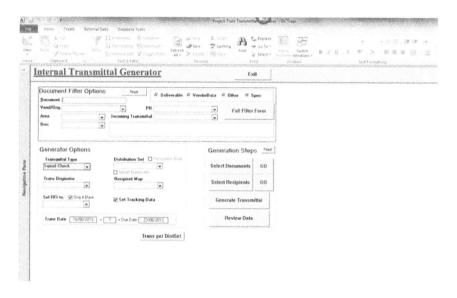

In Filter Options select the discipline for your document(s) – 1 Mechanical, 1 Structural, and 1 Process

Under Generator Options select Distribution Set and Recipient Map

Under Generation Steps select Documents then All and Continue

Then Select Recipients and All then Continue

Generate Transmittal (This is quick and you may not see anything happen at all)

Review Data

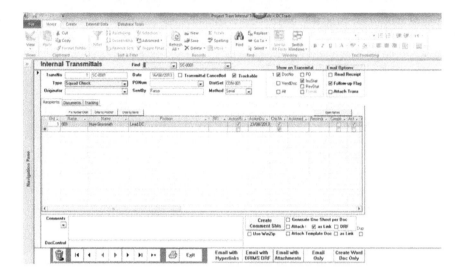

Click Email with Attachments – on a network we would use Hyperlinks for internal people and attachments and check the WinZip box tool.

When you click Email with Attachments Outlook or your email application will open, check the information and press save or send – please DO NOT send if the email address is real and the recipient might become angry or confused.

You have just sent an Internal Review Transmittal.

Exit and Exit

NOTE Because the documents are in 3 disciplines you should have 3 internal transmittals. This is being addressed as only 1, based on the Matrix, may be necessary.

Select 3 Transmittals and 0 Generate under External Transmittals

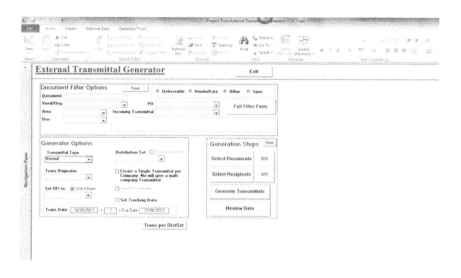

Select the Distribution Set CON-001

Check the Create a Single Transmittal per Company and Check Tracking Data

Select Documents, All, Continue

Select Recipients, All, Continue

Select Generate Transmittals

Select Review Data

Click the Green < Button, Email with Attachments (Send or Save the Outlook email message)

Click the Green > Button, Email with Attachments (Send or Save the Outlook email message)

REPEAT FOR Distribution Set CON-002

Exit, Exit and return to the main menu

NOTE we have done this for practice. It is rare to send documents to a third part for review but does happen for example some government departments/regulators require Vessel drawings sent to a nominated specialist to be reviewed.

You have just raised two external transmittals for your documents

From the main menu select 1 Document Form

Note in the Revision History the Internal Transmittal is shown.

Select the IntTran Tab and you will see more detail on the Internal
Transmittal you raised.

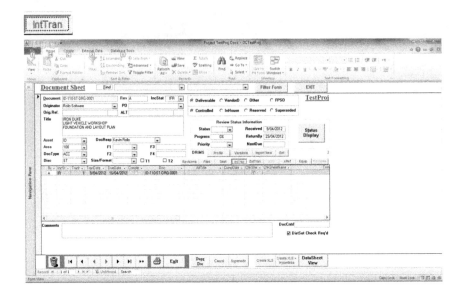

Select the ExtTran Tab and you will see the details for the External
Transmittals you raised.

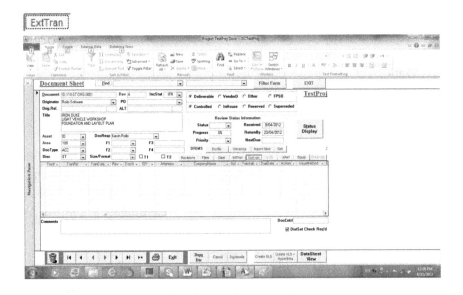

We just Disseminated Up to Date Information (DUI)

13.00 Tender Documents / Process

The Engineering and Procurement team will build between them all the documents necessary to go out in Tender Packages (the first part of the ongoing evolution of our External Matrices). There MUST be in that package a list of all the controlled documents that are to be transmitted (be careful they often get the Rev No's wrong – you will need to correct the list – on a copy – and give it back), with the contract documents (sometimes but not always managed by DC), and a list of who they are to be sent to. There is usually a version of the Vendor Drawing and Data List for documents the tenderers are to submit with the tender.

It is rare, but sometimes happens that DC has to manage the documents on that list in the Tender phase. I prefer it to happen for one main reason – if the tenderer does not submit what they were asked for or were not given some form of exemption from submitting those documents via an RFI or controlled request then will they manage to submit what they are told as a part of the actual Contract/PO if awarded? When DC is involved we can add the document list to our database with, for example, a T (to denote Tender) preceding the Sequence No and the date due. We can identify to the Package Engineering and Procurement non-conforming tenders i.e. those that did not submit what they were asked for.

Having dealt with many vendors for many years I also like to be involved in the tender review process too. Any DC who has worked with vendors gets to know them and how they operate when it comes to vendor data quite well. Vendors vary wildly with what and when they submit:

> Some are excellent they submit good, few or no mark-ups needed, data on time.

> Some are very good thy submit, few or no mark-ups needed, data but only after a reminder or two (which is why having an early reminder is a good idea)

Some are OK and submit reasonable quality data, some mark-ups, but on time

Some are OK and submit reasonable quality data, some mark-ups, but late

Some are awful and either submit very late or send in material that gets heavily marked up.

NOTE: Due to changes in personnel or ownership I have seen some vendors who were excellent with VD go bad and others come good sometimes we may have to sound our warning and accept that the people who make the final decisions will go with what they think best for the business.

Often there is very little difference between them all in the way of pricing. Cost people will most likely go for the cheapest but this can be a problem. Let's say the cheapest quote was $20,000 cheaper than the next one but the Vendor is one that has to be expedited often and sometimes submits material that is heavily marked-up. Also say the one that is $20,000 dearer is one that submits good material on time and is rarely expedited. The "not so good" vendor can cost us the $20,000 price difference in time/review/re-review and/or expediting overdue data or more $ quite quickly therefore not really creating any cost saving at all. The "materials" controllers may also want a say too – some vendors may have a reputation for late delivery or equipment that passed inspection but is of not great quality.

I always try to be involved and will always ask that an award is made to a vendor who I know will not have to be expedited on a regular basis or submit poor quality data. In the end if the award was made to the cheapest it could cost us the saving in expediting alone. Where not permitted to be involved directly in the Tender Evaluation process you will know from having raised the transmittals to the vendors who they are and who the package Engineer is if you have a concern about one or more of the vendors raise that concern with the Package Engineer and Contracts Administration and any expeditor.

14.00 Progress and Other Reports

Reports such Expediting Reports – discussed above – are standard in a majority of DC applications. We may also, rare, be required to produce progress reports. This is often done by setting a progress value against each status code. Often this means a very steep initial curve because, in the main, an IFR document is 60% complete so we may have to put in some other status codes, pre IFR, and print manual reports for the Lead Discipline Engineers to complete and return. In the example below we will accept the steep curve.

DocStatCode	DocStatName	ProgVal
1	Reviewed No Comment	90.00%
2	Reviewed with Comment	80.00%
3	Do Not Proceed	60.00%
4	Accepted as Final/IFC	95.00%
5	Accepted as As Built	100.00%
AB	As Built	100.00%
CAN	Cancelled	0.00%
IFI	Issued For information	0.00%
IFT	Issued For Tender	85.00%
IFU	Issued for Use	100.00%
IFR or INR	Issued for Review OR In Review	60.00%
RES	Reserved/In Preparation	0.00%

Most DC applications have a similar function and the reports are standard. In very rare cases we may also be required to "manage" budget hours against each deliverable for Engineering and Drafting. DrawCon can do this but the fields are hidden in our worked example version. DrawCon will also link to another Rollosoftware product where hours are recorded against each deliverable when they are worked on (most of the big EEDMS tools do this automatically). Again, the reports are in the system but sometimes have to be changed. For example, the most common method of calculating earned man-hours is to multiply the total budget hours by the progress percentage. For example, a 100 hour P&ID has been Issued for Review it has Earned 60 hours (60% x 100). Where the lead engineer is reporting more hours to complete than they have left in the budget (earned hours plus time to complete) or the actual progress is not where it should be based on the hours used we can highlight problems. However, sometimes this can become even more complicated, and another field added to your document profile for weight. Often, for example, a P&ID will have greater weight than a simple electrical drawing which will be produced from a rebadged standard drawing. The earned man-hours then could be something like Total Budget Hours x Percentage Complete x Weight. So be prepared this may happen. It can also be very confusing because you then have to know at what weighted percentage/earned man-hours = 100% completion for a discipline as it may never directly add to 100% for each discipline and more than 100% when the disciplines are summed up. I get why it is done but it's a serious pain.

Where we use a Proactive database the most commonly used dates are IFR or IFT and IFC (usually only two of them IFR and IFC). For a scheduling tool these may be reported as early start (IFR) and late finish (IFC) dates. Again, DrawCon has these fields available and are hidden in the worked example version they can be added by yourself using either F3 and F4 or by myself or Rollosoftware to the main profile. All this data can be exported in a format that can be imported to Primavera P6 or Drawcon can be directly linked, via ODBC, to Primavera P6.

In the main the most common reports we produce are Document Registers (becoming rarer with multi-access EEDMS tools) and expediting reports.

14.01 Practical

Open DrawCon

Select 3 Transmittals and Under Internal Select each of the 3 reports in turn to familiarise yourself with the reports that can be produced to expedite or forecast expediting from. The 7 Expediting Report may not open as we currently have no overdue material (you could forward date your PC/Laptop by 7 days to obtain some reports). Do the same thing for the reports under External Reports the same note applies.

Return to the Main Menu

Select 8 Report Menu under Menu's. Open each report to familiarise yourself with the reports that can be produced. Particularly the document register – click continue when the filter pops up we do not have enough documents to worry about a filter.

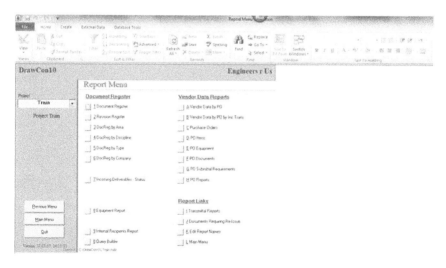

15.00 Engineering Change Requests

During the Engineering Lifecycle, as we discussed, documents are frozen at a specific revision/status – once a document is IFC the correct process for making change is for the Originator to submit an Engineering Change Request. This goes through a number of people, on a workflow or transmittal from DC, including Contract Administrators/Schedulers (cost and time involved) for approval.

An example of this could be an IFC datasheet that shows the acceptable pressure in a section of pipe as 100 bar (atmospheres) that should have been 10 bar – a simple thing to overlook. When someone checks it thoroughly the error is noticed. An ECR should be raised to change the datasheet to Rev 1 to correct the error. In this case, if the plant is close to pre-commissioning or commissioning, the datasheet may be changed in a hurry and the ECR raised after.

Unfortunately, this does not always happen and some documents are changed on the fly. Those changed as a result of either a TQ, RFI or something seen in the field during construction which requires some form of change should have that number recorded in the Rev History box for reference. Often people with construction and/or maintenance experience are not included on reviews and notice problems with the design when they come to construction and changes have to be made. Sometimes site conditions, possibly unexpected, can cause change. Remember well that just because something can be drawn does not mean it is easy or even can be done with concrete, bricks, steel and glass etc.

Once approved the document can be revised and should show the ECR number in the revision history.

In operations, As Built or handed-over documents are changed by a Management of Change Process. Similar to an ECR however, because of Operations, some are done post change in the field.

16.00 Final Documentation / As Built

Using our Document Classification Spread-sheet lets identify the types of documents that might need to be "As Built" Document Classification.xlsx . Hint Everything Electrical and Instruments is to be As Built there are others too.

As Built Definitions / Possible Phases

As Delivered – is an As Built for a particular item of equipment delivered by a Vendor that will become part of a larger whole for example a pump or motor going into a pump skid that might be being constructed by another party i.e. we provided the pump from Vendor A to Vendor B to build the pump skid.

As Constructed – the first pass of mark-ups done on site, usually prior to any form of commissioning, when construction in that area is complete sometimes known as As Mechanically Complete. Or in the example above Vendor B submits his drawing showing the completed skid.

As Pre-Commissioned – mark-ups done onsite or in a vendors yard for, usually but not always, pre-assembled modules that are to be shipped to site for final construction where (other than electrical kit such as transformers) commissioning work is done with water instead of product/gas.

As Commissioned – mark-ups done on site during the commissioning process where changes can often be made to electrical equipment such as fuses/circuit breakers and instruments. This form of commissioning might also be done in a Vendors (often Electrical Equipment) workshop.

As Handed Over – final set of mark-ups done onsite after, if we are responsible for it, a trial plant run period of, say, 3 months where changes can also be made.

Often, not always, designers (drafters) are sent to site to do this work onsite. Many current PMC/EPCM companies try to avoid signing contracts where they are responsible for operational commissioning and/ or performance guarantees on the plant as a whole. This has, thankfully, created a whole new field of specialised commissioning and hand-over companies but they may not have any responsibility for handing over documents other than mark-ups back to the owner/operator or PMC.

16.01 Hand-Over Methodologies

Try to meet the client's needs (remember the saying the client is seldom right but NEVER wrong)

It is for them and, to a degree, and for us easier to hand documents over on a system by system/area by area basis this is progressive, and it may mean some parts of the plant E.g. Crushing can be made operational before others.

The best we can hope for is a full electronic hand-over either in phases or at the end of the project.

The tip truck method means we "stockpile" everything and give them the lot in one go at the end easier for us but, in the printed world, can destroy space – Manuals and MDR's eat up a lot of space especially if the client needs 4 or more copies of each – often the MDR goes straight to archive but Manuals can end up in an Asset Library onsite and in the CBD operations office and in the Operations Control Room(s) on the Asset.

The simplest method of keeping track of what must be done with ALL project documents is to have, as part of the document profile, 4 simple check boxes: To Be As Built (remember not everything is); To Be Handed-over (again not everything is); Include in IOM (your project may be responsible for compiling a single Ops and Maintenance Manual from those received from vendors etc.); and Include in MDR (as for manuals). There is, or was in the marketplace software that could be "integrated" to DC tools (via ODBC or an API suite) that, when activated, by you and provided information as to what sections the Manual or MDR was to have and in what order (the system asks). It then proceeded to, based on the check boxes in your system and linked files, find the files and appropriate sections and place them all in the right order in to one much larger file that, when complete, is ready to send out to print or burnable/copiable on to CD/DVD/Memory Stick/External HDD.

Also note that where we have an As Built check box that documents that do not need to be As Built can be "progressed" to 100%.

With these check boxes we can also design reports for the documents needing to be As Built and expedite on those reports and can send registers of documents to be handed-over to operations in excel format for guidance on when they will be required.

In DrawCon from the Main Menu select 8 Report Menu
Then Select 0 Query Builder

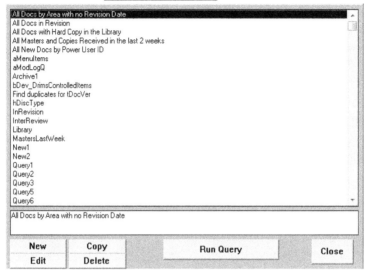

Select New
Select Simple Query Wizard

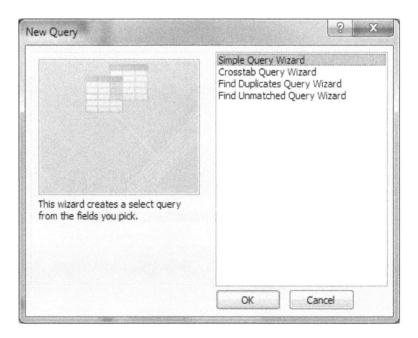

and OK

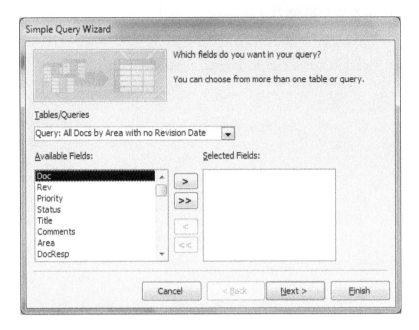

From the Drop Down Select Table: tDoc

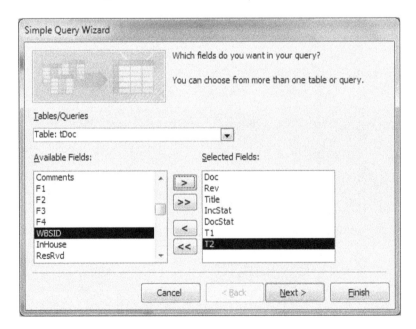

Select the fields shown as below

Click Next

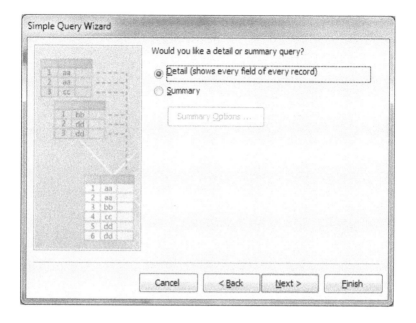

The Next again

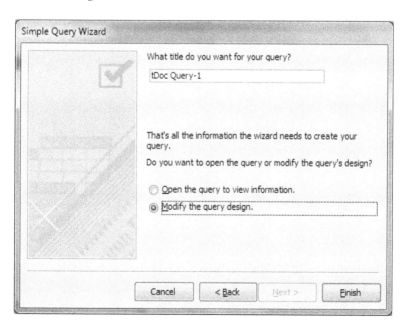

Change the name as shown

Also change the radio button to Modify the query design

Click Finish

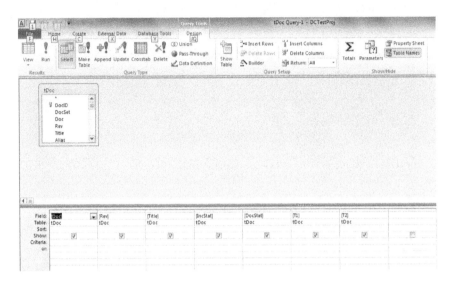

In Criteria in T1 and T2 type the word Yes

From the Menu Ribbon click Show Table

Show
Table

Add the tables tIncStat and tDocStat the relationship connections will appear automatically.

From the table tIncStat drag IncStatName to the field next to IncStat and check IncStat off.

From the table tDocStat drag DocStatName to the field next to DocStat and check DocStat off.

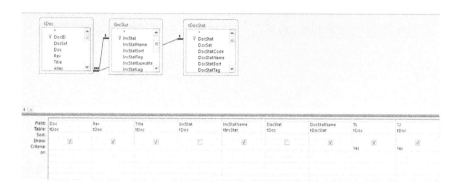

Click the Run Button

Run

The result will be something like:

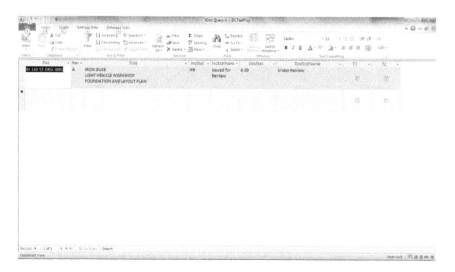

Click the Save Button

Copy the Query result to Excel. This is a register of Documents that are To Be As Built and To be Handed-over.

Click the View Design Button

De-Select T2 = Yes in the Criteria. Run the query, copy the results to a new worksheet in your Excel file and in Access select File Save As and change the name to tDoc Query-2.

Click the View Design Button again and this time De-Select T1 = Yes and Select T2 = Yes in the Criteria. Run the query, copy the results to a new worksheet in your Excel file and in Access select File Save As and change the name to tDoc Query-3.

You now have individual Queries for To Be As Built and To Be Handed-over.

The version of DrawCon provided does not have a Report Wizard function.

It is possible in Excel to filter the values given to produce the same results from the original export/copy.

17.00 Document Retention

17.01 Retention Periods and Methods

To comply with the law all organisations must have a document retention schedule set out by the document types we classified earlier.

In a majority of cases current Engineering Documents are kept for the Life of the Plant plus 5 years or until the plant is demolished or otherwise disposed of. Superseded Engineering Documents are kept, usually, for 5 to 10 years just in case something goes horribly wrong and we need to see how the final design was arrived at.

Engineering correspondence, for example, Technical Queries are usually kept for 5 to 10 years.

Letters and general correspondence is usually kept for 5 years and financial records for 7 years (or whatever period the law requires).

Archiving can be done in one of three ways – Hard Copy, Electronic or a Hybrid of both.

17.02 Electronic vs Hard Copy Archives

17.02.1 Hard Copy Archiving the Catch-22's

Hard Copy archives normally consist of a collection of all related records, for example all the superseded copies of a drawing, stored in an archive box with a detailed contents list. The contents lists can be built using our Registers if we have the fields necessary to record this information.

Depending on the space available and onsite fire systems etc. there is often a storage facility onsite where boxes are kept for between 3 and 6 months. A method of recording if any of the box contents has been referred to is implemented and once the initial storage period has elapsed the box(s) are reviewed and either sent offsite or kept for another 3 to 6 months. Offsite storage facilities are specialised companies. Your organisation may choose to rent its own space in a warehouse or somewhere else to do this but the systems of storing, ensuring protection from fire or flood, recalling etc. must be very robust and it is often no cheaper to do than using a specialised service.

The Catch-22's of a purely hard copy archives are:

Hard Copy printing all "outputs" from CAD applications; and

The law varies from place to place. In Western Australia pretty much anything that has had a pen put on it has to be kept, it's often not and DC's will instruct Engineers to either Electronically Sign or mark everything. Archiving is a huge bone of contention and a massive expense and brings its own Catch-22 with it. For example:

An archive box may cost, say, $3.00 a year to keep. [Not allowing for any inflation]

Most Engineering material has to be kept for Life of Plant (Usually 20 years) Plus 5 years. 25 years at $3 = $75 per box, they can number into the thousands.

At the 25 year mark it is unlikely anyone involved will be around to review the content but let's say there is. On today's prices to bring a box out of archive for review costs $30 and to destroy the contents with a certificate another $30. If that path is taken the box has cost $135 over its life. The Catch-22 is that the $60 to review/destroy will buy another 20 years in store and guess what happens! The box stays in the store and turns in to expensive dust.

Specialised archive stores can be massive:

They have to have climate control systems to keep the paper dry and usually Halon (certainly not water due to the damage it can do) fire systems too. Note too that they have to have a special storage facility for electronic media in particular CD's/DVD's – there are now bacteria that eat them. Other electronic media must be kept protected from any risk of Electro-magnetic pulses or radiation or they too become useless.

17.02.2 Electronic Archiving and ISO15489

Where the law allows it, it is best to electronically archive. The only catch here is that all electronic systems must be ISO 15489 compliant i.e. backwards compatible otherwise the files have to be recalled and converted. This can be true for documents created in Pre 95 versions of Office and for some CAD applications too. Conversion is then quite painful for old office files we will have to ask IT to install a PC with Windows and Office XP (or run multiple boot/virtual PC) open every file save it to XP format then re-open it in a later version of Office and save to that format. Where CAD files are involved we will either have to have an older version of the software installed re-open and save in that format then re-open and save in the current format. We might also send the whole lot out to a specialist company/contractor to convert.

NOTE this might not be a problem with either Office or the CAD application but could be a problem with how your EDMS works with those applications. This too will need to be tested and if the EDMS is found to be at fault your software provider will need to be contacted for a solution to the problem.

Where backward compatibility cannot be assured mechanisms must be put in place to provide us with a warning that old files will need to be converted and act upon it.

Similarly, the company may choose to change its toolset completely. If the system is not going to retain the old toolset indefinitely to allow access to data created in those tools a conversion project must be implemented – the new software provider may provide this service.

From a quality perspective you should also note that intelligence in some documents, for example hyperlinks and Tables of Contents, may not work when the document is stored in an EEDMS / EDMS and this may need to be tested. Documents may need to be updated – hyperlinked documents should also be stored in the same system and it should be possible to build a hyperlink or paste in the document a shortcut to where it is stored in the EDMS application. If you are using an EDMS that is NOT integrated to a CAD tool you might also find any intelligence that is in the CAD files, for example Intelligent P&ID's, also becomes broken or will not work. Where the EDMS is being used in this instance as a back-up to the files in the CAD tool itself this is not a huge issue however, if the EDMS is the sole repository for CAD data post hand-over etc. and the CAD tools with the data in them is not archived off securely this could become a huge problem area.

Electronic archiving also must be done to a standard which meets any company or client Business Recovery Criteria and where storage media such as CD's/DVD's, Memory Sticks or External HDD's are used how they are stored to keep them for degenerating or recalled for renewal, copy to another media, is an issue to be resolved. Where storage media is used they also may be sent to an offsite storage facility and rapid recovery may prove costly. Note there does happen to be bacteria that can and do eat CD's and DVD's and any storage method must be able to prevent this from happening. The facility must also have some protection against fire and against potential electromagnetic disturbance of your material too such as lightning protection and not storing any near power supplies.

EEDMS and our Excel registers need to record where an electronic file has been stored if stored off network e.g. a disk number and on/offsite storage and retention period.

Where a paper only copy exists a decision must be reached as to whether or not it is worth scanning, at best possible resolution with some quality checking of the scan (e.g. 1's and I's, 0's and O's, 8's and B's) and then electronically archiving and destroying the paper.

Sometimes a duplicate or hybrid system of both hard copy and electronic is used. On rare occasions documents may also be microfisched but they too have a limited life and specialised storage is required.

You may also need to ask any end user/client what their retention schedule is. If it does not match your own and your employer is not prepared to store material per the client's schedule you may be forced to hand over everything – squad check copies etc. etc.

17.03 Backing-Up Electronic Files

CAD Systems – most have roll back if a mistake is made. If they do NOT have this function the file(s) – where files are usually zipped (with all X-Refs bound on to the respective drawing files) – must also be given to DC or the Admin person managing correspondence to include, link to, in their register.

Whole network back-up and disaster recovery is done in a number of ways and methods:

Offsite mirror servers – the main server will either copy data to the mirror live or as outlined below tapes.

Tapes (Usually stored onsite for 1 day then sent offsite to fireproof store)

Differential back-up, only changed/new files, at midnight Monday to Saturday to an offsite server/tape or portable hard disk.

Full back-up entire network Sunday midnight to an offsite server/tape or portable hard disk.

It is not a document control function to back-up entire systems. If your company uses a SaaS DC tool it must assure itself of the providers disaster recovery procedures.

What you should know, discussed in greater detail later, is that in some cases remote sites lack bandwidth and may struggle to access local or SaaS servers during the day. Often when this happens a server is deployed to site and it is updated via a filtered for that asset differential back-up (usually Monday to Saturday) and a full back-up (Sunday) overnight often at midnight when bandwidth is not as heavily consumed.

There may be a requirement to hand over your entire DC database (or at least for the up to date and handed-over records) and all the related files. When you create your hand-over transmittals(s) there must be a function that permits you to copy all the corresponding files to a nominated device (DVD Burner, Memory Stick, Portable Hard Drive).

Where there is a requirement to hand over the entire CAD database that is for the System Administrator for that system to do but you will still need to create a transmittal for everything in it (i.e. deliverables).

17.04 Workshop

Using our Document Types Table define what documents are to be kept, how and for how long, this includes Superseded material. Current material is Life of Plant which will be 30 years. The law requires us to add another 5 years on top of that and also for all superseded material too. We will pretend that there has been or will be no litigation which could extend the time in archive.

Document Classification.xlsx

Update the data in the Retention worksheet.

Open DrawCon and your DCTrain database. For this exercise we will "pretend" that the project has ended and all the material in your database is to be archived physically.

From the Main Menu select 6 Archive Box

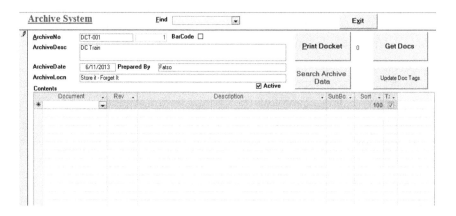

Select ALL the documents in your DCTrain Database. Print and PDF a Docket.

Re-open the Document Classification spread-sheet and update the column with the Box No and Offsite storage.

18.00 Document Control Staff and Organization

This does vary from employer to employer / project to project and can be affected by how the design is to be done e.g. almost entirely 3D with very few 2D drawings but most common is:

Project Controls Manager

Information Management Coordinator

Document Control Manager (DCM)

Lead Document Controller(s) (LDC) [on mega projects this can be one for each of Internal Design, Vendors and Site(s)] OR one, or more, for each large asset (let's say there are 4 gas platforms [3 well offshore and 1 inshore] and an onshore plant) due to the complexity of the whole there will most likely be 5 or 6 LDC's – possibly (where communications get messed up badly 2 for each asset (one for Design and one for Vendors) and where the EPC is also doing the construction 3 for each asset (one design, one vendor, one onsite) a big onshore plant may be split in two and have 2 (one for each section), 4 (design/vendor split across the sections) or 6 (including 2 onsite) LDC's.

Senior Document Controllers (SDC) – often, not always, 2 per LDC

Document Controllers (DC) and Junior Document Controllers (JDC)/File Clerks

Depending on whether document controllers have to manage hard copy, electronic copy (native, renditions and scans) and who may do the scanning work etc. the numbers will vary. If we are managing all types and doing scanning, copying, filing etc. on an 18 month project that produces around 100,000 documents there will be at peak load 1 DCM, 3 Leads (assuming a site), 3 Seniors, 6 to 8 DC's and JDC's – I've certainly done it with less in a primarily paper based system.

As an example a major Oil/Gas operator in Perth was going to run its own Document Control on a mega project, i.e. they were going to be the PMC as such, that originally involved 3 Offshore platforms, an Inshore platform and a land based LNG facility with port.

There would have been – 1 Lead Information Management Coordinator, 5 Information Management Coordinators (1 for each major asset), 5 Lead Document Controllers (not a lot of hands-on work – more like a DCM), 10 Senior Document Controllers and at peak up to 30 Document Controllers.

Some companies also bring in Documents for Operations Coordinators. In my opinion a good IMC and/or DCM/LDC negates this need they should ascertain Operations needs prior to project DC set-up and work to them.

Rule of thumb at peak, assuming a Proactive DC register, 1 DC per 5000 to 10000 documents over a 3 to 6 month period. This also assumes little or no training needs to be provided.

Manpower requirements depend heavily on the method of DC to be deployed – will we manage electronic files and make renditions or scans, will we be looking after paper, what is the total number of drawings and documents, including vendor we may expect to see and over what time period. Compressed times mean more people to process the information but for a shorter period of time on the project. The more "relaxed" the schedule the fewer DC's will be necessary.

Training and the systems deployed for doing document control and providing access to documents for team members are crucial to manpower numbers for DC's.

Where a DC database tool only is used it is critical to be able to give read only access to all non DC team members and that the documents, or at least the latest PDF, are mapped in the system and team members shown how to apply filters and find what they need.

If the system does not support mapping to documents then the paper based filing system must be simple enough for everyone in the team to follow. For drawings this may mean simply having coloured A3 landscape files (use the same colour for each discipline as their mark-up colour) and have a big sign with a clear explanation as to which colour is for which discipline – a lot of people, no matter how well they are labelled, do not read or absorb information on file labels and come and ask DC where stuff can be found.

Where a collaboration tool or EDMS/EEDMS is deployed it is also critical to regularly train and/or update training for non DC team members.

No matter what system is deployed the entire non DC team must understand the applications and processes DC use.

If your DCC is constantly being bombarded by team members looking for documents or asking how something must be done then the training is inadequate and needs to be addressed immediately. There is NO point throwing more DC resources at the problem because others are being distracted from their work see the Project Manager or other superior and organise immediate training for the non DC team.

I assure you that the number of people asking questions of this nature of DC increases dramatically as projects hit peak and there is nothing worse than trying to process '000's of documents and having to answer questions every 15 minutes or so – this is when mistakes are made. I have had to deal with sort of thing a number of times and you would be surprised at the number of times I worked a Sunday or Public Holiday to get stuff done that should/could have been done during the week had the non DC team members been adequately trained and were able to find documents or knew how to get them in to DC etc.

19.00 Quality Management System

19.01 Document Hierarchy

The Document Hierarchy in a Quality Management System is something like:

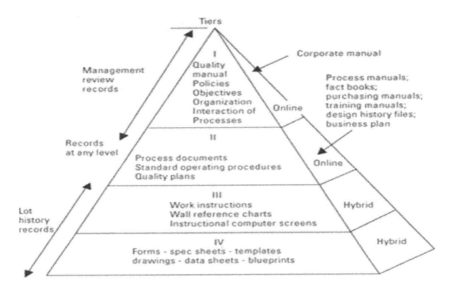

NOTE WELL

The Quality Manual shown at the top of the pyramid is usually made up of the documents also shown in Level i and, often, those at Levels ii and iii.

This system although it looks top heavy is driven from the bottom up. The documents in Level iv are those we must have, the documents in Level iii e.g. Work Instructions, Guidelines and Instructional "Computer Screens" and/or video to be able to do our job correctly. They are a document that is critical to "Business Continuity".

In more recent times I've come across Quality and HSE systems that do not require manuals, but do have a plethora of checklists etc to be completed to assure compliance with the law/standards. This can get confusing for some of us who tend to go looking for a manual!

20.00 Writing a Guideline and/or Work Instruction

Guidelines and Work Instructions are the most important document(s) in the hierarchy.

To build or write a Guideline/Work Instruction the simplest methods are:

> Do a mind map on a whiteboard then convert it to a flowchart on a whiteboard then write dot points, KISS, to expand upon

> If you have it use, Camtasia or a similar tool, to make videos. This is best done with someone next to you who has limited knowledge of the subject matter. They can ask questions as you go, its actually quite difficult talking to yourself, and that person will force you to slow down.

We will do our exercise with basic mind-maps and flowcharts. These techniques are absolutely essential to problem solving. If a problem with respect to how Document Control is being done presents itself remove yourself to a quiet meeting room with a whiteboard and mind map/flow chart the current process then step back and see if there is a simpler process flow that can be implemented – change your flowchart then take your idea to the person who signs off on the DC procedure and discuss it out (or take that person to the white-board and explain).

If you are not used to using, developing or thinking in flow-charts the first step is to do a mind map – there are a number of websites where free trials or free mind mapping software can be found, I'd actually recommend against using software for a brain dump/mind map – use a blank piece of A3 (or larger) paper or a whiteboard then use the software - the software itself unless you are an expert user can distract your thought processes and a mind map is meant to be a straight brain dump. Not a great example but I can type nearly 100 words a minute and I still cannot keep up with my thinking even in Word. I then also find, no matter how often I turn it off, that the auto-formatter or even the spell-checker distracts me from my train of thought. Fortunately for me it's still better than trying to write down what I am thinking by hand.....

This is an example of a mind map that should be referred to later on when we discuss why there is a lot of resistance to any form of change.

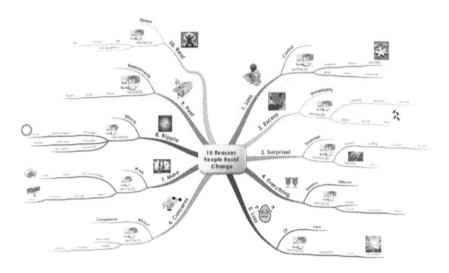

20.01 Basic Flow Chart Symbols

The basic shapes in a flow chart are:

Start - Oval Shape, Action - Rectangle – single connector – line with arrow to indicate flow direction, Decisions -Diamonds, 2 (or more – not recommended) connectors –– line with arrow to indicate flow direction

The chart must flow from start to end i.e. there must be connectors between all the boxes

Flow charts can also be done in Swimming Lanes by "responsibility" with words down a lane on the left and just the symbols in each lane.

Ours will be a straight flow chart on a page we will not try to build it in to anything more at this stage.

All flow charts have a start point and an end point or points. Some may extend to more than one page and therefore a connector is also required to show what page the chart extends to. Flow charts all have actions and decisions.

The basic flow chart symbols we will use are:

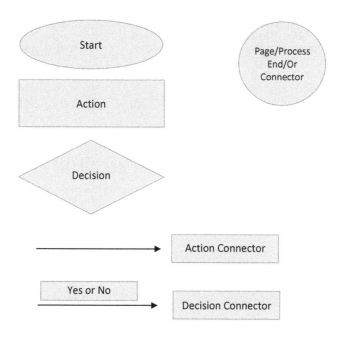

Flowcharts of processes are important – quite often people find them easier to follow than the written word. Pictures do paint a thousand words and sometimes referring to the flowchart and then the written word can make things much much clearer. Even using colours for different processes in the flowchart can help – it's not too difficult, when you think about it, to find the right part of the process in the chart and then follow the applicable coloured connections (e.g. follow the blue one, then the red one, then the green one …..).

20.02 Exercise

Intended as a demonstration of how difficult it can be to write or video work instructions.

Go to Appendix 9 and follow the written instructions first – DO NOT watch the video first.

How easy or difficult was it for you to follow those instructions?

Now download the For Free Patterned Sheet Download <u>Click Here (PDF File)</u>

Did the Patterned Sheet make it simpler for you to make the plane?

Now view the video Folding Instructions <u>Click Here (YouTube Video file)</u>

Did this video make making the plane any simpler?

Did you need to use one, two or all three of the actual instructions provided?

In the authors opinion and no offence is at all intended the actual work instruction in Appendix 9 (not altered) is difficult to follow. The video does not have a voice over and is too fast. Without the Work Instruction, Video and pattern sheet it is very difficult to make this plane.

The point here is that if you have to write work instructions you must write them from the perspective of doing so for someone with no knowledge of your profession or trade and when you make video have someone sit with you who has limited knowledge who will slow you down as you work and ask questions too – it makes for big video files but the more detailed the better. That said keep the language simple – two great examples:

<u>http://www.virtualeconomics.co.uk/2010/12/googles-reading-age-tool-comparing-uk-newspapers.html</u> The average reading age of most UK newspapers is 10.

<u>http://www.abrahamlincolnonline.org/lincoln/speeches/gettysburg.htm</u> count the words of one syllable.

Very detailed video or written (with lots of screen shots) working instructions are a necessary evil but there is NO reason for not following the KISS principle.

20.03 Practical

Now that the majority of what we have to do and how has been explained to you try to build your own flowchart – for processing Vendor Drawings from beginning to end – build in a "loop" that allows for "Revise and Resubmit" use different colour connector(s). This can be done in Word, OpenOffice, Visio or by hand. HINT: do a Mind Map first.

Write a Work Instruction for the Flowchart too. If you have access to Camtasia or something similar record everything you do on your desktop in DrawCon.

21.00 Document Control Procedure

Our Document Control Procedure for our Project must incorporate:

A base level flow chart

Our "Nutshell" Requirements - It MUST answer all the ISO9001 questions.

Meeting Operations / Client Requirements

Classification of Documents, Numbering and Title Conventions

Cross references to any other related document such as the Work Instruction(s) and Law (quote those that apply)

Sometimes the Document Numbering and Title Conventions are published in a separate procedure.

21.01 Practical

There are loads of downloadable, some are not free, DC procedures on the internet see if you can find one and try to write your own based upon it for the processing of Vendor Data from end to end include expediting – your references must include one of the two VDDRL examples provided (does not need to be completed), your work instruction with flowchart(s) and one law.

22.00 A Our Document Control Practical Exercise (Mining)

This chapter and Appendix 2 will also be available with fully worked examples for Oil/Gas and Civil. This is still a useful exercise for anyone in DC to do regardless of the industry you are employed in.

Using the information below let's revisit our Document Control flow chart and also open DrawCon add a new project (DCFEG) and set-up the valid codes and library tables, then add/reserve the documents.

Assumptions:

1. We are using Pro-Active Document Control methods.
2. You are all DCM or LDC's – you have been promoted. I am your IMC and above me is the project controls manager and then (those we work with) an Engineering Manager, a Drawing Office Manager, a scheduler and a QA/QC Manager plus a Lead Discipline Engineer for each Discipline.
3. The project has received a Final Investment Decision from Pre-Feed and FEED documentation etc. and has been given the go ahead.
4. The answers to our questions are Yes.
5. We are "Project Managing" the Project.
6. Our company can obtain better prices on some of the materials and other equipment needed and we will be placing the Purchase Orders and Contracts for those items.
7. We are also to be the operator and have "operations" Information Hand-Over Guide.
8. ALL documents and drawings produced, including Shop Detail Drawings, will have some form of review.
9. There has been a "Registration of Interest" process during FEED and all potential tenderers for every P/O have been identified but no letters of intent have been sent to any Vendor.
10. We are building an Iron Ore Plant. No contracts have been awarded but the FEED team identified a list of potential EPC's and Vendors.

a. The Plant/Mine will include:
   i.   The Mine itself – open cut
   ii.   A RoM Area with a Grizzly (which includes a Rock Breaker) and a Chute
   iii.   The Chute will pass ore to a plate feeder
   iv.   The plate feeder will pass ore in to a Jaw Crusher
   v.   Crushed Ore will be sent over screens
   vi.   Oversized ore will be sent via a conveyor system to a cone crusher
   vii.   Undersized ore will be sent to a stacker stockpile system for which a fines circuit will be developed at a later stage
   viii. Ore passing the screen size grade will pass via conveyors to cyclones for removal of any overburden or loose material. Slurry from this system will be sent to a tailings dam.
   ix.   Wet ore will be passed through a dryer
   x.   After drying the ore will be sent overland via conveyors to a stacker (luffing) where it will be stacked over a purpose built tunnel which fills trains
   xi.   The tunnel is a concrete box approximately 50 metres long and will have special gates that open and close when ore trucks are below
   xii.   There will be a rail loop through the tunnel and a spur line to an already existing line that will take the trains to a port facility
   xiii. We will not need to upgrade the port facility or existing rail system to cater for extra traffic as another mine will go offline when ours is functional.
   xiv. The tailings dam must have an evaporator facility to reduce water levels – water is not to be pumped directly on to the ground or into any water coarse

11. We are doing ALL the design work except for the Accommodation camp and Airport (for FI/FO workers) which are to be awarded on P/O's and we will manage the review process.

12. With some exceptions the project team is in place and we have a "telephone list", see below, of names and positions to add to our database (dream them up).
13. We IMC/DCM/LDC and expeditor will be at contract/PO kick-off meetings to discuss drawing and data requirements and the "VDDRL" and will only leave when the list, dates in particular, is agreed and the contractors and vendors agree to the procedure for Contractor/Vendor drawings and data.
14. Only Piping (not Iso's) i.e. the model, Electrical, Instrument and Process drawings and documents will be As Built
15. Only an MDR, IOM and Vendor Drawings from Vendors will be handed over to operations by us. ALL design documents will be handed over at the final revision. TQ's, RFI's and ECR's will not be handed over but kept for 5 years.
16. The entire project document system will be 100% electronic we will not be accepting paper drawings/documents/mark-ups from anyone a tracer or junior engineer will be employed to assist those who prefer to work with paper to bring up to date electronic copies.

We have 18 months until first ore is to be sent by train to the port.

We have identified a specialist commissioning company who will also run the plant and train our operators for the first three months. They will do mark-ups for As Builts but not the As Builts themselves and will be verifying some data such as Equipment Numbers and providing a GPS location but they will not be doing the document hand-over it is our problem.

The questions you must ask with me are:

1. Are there any documents and data to carry over from the FEED?
2. Will these documents have document numbers that need to change (NO)
3. Is the data in the document profiles up to date and correct? (We will DQ Audit it anyway)
4. Is the project to be done almost entirely in 3D CAD?

5. Do we have a rough procurement schedule for items to be purchased by us?

Firstly we open a new project and either manually add all the "valid" codes or import them from a library source (FEED) in this case from scratch.

We add all the "telephone list" of project team members to the database. Each "Lead" engineer is also the "package engineer" for their respective discipline. Our database does not have workflows, but the system will send links to .pdf files for mark-up via outlook when an internal transmittal is raised and, because there are no nested workflows, or unless we are directed otherwise the leads for each discipline are the reviewers.

We add to our database the list of contracts and P/O's.

We import, after any necessary Data Quality (DQ) Audit/Desk topping, the documents and data from FEED into our project database – current revisions only with no transmittal history. Regardless of what we are told we WILL DQ Audit ALL data associated with any documents to be imported in to our project.

We print off any Process Flow Diagram(s) and any P&ID's.

Working with both the Engineering Manager (EM), Scheduler (Sch) and Drawing Office Manager (DOM) and our list from procurement we develop, in Excel, a rough (it can never be 100% right) deliverables list with some IFR, IFT and IFC delivery dates and then import it into our database.

Let's say (nowhere near a complete list and in some cases barely even close but for this exercise a good start) we will have, prior to receiving Vendor Drawing Lists for the items we are purchasing:

1 Overall 3D Model

10 3D model sections each to be delivered based on the schedule dates/procurement dates for the respective "plant areas/systems"

There will be no Mechanical, Piping (other than Isometric and Vendor Drawings) in 2D.

There will be approximately 8 Structural GA, 16 Elevation and 126 Detail type drawings – chutes above the train load-out tunnel. These chutes will NOT be designed in 3D

There will be approximately 20 "Architectural" drawings for the Camp and 5 for the Airport facility to be done by a design contractor.

There will be approximately 10 P&ID's (1 per area/system)

There are 8 PFD's to be updated – 1 overall and 1 for each "working area (300 to 900)"

There will be approximately 25,000 Structural Shop Detail Drawings for the load-out chutes to be done externally by the fabricator (6250 per chute) – when you reserve these if you know how to use queries in Access create an update query with tDoc as the table and update F1 to SDD and F2 to D06 – note if you do not know how to use queries skip this data but you must reserve the drawings. They will have V numbers. The Po No is 007 and the vendor is Steel Stuff.

There will be approximately 10,000 Instrument Loop Diagrams – 1000 each area (rare in Mining & Run of Mine would have limited numbers too)

There will be approximately 11 Instrument Layout/GA drawings – 1 overall, 1 each area

There will be approximately 1,000 Electrical Drawings (use 001, 100, 200, 300, 400, 500, 600, 700, 800, 900 – not normal but close enough for this exercise – 100 each for this exercise call them all Single Line Diagrams)

There will be approximately 155 Civil Drawings (45 in Load-out – Rail and 30 in Port Rail), none in Mine, 10 each in other areas)

There will be approximately 10 drawings associated with the mine itself

There will be approximately 20 Scope of Work Documents (3 Contracts and 17 P/O's to be awarded – use 099 Area Code & General Disc Code [not 100% correct but good enough for this exercise])

There will be approximately 100 Specifications for the contracts/PO's – (use 099 Area Code and the General discipline code [not 100% correct but good enough for this exercise])

There will be approximately 900 Datasheets (100 each area ending 00, 50 Elec and 50 Mech)

There will be approximately 50 Calculation "Documents" in each area ending 00 in Mechanical and Electrical plus 50 in structural – area 700.

We will not yet be reserving numbers for Piping Iso's. The System Administrator for the CAD Model tool will give us a .CSV file for all Piping Iso's when they are issued and we will accept the numbers that are on them. We can expect to receive them within 5 working days of each model file being frozen.

Note there would likely be a number of civil and structural drawings in the RoM area and structural drawings associated with the Grizzly and Chute to the plate feeder. These areas are generally "built-up" and require a lot of "fill" dirt (usually overburden from the mine that may have been crushed down by a mobile crusher) and concrete retaining walls etc. The same applies to the train load-out tunnel where the tunnel is built and then the chutes added and the area around them filled with dirt.

There will be 2 Contract "Vendor Drawing and Data Requirements Lists" and 17 P/O "Vendor Drawing and Data Requirements Lists" these are in a form that the Contractors and Vendors are to revise/add their information to and submit back to us at the next revision. Use Area 099 and General Disc Code.

We will be using all Corporate "Plans", "Policies", "Procedures" and "Standards" except where shown above. They will be "issued to us" by Corporate Information Control and we will add them to our database with their existing numbers and we will NOT be revising any of them. These standards include an Equipment/Tag Numbering standard and the 3D CAD application will assign Tag Numbers and will track Tag to Document and Document to Document relationships.

There will be two major contracts, EPC and Camp/Airport, and 17 P/O's for piping, instruments, mechanical equipment such as pumps, various (Mechanical and Instrument/Process Controls) valves, steel, stackers, conveyors, load-out gates etc. The contractors have been identified and there will not be a tender process for these contracts.

In DrawCon they will be:

FLY01   -   Airport Experts (Make up an address); and

CAMP1   -   Camps and Messing (Make up an address)

The two contracts are almost complete and will be based on FEED documents we are importing in to our system they become Distribution Matrix CON-001 the intent is to award in 4 weeks and the contractors must produce their Drawing and Data List within one week of award. Their document numbers will come from our system but will NOT be badged V or F. Let's say the award will be 1 August 2014.

There are a number of "long lead" items for which a "tender" process of sorts took place during the FEED stage and this will be awarded on or around 15 Aug 2014. In DrawCon they are:

GATES - Clamshell Gates r Us - Load-out Tunnel Clamshell Gates

CONV1 - Conveyors r Us   - Overland Conveyor

CRSH1 - Crushers r Us   - Jaw (Primary) and Cone (Oversize) Crushers

STKR1 - Stackers r Us   - Luffing Stackers (2)

STL01   - Steel Stuff   - Load-Out Chutes (inc Shop Detailing)

Make up addresses DO NOT USE (unless it's your own) real email addresses

★★ For the Contracts and Vendor Documents we have or will reserve some document numbers. We do need to obtain from FEED the VDDRL for each one. Only one will appear in the worked examples. You will need to add the document to DrawCon, review it, update it with document numbers and reserve those numbers in DrawCon.

Note the Company list should also include Iron1 – Iron Monarchy as the client. Make up an address

The remaining P/O's will have their documentation developed by us and will be issued for tender (IFT) at 2 P/O's the second month after the first contract is awarded let's say 1 Oct 2013, and then 1 per month there-after for the remaining 7 let's say on the 1st of each month. Awards are intended for 2 months after the initial IFT date. E.g. the first award is scheduled for 1 Dec 2014.

All the "Vendors" will have 7 days post award to submit their drawing and data lists and we will be assigning them numbers (with some spares) from those lists with a V pre the sequence number and there will only be one database for the project (not recommended it is usually much simpler to have a separate database for Vendors).

For the purposes of this exercise for Design documents (non V) we are using a hybridised method and are not recording Due Dates for IFR, IFT or IFC we will initially build our list in Excel then Reserve all the Numbers in DrawCon. For vendor documents that have been reserved against the VDDRL we will record the date due in the Next Due date field in the Status SubForm in the Document Profile.

We check for the document numbers already in use and assign new numbers in our spread-sheet for the documents outlined above. Note that the PFD's and P&ID's already exist but in FEED format which is not as complete as a fully engineered drawing.

We (EM, Sch, DOM and DCM/LDC(s)) are all agreed on the spread-sheet and it is imported in to our database. Note we will not bother with a spread-sheet for our practical and reserve numbers as shown above.

We will be managing budget hours against deliverables. The "progress curve" if when we produce one is very steep as it goes from 0% directly to 60% at IFR. In a full CAD/EEDMS application other milestones precede IFR and budget hours are recorded for each deliverable and the system automatically tracks progress based on a drawing or document template being opened from a "place-holder" our database puts in it and the amount of actual work done in the template (not time based but time open is recorded) these systems tend to "version" these as, for example, A1, A2 and so on until Revision A is released IFR. We do not see the versions in our database we only deal with released/issued for ….. documents.

There will be an expeditor for vendor data/contractor data. The system has 4 levels of expediting reports:

1. Due within the next 5 working days – a friendly reminder – auto emailed to the contractor or vendor and expeditor
2. Due today – a friendly reminder– auto emailed to the contractor or vendor and expeditor
3. Due 5 working days ago – auto emailed to the Engineering Manager and/or expeditor to send on due to the nature of the possibility of liquidated damages being applied
4. Due 10 working days ago – auto email to the Project Manager who will forward on and includes scheduler, cost controller, contracts admin, accounts – progress payments are to be withheld and liquidated damages applied to the payments when made.

DCM/LDC's will expedite all internal design data – there will be in place a "Yellow Card" (first strike) and "Red Card" (second strike) system. That system will automatically generate an expediting email for overdue new data and overdue reviews. A Yellow Card is issued at 5 working days overdue and the Engineering Manager will receive a copy, a Red Card is issued at 10 working days overdue, and the EM and Project Manager receive a copy. We WILL NOT be required to change any dates for internal design data or vendor data.

There is a Vendor Drawing and Data Requirements Spread sheet that also provides DC with the review team matrix. For our purposes the matrices will be CON-001, CON-002, PO-001, PO-002 and so on. There will be both Internal (Map) and External Distribution matrices.

We will NOT be managing Tender documents submitted. (Not recommended but most common)

We will update our external distribution matrices at the whole package ready for IFT.

We will update our internal distribution matrices on the fly but the original set-up will be, for example, for Mechanical Docs/Drgs – Lead Mechanical Engineer, Lead Piping Engineer, Lead Process Engineer, Lead Structural Engineer, Lead Electrical Engineer, Lead Instrument Engineer, Lead Mechanical Engineer – Operations, Lead Mechanical Engineer. Switch the first and last reviewer around for each discipline and change the Operations Lead for each discipline they are on our "Telephone List".

Our database has a viewer/redlining tool and allows parallel reviews which means more than one Lead can open any document (always a copy but it looks real) at any time and comment and see others comments live.

When we receive the VDDRL from the contractors and vendors, in our excel spread-sheet format, they will immediately go on a 5 day review while the review is taking place we will start to assign document numbers in our copy of the spread-sheet. When the review is complete will we make any necessary changes per mark-ups and import the sheet in to our Database with all the numbers and IFR, IFC due dates.

Because we can plan due to having a Pro-Active register we will have all our DC's in place and trained ahead of need. We will assign 2 LDC's (1 for "Design" and 1 for Vendors), 2 DC's and 1 SDC per contract and 1 DC per major vendor there will also be an SDC onsite. They will be rotated around so they gain experience of all the roles. We do not need, because Operations have an IHOG, Documents for Operations Coordinator or DC but the DCM will include Operations personnel in the internal review matrices as above.

When we receive a package of drawings/documents from the respective lead engineer for IFR we open and update our database with Rev A and the path to the file, note we will only be doing Squad Check (Inter discipline) reviews Intra discipline reviews will be done on a "no revision" document prior to hand-over to DC for IFR, the system will automatically add the received date and we update the internal distribution map based on the discipline. For KISS we will call these AA-001, CI-001, MM-001 and so on. When the update is complete we raise our Internal Transmittal to the Map and send it electronically (hyperlinks). The system will expedite tardy reviewers based on our Yellow/Red Card system and we will also print off expediting reports and go and talk to anyone who looks like or is overdue to return review documents.

When we receive notification back from the responsible lead that a review is complete we will open the files and note what is in the Review stamp and update our database with the Review Status.

Unless a document has completely failed review on the first pass (code 3) there will be no second review. As we are the client there is no need to Issue documents for approval to the client/operators representative.

The respective lead engineer will take responsibility for striking out or incorporating all mark-ups and Rev B will be the IFT document.

When we receive those we will update our database and when instructed issue them to the potential contractors or vendors for Tender.

During the tender process we will be managing TQ's and RFI's the review matrix for each will be the Lead Discipline Engineer, Scheduler, Cost Controller, Contracts Engineer and Expeditor.

Usually after a "preferred" contractor or vendor is identified there is correspondence and meetings between them, the Lead Discipline Engineer, Scheduler, Cost Controller, Contracts Engineer and Expeditor. Often there are, by necessity, design changes to be made to the IFT documents. Those are issued to us at Rev 0 as either IFC or IFU. We update our distribution matrix then deactivate the failed bidders and add site and other necessary recipients of the documents. We update our database to Rev 0 and issue the documents per the updated matrix.

Ideally, this is not always done, the design is then frozen and to make subsequent changes to IFC/IFU documents and drawings requires an Engineering Change Request process. We will manage ECR's and the matrix for those will be the Lead Discipline Engineer, Scheduler, Cost Controller, Contracts Engineer and Expeditor. Approved ECR's will trigger design change and a review of the revised document at Rev 0A we will update our database and activate an internal review transmittal per the matrix. Once the review is complete the respective lead engineer will take responsibility for striking out or incorporating all mark-ups and Rev 1 will be the IFC/IFU document with the ECR No shown in the revision history. We will update our database and activate an external transmittal per the matrix.

As the project winds down and when design and construction of each area/system is complete the DCM/IMC will open an operations database and documents not requiring As Built will be imported in to the operations database after some final document and data quality checking by the LDC's/DCM. A transmittal is raised to operations usually someone in-house and on the vessel for these documents. System by system, where possible, is preferred otherwise they could be dealing with a lot of material in a very short time frame.

There will be a team in the field doing necessary As Constructed Mark-ups. Rev 1A – we will update our database on receipt but no further action is required

The "hydro" commissioning contractor will do As Commissioned Mark-ups with the aid of some drafters. Rev 1B – we will update our database on receipt but no further action is required

The "operations" commissioning contractor will do "As Handed-Over" Mark-ups. Rev 1C – we will update our database on receipt but no further action is required.

Rev 2 will be the As Built Revision. We will update our database do a final data/document quality check then export to the operations database. A transmittal is raised to operations usually someone in-house and on the vessel.

An operations portal will be built by an external professional firm from the operations database and final CAD application data. A transmittal is raised for the portal to operations and the vessel. The portal will be completed before it becomes fully operational and may need some final updating post operations with As Builts from the Operations Commissioning Team.

We will not need to do any data cleansing/massaging for Operations Computerised Maintenance System, e.g. SAP, a copy of the CAD application used with only the final documents and drawings will be integrated to SAP by others.

ALSO

Create an Internal Map from your Telephone List (see below)

Position	DocRespName	Location
Project Manager	Fred Bloggs	Site/CBD
Deputy Project Manager	Joe Bloggs	CBD
Site Manager	John Smith	CBD
Engineering Manager	Jane Doe	CBD
Contracts/Procurement Lead	Anthony Buyer	CBD
Lead Mechanical Engineer	Jim Mech	CBD
Lead Process Engineer	Heather Heat	CBD
Lead Piping Engineer	Eddie Tube	CBD
Lead Civil/Structural Engineer	Manny Steel	CBD
Lead Instrument Engineer	Jenny Gauge	CBD
Lead Electrical Engineer	Andrew Spark	CBD
Lead Mining Engineer	Ditch Digger	CBD
Lead QA/QC	Greg Right	CBD
Lead HSE	Steve Safe	CBD
Information Management Coord	Huw Grossmith	CBD
Project Controls Manager	Peter Perfect	CBD
Scheduler	Ian Planner	CBD
Expeditor	Jill Chaser	CBD
Materials Controller	Neil Stuff	CBD
Drawing Office Manager	Ina Draft	CBD
Site DC	Jesse Record	CBD
Lead Facilities Engineer	Veronica Camp	Site/CBD

We will also have a rudimentary Equipment List. These are generally developed partly on the fly and partly by importing data we can obtain from either the CAD system administrator or engineers such as the major equipment list, instrument index and cable schedules (not many people add cables to this information but I like to if it is readily available).

For the time being it should look like this:

fEquipSub			
Equip No.	**Description**	**Area**	**P/O**
301-GR-001	RoM Grizzly 1	301	
301-GR-002	RoM Grizzly 1	301	
301-RB-001	Rockbreaker - Grizzly 1	301	
301-RB-002	Rockbreaker - Grizzly 2	301	
500-CR-001	Jaw / Primary Crusher	500	PO-002
500-CR-010	Cone/Recycle Crusher	500	PO-003
500-CV-001	Crusher Recycle Conveyor	500	PO-005
500-MT-001A	Screen 01 - Motor 1	500	PO-008
500-MT-001B	Screen 01 - Motor 2	500	PO-008
500-MT-002A	Screen 02 - Motor 1	500	PO-008
500-MT-002B	Screen 02 - Motor 2	500	PO-008
500-SC-001	Screen Unit 1	500	PO-008
500-SC-002	Screen Unit 2	500	PO-008
600-CV-001	Stockpile Conveyor	600	PO-004
600-ST-001	Stockpile Stacker - 01	600	PO-001
600-ST-002	Stockpile Stacker - 02	600	PO-001
701-CH-001	Load-out Chute - 01	700	PO-007
702-CH-001	Load-out Chute - 02	700	PO-007
703-CH-001	Load-out Chute - 03	700	PO-007
704-CH-001	Load-out Chute - 04	700	PO-007
775-CG-001	Clamshell - 01	700	PO-006
776-CG-001	Clamshell - 02	700	PO-006
777-CG-001	Clamshell - 03	700	PO-006
778-CG-001	Clamshell - 04	700	PO-006

The worked example shows Document to Tag relationships for some of the equipment on this list. It is optional for you to try.

You should also try to associate, where the data is available, documents to documents – see the example below:

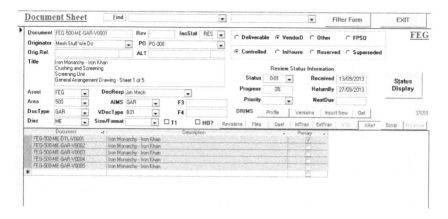

Create 2 Distribution Sets using 4 Distribution Sets from the Main Menu

The first Set is for the Camp Drawings you have reserved (apply a filter) the internal reviewers are as below and the external recipient will be Camps and Messing.★

The second Set is for the Airport Drawings you have reserved (apply a filter) the internal reviewers are as below and the external recipient will be Airport Experts.★

★These lists grow and will include your own site DC plus others- this is being abbreviated for this exercise ordinarily the list would show all bidders and the losing bidders are made inactive as we progress.

The Review of documents related to facilities the order is:

fDSet-Int						
Order	Recipient	Position	Location	IntRFI	FormatNote	Comments
1.00	Veronica Camp	Lead Facilities Engineer	Site/CBD	REV		
2.00	Manny Steel	Lead Civil/ Structural Engineer	CBD	REV		
3.00	Ina Draft	Drawing Office Manager	CBD	REV		
4.00	Andrew Spark	Lead Electrical Engineer	CBD	REV		

fDSet-Int						
Order	Recipient	Position	Location	IntRFI	FormatNote	Comments
5.00	Jenny Gauge	Lead Instrument Engineer	CBD	REV		
6.00	Jim Mech	Lead Mechanical Engineer	CBD	REV		
7.00	Eddie Tube	Lead Piping Engineer	CBD	REV		
8.00	Heather Heat	Lead Process Engineer	CBD	REV		
9.00	Jane Doe	Engineering Manager	CBD	REV		
10.00	Veronica Camp	Lead Facilities Engineer	Site/CBD	REV		

Use a similar structure but change the order for the Screens PO (see below) – hint the screen package is Mechanical.

Update all the Drawings to Rev A for the two packages above. The IncStat will be IFR, the DocStat will be 20 On Review/Squad Check. The Budget Hours for each of these drawings is 40.

Press F11 in DrawCon and select the Forms drop down on the left. Find the form fWBS and add 2 WBS's: Arch-001 – Architectural Design Camps and Arch-002 – Architectural Design Airport. Close the form.

From the main menu open the Document Form and filter on AA.

Set the WBS to Arch-001 for all Camp drawings and Arch-002 for all Airport Drawings

Create an Internal Transmittal for both sets.

We will "pretend" the review is completed the same day. Log todays date (space bar) in Log Action Complete against ALL documents on both Internal Transmittals.

Update the Review Status Information Status to 0-10 Reviewed no Comment for ALL the documents from FLY01 and CAMP1.

Generate a transmittal for the relevant documents back to each contractor with the new status code RFI Reviewed no Comment.

Check your DrawCon Document Profiles under both the IntTran and ExtTran buttons for the data.

Go back to transmittals and log acknowledgements as todays date.

Do a google search and/or create 4 companies for a tender package for Screening Units – DO NOT use real email addresses.

Add a new PO – SCRN 1 with a date of award as 1/11/2014 DO NOT check the awarded box the RFQ date is today.

The IFR Date on the VDDRL is date of award, 1/11/2014, plus 7 days

We will send to them to complete approximately 50 Datasheets to complete and return. They will need to see ALL P&ID's at IFT and IFC for Area 500. Add the data-sheets – 20 Mechanical, 20 Electrical (5 are for Motors), 10 Instruments they will all be in Area 500. Make them all Rev B Inc Stat IFT Status (in Review Status is IFT), budget hours are 10 each. Rev the model file for this area up to B same status codes budget hours 200. Add a Scope of Work Document, a specification (screens) and an Engineering Requisition all at Rev B IFT with 50 budget hours each also add a specification (general – Site Conditions) at Rev B IFT 50 budget hours. Add a VDDRL at Rev B IFT 10 budget hours.

Create an internal distribution matrix for ALL the documents in this package with the Lead Mech Eng first and last on the review team. Create an external distribution matrix for ALL the "design" documents only to all 4 companies.

Raise an external transmittal to all 4 companies for the non V documents you have just reserved and the model as IFT.

Once the transmittal is raise use todays date to acknowledge. Then deactivate 3 of the vendors and go back to the PO table and check award and use todays date.

Revise all the documents to 0 the model and any drawings/documents will be IFC. The datasheets and VDDRL will be IFP there will be details the vendor needs to complete.

Raise a transmittal to the active vendor for ALL the documents. Acknowledge as a today.

The Vendor submits the VDDRL are Rev 1 – IFR. Put it on an internal review. At the same time create:

| 10 | V | Mechanical Drawings (5 GA's, 5 Details) |
| 10 | V | Structural Drawings (5 GA's, 5 Elev/Details) |

10	V	Electrical Drawings (SLD)
5	V	Electrical Drawings (Motor GA's)
1	V	Instrument Layout
1	V	P&ID
1	V	Piping GA
1	V	Civil (GA)
1	V	IOM Index
1	V	IOM
1	V	MDR Index
1	V	MDR
1	V	ITP
1	V	Factory Acceptance Test Procedure
1	V	Noise Data Sheet
1	V	Weight Report
1	V	Shipping Procedure

There would ordinarily be a bit more than this but its close enough.

The internal review is completed on the VDDRL in 5 working days – update the Internal Review transmittal – Actioned. Update the Doc/Review Status to 1 – Reviewed no Comment. Transmit to vendor.

When you do your Set-up in DrawCon the project will be FEG. T1 is ASB?, T2 is HO?, F1 is AIMS, F2 is VDocCode, F3 AND F4 leave open.

You will note in the worked example there are some other PO's that have been "awarded"

	fPOList
PONum	PoName	Combo 130	PO Engineer	PO Group	Po Sort	Vendor Data	Po Tag	Poid	Text 93	Text 95
-------	--------	-----------	-------------	----------	---------	-------------	--------	------	---------	---------
CON-001	Camps (Permanent and Construction)	CAMP1	022		100.00	-1	-1	8.00	13/09/13 12:07PM	
CON-002	Airport	FLY01	022		100.00	-1	-1	9.00	13/09/13 12:07PM	

									fPOList	
PONum	PoName	Combo 130	PO Engineer	PO Group	Po Sort	Vendor Data	Po Tag	Poid	Text 93	Text 95
PO-001	Luffing Stackers (2x)	STKR1	006		100.00	-1	-1	1.00	13/09/13 12:07PM	
PO-002	Jaw Crusher	CRSH1	006		100.00	-1	-1	2.00	13/09/13 12:07PM	
PO-003	Cone Crusher	CRSH1	006		100.00	-1	-1	3.00	13/09/13 12:07PM	
PO-004	Stockpile Conveyor	CONV1	006		100.00	-1	-1	4.00	13/09/13 12:07PM	
PO-005	Crusher Re–Cycle Conveyor	CONV1	006		100.00	-1	-1	5.00	13/09/13 12:07PM	
PO-006	Clamshell Gates (4x)	GATES	006		100.00	-1	-1	6.00	13/09/13 12:07PM	
PO-007	Steel Stockpile Chutes (Train Load-Out)	STL01	009		100.00	-1	-1	7.00	13/09/13 12:07PM	

Some of this equipment as mentioned is on the Long Lead item list. With 18 months to build a simple mine this would be most uncommon. I have NOT in this screen shot shown the new PO you are to raise but it will be in the worked example.

22.00 B Our Document Control Practical Exercise – Oil/Gas

Using the information below let's revisit our Document Control flow chart and also open DrawCon add a new project and set-up the valid codes and library tables, then add/reserve the documents.

Assumptions (remember what I said above Assumptions are Dangerous at best):

1. We are using Pro-Active Document Control methods.
2. You are all DCM or LDC's – you have been promoted. I am your IMC and above me is the project controls manager and then (those we work with) an Engineering Manager, a Drawing Office Manager, a scheduler and a QA/QC Manager plus a Lead Discipline Engineer for each Discipline.
3. The project has received a Final Investment Decision from Pre-Feed and FEED documentation etc. and has been given the go ahead.
4. The answers to our questions are Yes.
5. We are "Project Managing" the Project.
6. Our company can obtain better prices on some of the materials and other equipment needed for the conversion and we will be placing the Purchase Orders and Contracts for those items.
7. We are also to be the operator and have "operations" Information Hand-Over Guide.
8. ALL documents and drawings produced, including Shop Detail Drawings, will have some form of review.
9. There has been a "Registration of Interest" process during FEED and all potential tenderers for every P/O have been identified but no letters of intent have been sent to any Vendor.
10. We are building an FPSO. No contracts, including for the hull have been awarded but the FEED team identified a suitable hull (an old oil tanker) that is currently available for sale through a company that specialises in hull conversions for FPSO's, that

company does have a letter of intention to award a contract for the purchase of the hull and conversion.

11. We are doing ALL the design work except for the Accommodation modules which is to be awarded on a P/O and the hull conversion contractor will be included in the review process.

12. With some exceptions the project team is in place, and we have a "telephone list" of names and positions to add to our database.

13. We IMC/DCM/LDC and expeditor will be at contract/PO kick-off meetings to discuss drawing and data requirements and the "VDDRL" and will only leave when the list, dates in particular, is agreed and the contractors and vendors agree to the procedure for Contractor/Vendor drawings and data.

14. Only Piping (not Iso's) i.e. the model, Electrical, Instrument and Process drawings and documents will be As Built

15. Only an MDR, IOM and Vendor Drawings will be handed over to operations from Vendors. ALL design documents will be handed over at the final revision. TQ's, RFI's and ECR's will not be handed over.

16. The entire project document system will be 100% electronic we will not be accepting paper drawings/documents/mark-ups from anyone a tracer or junior engineer will be employed to assist those who prefer to work with paper to bring up to date electronic copies.

The conversion will take 18 months and will be done in ship yards in Singapore.

The ship is scheduled to sail to its "anchor" point in 23 months allowing for "hydro" pre-commissioning which will be done in the shipyard.

We are responsible for "commissioning" at the anchor point and that will take, with some limited operation time 3 months.

The FPSO will be fully operational in 26 months.

The questions you must ask with me are:

1. Are there any documents and data to carry over from the FEED?

2. Is the data in the document profiles up to date and correct?
3. Is the project to be done almost entirely in 3D CAD?
4. Do we have a rough procurement schedule for items to be purchased by us?

Firstly, we open a new project and either manually add all the "valid" codes or import them from a library source.

We add all the "telephone list" of project team members to the database. Each "Lead" engineer is also the "package engineer" for their respective discipline. Our database does not have workflows therefore unless we are directed otherwise the leads for each discipline are the reviewers.

We add to our database the list of contracts and P/O's.

We import, after any necessary Data Quality (DQ) Audit/Desk topping, the documents and data from FEED into our project database. Regardless of what we are told we WILL DQ Audit ALL data associated with any documents to be imported into our project.

We print off any Process Flow Diagram(s) and any P&ID's.

Working with both the Engineering Manager (EM), Scheduler (Sch) and Drawing Office Manager (DOM) and our list from procurement we develop, often in Excel, a rough (it can never be 100% right) deliverables list with some IFR, IFT and IFC delivery dates.

Let's say (nowhere near a complete list) we will have, prior to receiving Vendor Drawing Lists for the items we are purchasing:

1 Overall 3D Model

20 3D model sections each to be delivered based on the schedule dates/procurement dates for the respective "plant areas/systems"

There will be no Mechanical, Piping (other than Isometric and Seabed/Riser Piping), or Marine Drawings in 2D.

There will be approximately 100 Structural GA type drawings. 50 for the Turret and 50 for the Helipad

There will be approximately 20 "Architectural" drawings as the entire accommodation facility will be demolished and enlarged for a permanent (FI/FO) crew.

There will be approximately 20 P&ID's (2 per area/system)

There are 10 PFD's to be updated – 1 Overall and one each – areas 200 to 575

There will be approximately 25,000 Structural Shop Detail Drawings, which the 3D CAD system can produce, 10,000 hull, 10,000 turret, 5,000 helipad

There will be approximately 10,000 Instrument Loop Diagrams, which the 3D CAD system can produce – areas 200 to 575

There will be approximately 20 Instrument Layout/GA drawings - – areas 200 to 575

There will be approximately 1,000 Electrical Drawings – across all but subsea

There will be approximately 10 Scope of Work Documents (10 Contracts and P/O's to be awarded) – use "General" system/area code (not right but close enough for the exercise)

There will be approximately 100 Specifications in various disciplines for the contracts/PO's – use "General" system/area code (not right but close enough for the exercise)

There will be approximately 1000 Datasheets –– use "General" system/area code (not right but close enough for the exercise)

There will be approximately 100 Calculation "Documents" across all disciplines - – use "General" system/area code and General discipline (not right but close enough for the exercise)

There will be 2 Contract "Vendor Drawing and Data Requirements Lists" and

We will be using all Corporate "Plans", "Policies", "Procedures" and "Standards" except where shown above. They will be "issued to us" by Corporate Information Control and we will add them to our database with their existing numbers and we will NOT be revising any of them. These standards include an Equipment/Tag Numbering standard and the 3D CAD application will assign Tag Numbers and will track Tag to Document and Document to Document relationships.

There will be two major contracts, hull and Sub-Sea EPIC, and 9 P/O's for piping, instruments, mechanical equipment such as pumps, various (Mechanical and Instrument/Process Controls) valves, steel, accommodation units etc.

The major contract is almost complete and will be based on FEED documents we are importing in to our system they become Distribution Matrix CON-001 the intent is to award in 4 weeks and the contractor must produce its Drawing and Data List within one week of award. Their document numbers will come from our system but will NOT be badged V or F. Let's say the award will be 1 August 2013

The remaining 9 P/O's will have their documentation developed by us and will be issued for tender (IFT) at 2 P/O's the second month after the contract is awarded let's say 1 Oct 2013, then 1 per month thereafter for the remaining 7 let's say on the 1st of each month. Awards are intended for 2 months after the initial IFT date. E.g. The first award is scheduled for 1 Dec 2013.

All the "Vendors" will have 7 days post award to submit their drawing and data lists and we will be assigning them numbers (with some spares) from those lists with a V pre the sequence number and there will only be one database for the project (not recommended it is usually much simpler to have a separate database for Vendors).

On our spreadsheet we assign dates IFR for documents 4 weeks prior to IFT – note this is usually not anywhere near this compressed but we need to secure the hull. IFT will be as above. IFC will be set for the same date as the award dates and the P/O's will go to the vendors with IFC documents.

We check for the document numbers already in use and assign new numbers in our spreadsheet for the documents outlined above. Note that the PFD's and P&ID's already exist but in FEED format which is not as complete as a fully engineered drawing.

We (EM, Sch, DOM and DCM/LDC(s)) are all agreed on the spreadsheet and it is not imported in to our database.

The law requires us to have a certain set of, expensive to buy, documents on the ship before it sails but post commissioning. We will assign document numbers (MAN) for those last – after the import of the data as above and design is complete, they will NOT get a V number. They will be on the ship prior to "hydro" commissioning.

Our settings for Progress against status in DrawCon will be:

DocStatCode	DocStatName	ProgVal
1	Reviewed No Comment	90.00%
2	Reviewed with Comment	80.00%
3	Do Not Proceed	60.00%
4	Accepted as Final/IFC	95.00%
5	Accepted as As Built	100.00%
AB	As Built	100.00%
CAN	Cancelled	0.00%
IFI	Issued For information	0.00%
IFT	Issued For Tender	85.00%
IFU	Issued for Use	100.00%
INR	In Review	60.00%
RSV	Reserved/In Preparation	0.00%

We will not be managing budget hours against deliverables therefore the progress milestones do not mean a great deal as we have little to actually report against. The "progress curve" if we were to produce one is very steep as it goes from 0% directly to 60% at IFR. In a full CAD/EEDMS application other milestones precede IFR and budget hours are recorded for each deliverable and the system automatically tracks progress based on a drawing or document template being opened from a "place-holder" our database puts in it and the amount of actual work done in the template (not time based but time open is recorded) these systems tend to "version" these as, for example, A1, A2 and so on until Revision A is released IFR. We do not see the versions in our database we only deal with released/issued for ….. documents.

There will be an expeditor for vendor data/contractor data. The system has 4 levels of expediting reports:

5. Due within the next 5 working days – a friendly reminder – auto emailed to the contractor or vendor and expeditor

6. Due today – a friendly reminder– auto emailed to the contractor or vendor and expeditor
7. Due 5 working days ago – auto emailed to the Engineering Manager and/or expeditor to send on due to the nature of the possibility of liquidated damages being applied
8. Due 10 working days ago – auto email to the Project Manager who will forward on and includes scheduler, cost controller, contracts admin, accounts – progress payments are to be withheld and liquidated damages applied to the payments when made.

DCM/LDC's will expedite all internal design data – there will be in place a "Yellow Card" (first strike) and "Red Card" (second strike) system. That system will automatically generate an expediting email for overdue new data and overdue reviews. A Yellow Card is issued at 5 working days overdue and the Engineering Manager will receive a copy, a Red Card is issued at 10 working days overdue and the EM and Project Manager receive a copy. We WILL NOT be required to change any dates for internal design data.

There is a Vendor Drawing and Data Requirements Spreadsheet that also provides DC with the review team matrix. For our purposes the matrices will be CON-001, CON-002, PO-001, PO-002 and so on. There will be both Internal (Map) and External Distribution matrices.

We will NOT be managing Tender documents submitted. (Not recommended but most common)

We will update our external distribution matrices at the whole package ready for IFT.

We will update our internal distribution matrices on the fly but the original set-up will be, for example, for Mechanical Docs/Drgs – Lead Mechanical Engineer, Lead Piping Engineer, Lead Process Engineer, Lead Structural Engineer, Lead Electrical Engineer, Lead Instrument Engineer, Lead Mechanical Engineer – Operations, Lead Mechanical Engineer. Switch the first and last reviewer around for each discipline and change the Operations Lead for each discipline they are on our "Telephone List".

Our database has a viewer/redlining tool and allows parallel reviews which means more than one Lead can open any document (always a copy but it looks real) at any time and comment and see others comments live.

When we receive the VDDRL from the contractors and vendors, in our excel spreadsheet format, they will immediately go on a 5 day review while the review is taking place we will start to assign document numbers in our copy of the spreadsheet. When the review is complete will we make any necessary changes per mark-ups and import the sheet in to our Database with all the numbers and IFR, IFC due dates.

Because we can plan due to having a Pro-Active register we will have all our DC's in place and trained ahead of need. We will assign 2 LDC's (1 for the hull conversion and 1 for sub-sea), 2 DC's and 1 SDC per contract and 1 DC per vendor. They will be rotated around so they gain experience of all the roles. We do not need, because Operations have an IHOG, a Documents for Operations Coordinator or DC but the DCM will include Operations personnel in the internal review matrices as above.

When we receive a package of drawings/documents from the respective lead engineer for IFR we open and update our database with Rev A and the path to the file, note we will only be doing Squad Check (Inter discipline) reviews Intra discipline reviews will be done on a "no revision" document prior to hand-over to DC for IFR, the system will automatically add the received date and we update the internal distribution map based on the discipline. For KISS we will call these AA-001, CI-001, MM-001 and so on. When the update is complete we raise our Internal Transmittal to the Map and send it electronically (hyperlinks). The system will expedite tardy reviewers based on our Yellow/Red Card system and we will also print off expediting reports and go and talk to anyone who looks like or is overdue to return review documents.

When we receive notification back from the responsible lead that a review is complete we will open the files and note what is in the Review stamp and update our database with the Review Status.

Unless a document has completely failed review on the first pass (code 3) there will be no second review. As we are the client there is no need to Issue documents for approval to the client/operators representative.

The respective lead engineer will take responsibility for striking out or incorporating all mark-ups and Rev B will be the IFT document.

When we receive those we will update our database and when instructed issue them to the potential contractors or vendors for Tender.

During the tender process we will be managing TQ's and RFI's the review matrix for each will be the Lead Discipline Engineer, Scheduler, Cost Controller, Contracts Engineer and Expeditor.

Usually after a "preferred" contractor or vendor is identified there is correspondence and meetings between them, the Lead Discipline Engineer, Scheduler, Cost Controller, Contracts Engineer and Expeditor. Often there are, by necessity, design changes to be made to the IFT documents. Those are issued to us at Rev 0 as either IFC or IFU. We update our distribution matrix the deactivate the failed bidders and add site and other necessary recipients of the documents. We update our database to Rev 0 and issue the documents per the updated matrix.

Ideally, this is not always done, the design is then frozen and to make subsequent changes to IFC/IFU documents and drawings requires an Engineering Change Request process. We will manage ECR's and the matrix for those will be the Lead Discipline Engineer, Scheduler, Cost Controller, Contracts Engineer and Expeditor. Approved ECR's will trigger design change and a review of the revised document at Rev 0A we will update our database and activate an internal review transmittal per the matrix. Once the review is complete the respective lead engineer will take responsibility for striking out or incorporating all mark-ups and Rev 1 will be the IFC/IFU document with the ECR No shown in the revision history. We will update our database and activate an external transmittal per the matrix.

As the project winds down and when design and construction of each area/system is complete the DCM/IMC will open an operations database and documents not requiring As Built will be imported in to the operations database after some final document and data quality checking by the LDC's/DCM. A transmittal is raised to operations usually someone in-house and on the vessel for these documents. System by system, where possible, is preferred otherwise they could be dealing with a lot of material in a very short time frame.

There will be a team in the field doing necessary As Constructed Mark-ups. Rev 1A – we will update our database on receipt but no further action is required

The "hydro" commissioning team will do As Commissioned Mark-ups with the aid of some drafters. Rev 1B – we will update our database on receipt but no further action is required

The "operations" commissioning team will do "As Handed-Over" Mark-ups. Rev 1C – we will update our database on receipt but no further action is required.

Rev 2 will be the As Built Revision. We will update our database do a final data/document quality check then export to the operations database. A transmittal is raised to operations usually someone in-house and on the vessel.

An operations portal will be built by an external professional firm from the operations database and final CAD application data. A transmittal is raised for the portal to operations and the vessel. The portal will be completed before it becomes fully operational and may need some final updating post operations with As Built's from the Operations Commissioning Team.

We will not need to do any data cleansing/massaging for Operations Computerised Maintenance System, e.g. SAP, a copy of the CAD application used with only the final documents and drawings will be integrated to SAP by others.

ALSO

Create an Internal Map from your Telephone List - which is in your imagination but should have at least an/a:

Project Manager
Deputy Project Manager
Engineering Manager
Lead Mechanical Engineer
Lead Maritime (Hull Structure) Engineer
Lead SubSea Engineer
Lead Piping Engineer

Lead Structural (Non Hull) Engineer

Lead Electrical Engineer

Lead Instrument Engineer

Lead Process Engineer

for the Review of "Process" discipline Drawings the order is:

1. Lead Process Engineer
2. Lead Instrument Engineer
3. All other Leads
4. Lead Process Engineer

Select 10 P&ID's at Random and update the Revision to A, the Incoming Status to IFR and the Review Status to INR. Create an internal transmittal for the P&ID's to the Map.

When the transmittal is raised change the Review Status of the drawings to 1 Reviewed no Comment.

Create a company called FPSO's are us with a fake address in Singapore and your personal (or especially made-up free email address)

Create a company called Hull Conversion Constructors with a fake address in Singapore and your personal (or especially made-up free email address)

Create an external distribution set for all Process drawings to both new companies.

Find the 10 P&ID's and Revise them to Rev 0 IFC / IFC

Transmit the drawings to the Distribution Set.

Create a new Company called Pump Engineers Malaysia with a fake address in Malaysia and add your personal (or especially made-up free email address)

They have been awarded a pump package and will be delivering pumps and motors. They will need

50 V Mechanical Drawing No's

250 V Electrical Drawing No's

1 IOM No

1 MDR No

250 V Instrument Drawing No's

1 VDDRL (which we will send them to complete)

We will send to them to complete approximately 50 Datasheets to complete and return. They will need to see ALL P&ID's at IFT and IFC.

The Project Name/Code is FPSO1

F1 = AIMS Code, F2 = VDcNo

For a complete list and other settings/valid codes see Appendix 2B.

22.00 C Our Document Control
Practical Exercise – Civil

Using the information below let's revisit our Document Control flow chart and also open DrawCon add a new project and set-up the valid codes and library tables, then add/reserve the documents.

Assumptions:

1. We are using Pro-Active Document Control methods.
2. You are all DCM or LDC's – you have been promoted. I am your IMC and above me is the project controls manager and then (those we work with) an Engineering Manager, a Drawing Office Manager, a scheduler and a QA/QC Manager plus a Lead Discipline Engineer for each Discipline.
3. The project has received a Final Investment Decision from Pre-Feed and FEED documentation etc. and has been given the go ahead.
4. The answers to our questions are Yes.
5. We are "Project Managing" the Project.
6. Our company can obtain better prices on some of the materials and other equipment needed for the conversion and we will be placing the Purchase Orders and Contracts for those items.
7. We are also to be the operator and have "operations" Information Hand-Over Guide.
8. ALL documents and drawings produced, including Shop Detail Drawings, will have some form of review.
9. There has been a "Registration of Interest" process during FEED and all potential tenderers for every P/O have been identified but no letters of intent have been sent to any Vendor.
10. We are building an Advanced Water Treatment Plant. No contracts have been awarded but the FEED team identified a number of suitable constructors and other vendors such as the Reverse Osmosis equipment (a long lead item).
11. We are doing ALL the design work except for the site buildings (Offices/Control Room etc.) which are to be awarded on a P/O.

12. With some exceptions the project team is in place and we have a "telephone list" of names and positions to add to our database. The client (owner) and the client's contracted Operator will be on all reviews.

13. We IMC/DCM/LDC and expeditor will be at contract/PO kick-off meetings to discuss drawing and data requirements and the "VDDRL" and will only leave when the list, dates in particular, is agreed and the contractors and vendors agree to the procedure for Contractor/Vendor drawings and data.

14. Only Piping (not Iso's) i.e. the model, Electrical, Instrument and Process drawings and documents will be As Built

15. Only an MDR, IOM and Vendor Drawings will be handed over to operations from Vendors. ALL design documents will be handed over at the final revision. TQ's, RFI's and ECR's will not be handed over.

16. The entire project document system will be 100% electronic we will not be accepting paper drawings/documents/mark-ups from anyone a tracer or junior engineer will be employed to assist those who prefer to work with paper to bring up to date electronic copies.

The construction will take 15 months and the plant will be "trial run" for the first three months but us.

We are responsible for "commissioning".

The AWTP will be fully operational in 18 months.

The questions you must ask with me are:

1. Are there any documents and data to carry over from the FEED?

2. Is the data in the document profiles up to date and correct?

3. Is the project to be done almost entirely in 3D CAD?

4. Do we have a rough procurement schedule for items to be purchased by us?

Firstly, we open a new project and either manually add all the "valid" codes or import them from a library source.

We add all the "telephone list" of project team members to the database. Each "Lead" engineer is also the "package engineer" for their respective discipline. Our database does not have workflows therefore unless we are directed otherwise the leads for each discipline are the reviewers.

We add to our database the list of contracts and P/O's.

We import, after any necessary Data Quality (DQ) Audit/Desk topping, the documents and data from FEED into our project database. Regardless of what we are told we WILL DQ Audit ALL data associated with any documents to be imported in to our project.

We print off any Process Flow Diagram(s) and any P&ID's.

Working with both the Engineering Manager (EM), Scheduler (Sch) and Drawing Office Manager (DOM) and our list from procurement we develop, often in Excel, a rough (it can never be 100% right) deliverables list with some IFR, IFT and IFC delivery dates.

Let's say (nowhere near a complete list) we will have, prior to receiving Vendor Drawing Lists for the items we are purchasing:

1 Overall 3D Model

36 (No Car Park 3D) 3D model sections each to be delivered based on the schedule dates/procurement dates for the respective "plant areas/ systems"

There will be no Mechanical, Piping (other than Isometrics), in 2D.

There will be approximately 100 Structural GA type drawings. Split them evenly across each are – buildings, tanks etc.

There will be approximately 20 "Architectural" drawings for offices etc.

There will be approximately 36 P&ID's (1 per area/system)

There are 37 PFD's to be updated – 1 Overall and one for each area not including the car park.

There will be approximately 10,000 Structural Shop Detail Drawings split them among the main buildings e.g. RO Building, Microfiltration Building, Covered Rec Area

There will be approximately 10,000 Instrument Loop Diagrams, which the 3D CAD system can produce – 5000 for Water Quality Analysis split the rest evenly none in Admin/Car Park.

There will be approximately 20 Instrument Layout/GA drawings Split Evenly none in Admin/Car Park.

There will be approximately 1,000 Electrical Drawings – across all areas some in the car park

There will be approximately 15 Scope of Work Documents (15 Contracts and P/O's to be awarded) – use "General" system/area code (not right but close enough for the exercise)

There will be approximately 100 Specifications in various disciplines for the contracts/PO's – use "General" system/area code (not right but close enough for the exercise)

There will be approximately 1000 Datasheets -– use "General" system/area code (not right but close enough for the exercise)

There will be approximately 100 Calculation "Documents" across all disciplines - – use "General" system/area code and General discipline (not right but close enough for the exercise)

There will be 1 Contract "Vendor Drawing and Data Requirements List" and 14 P/O – Vendor VDDRL's.

We will be using all Corporate "Plans", "Policies", "Procedures" and "Standards" except where shown above. They will be "issued to us" by Corporate Information Control and we will add them to our database with their existing numbers and we will NOT be revising any of them. These standards include an Equipment/Tag Numbering standard and the 3D CAD application will assign Tag Numbers and will track Tag to Document and Document to Document relationships.

There will be one major contract, construction, and 14 P/O's for piping, instruments, mechanical equipment such as pumps, various (Mechanical and Instrument/Process Controls) valves, steel, admin buildings units etc.

The major contract is almost complete and will be based on FEED documents we are importing in to our system they become Distribution Matrix CON-001 the intent is to award in 4 weeks and the contractor must produce its Drawing and Data List within one week of award. Their document numbers will come from our system but will NOT be badged V or F. Let's say the award will be 1 Feb 2014

The remaining 14 P/O's will have their documentation developed by us and will be issued for tender (IFT) at 2 P/O's the second month after the contract is awarded let's say 1 Mar 2014, then 2 per month there–after for the remaining 7 let's say on the 1ˢᵗ of each month. Awards are intended for 2 months after the initial IFT date. E.g. The first award is scheduled for 1 May 2014.

All the "Vendors" will have 7 days post award to submit their drawing and data lists and we will be assigning them numbers (with some spares) from those lists with a V pre the sequence number and there will only be one database for the project (not recommended it is usually much simpler to have a separate database for Vendors).

On our spreadsheet we assign dates IFR for documents 4 weeks prior to IFT – note this is usually not anywhere near this compressed but we need to secure the hull. IFT will be as above. IFC will be set for the same date as the award dates and the P/O's will go to the vendors with IFC documents.

We check for the document numbers already in use and assign new numbers in our spreadsheet for the documents outlined above. Note that the PFD's and P&ID's already exist but in FEED format which is not as complete as a fully engineered drawing.

We (EM, Sch, DOM and DCM/LDC(s)) are all agreed on the spreadsheet and it is not imported in to our database.

Our settings for Progress against status in DrawCon will be:

DocStatCode	DocStatName	ProgVal
1	Reviewed No Comment	90.00%
2	Reviewed with Comment	80.00%
3	Do Not Proceed	60.00%
4	Accepted as Final/IFC	95.00%
5	Accepted as As Built	100.00%
AB	As Built	100.00%
CAN	Cancelled	0.00%
IFI	Issued For information	0.00%
IFT	Issued For Tender	85.00%
IFU	Issued for Use	100.00%
INR	In Review	60.00%
RSV	Reserved/In Preparation	0.00%

We will not be managing budget hours against deliverables therefore the progress milestones do not mean a great deal as we have little to actually report against. The "progress curve" if we were to produce one is very steep as it goes from 0% directly to 60% at IFR. In a full CAD/EEDMS application other milestones precede IFR and budget hours are recorded for each deliverable and the system automatically tracks progress based on a drawing or document template being opened from a "place-holder" our database puts in it and the amount of actual work done in the template (not time based but time open is recorded) these systems tend to "version" these as, for example, A1, A2 and so on until Revision A is released IFR. We do not see the versions in our database we only deal with released/issued for ….. documents.

There will be an expeditor for vendor data/contractor data. The system has 4 levels of expediting reports:

1. Due within the next 5 working days – a friendly reminder – auto emailed to the contractor or vendor and expeditor
2. Due today – a friendly reminder– auto emailed to the contractor or vendor and expeditor
3. Due 5 working days ago – auto emailed to the Engineering Manager and/or expeditor to send on due to the nature of the possibility of liquidated damages being applied
4. Due 10 working days ago – auto email to the Project Manager who will forward on and includes scheduler, cost controller, contracts admin, accounts – progress payments are to be with-held and liquidated damages applied to the payments when made.

DCM/LDC's will expedite all internal design data – there will be in place a "Yellow Card" (first strike) and "Red Card" (second strike) system. That system will automatically generate an expediting email for overdue new data and overdue reviews. A Yellow Card is issued at 5 working days overdue and the Engineering Manager will receive a copy, a Red Card is issued at 10 working days overdue and the EM and Project Manager receive a copy. We WILL NOT be required to change any dates for internal design data.

There is a Vendor Drawing and Data Requirements Spreadsheet that also provides DC with the review team matrix. For our purposes the matrices will be CON-001, CON-002, PO-001, PO-002 and so on. There will be both Internal (Map) and External Distribution matrices.

We will NOT be managing Tender documents submitted. (Not recommended but most common)

We will update our external distribution matrices at the whole package ready for IFT.

We will update our internal distribution matrices on the fly but the original set-up will be, for example, for Mechanical Docs/Drgs – Lead Mechanical Engineer, Lead Piping Engineer, Lead Process Engineer, Lead Structural Engineer, Lead Electrical Engineer, Lead Instrument Engineer, Lead Mechanical Engineer – Operations, Lead Mechanical Engineer. Switch the first and last reviewer around for each discipline and change the Operations Lead for each discipline they are on our "Telephone List".

Our database has a viewer/redlining tool and allows parallel reviews which means more than one Lead can open any document (always a copy but it looks real) at any time and comment and see others comments live.

When we receive the VDDRL from the contractors and vendors, in our excel spreadsheet format, they will immediately go on a 5 day review while the review is taking place we will start to assign document numbers in our copy of the spreadsheet. When the review is complete will we make any necessary changes per mark-ups and import the sheet in to our Database with all the numbers and IFR, IFC due dates.

Because we can plan due to having a Pro-Active register we will have all our DC's in place and trained ahead of need. We will assign 2 LDC's (1 for the hull conversion and 1 for sub-sea), 2 DC's and 1 SDC per contract and 1 DC per vendor. They will be rotated around so they gain experience of all the roles. We do not need, because Operations have an IHOG, a Documents for Operations Coordinator or DC but the DCM will include Operations personnel in the internal review matrices as above.

When we receive a package of drawings/documents from the respective lead engineer for IFR we open and update our database with Rev A and the path to the file, note we will only be doing Squad Check (Inter discipline) reviews Intra discipline reviews will be done on a "no revision" document prior to hand-over to DC for IFR, the system will automatically add the received date and we update the internal distribution map based on the discipline. For KISS we will call these AA-001, CI-001, MM-001 and so on. When the update is complete we raise our Internal Transmittal to the Map and send it electronically (hyperlinks). The system will expedite tardy reviewers based on our Yellow/Red Card system and we will also print off expediting reports and go and talk to anyone who looks like or is overdue to return review documents.

When we receive notification back from the responsible lead that a review is complete we will open the files and note what is in the Review stamp and update our database with the Review Status.

Unless a document has completely failed review on the first pass (code 3) there will be no second review. As we are the client there is no need to Issue documents for approval to the client/operators representative.

The respective lead engineer will take responsibility for striking out or incorporating all mark-ups and Rev B will be the IFT document.

When we receive those we will update our database and when instructed issue them to the potential contractors or vendors for Tender.

During the tender process we will be managing TQ's and RFI's the review matrix for each will be the Lead Discipline Engineer, Scheduler, Cost Controller, Contracts Engineer and Expeditor.

Usually after a "preferred" contractor or vendor is identified there is correspondence and meetings between them, the Lead Discipline Engineer, Scheduler, Cost Controller, Contracts Engineer and Expeditor. Often there are, by necessity, design changes to be made to the IFT documents. Those are issued to us at Rev 0 as either IFC or IFU. We update our distribution matrix the deactivate the failed bidders and add site and other necessary recipients of the documents. We update our database to Rev 0 and issue the documents per the updated matrix.

Ideally, this is not always done, the design is then frozen and to make subsequent changes to IFC/IFU documents and drawings requires an Engineering Change Request process. We will manage ECR's and the matrix for those will be the Lead Discipline Engineer, Scheduler, Cost Controller, Contracts Engineer and Expeditor. Approved ECR's will trigger design change and a review of the revised document at Rev 0A we will update our database and activate an internal review transmittal per the matrix. Once the review is complete the respective lead engineer will take responsibility for striking out or incorporating all mark-ups and Rev 1 will be the IFC/IFU document with the ECR No shown in the revision history. We will update our database and activate an external transmittal per the matrix.

As the project winds down and when design and construction of each area/system is complete the DCM/IMC will open an operations database and documents not requiring As Built will be imported in to the operations database after some final document and data quality checking by the LDC's/DCM. A transmittal is raised to operations usually someone in-house and on the vessel for these documents. System by system, where possible, is preferred otherwise they could be dealing with a lot of material in a very short time frame.

There will be a team in the field doing necessary As Constructed Mark-ups. Rev 1A – we will update our database on receipt but no further action is required

The "hydro" commissioning team will do As Commissioned Mark-ups with the aid of some drafters. Rev 1B – we will update our database on receipt but no further action is required

The "operations" commissioning team will do "As Handed-Over" Mark-ups. Rev 1C – we will update our database on receipt but no further action is required.

Rev 2 will be the As Built Revision. We will update our database do a final data/document quality check then export to the operations database. A transmittal is raised to operations usually someone in-house and on the vessel.

An operations portal will be built by an external professional firm from the operations database and final CAD application data. A transmittal is raised for the portal to operations and the vessel. The portal will be completed before it becomes fully operational and may need some final updating post operations with As Built's from the Operations Commissioning Team.

We will not need to do any data cleansing/massaging for Operations Computerised Maintenance System, e.g. SAP, a copy of the CAD application used with only the final documents and drawings will be integrated to SAP by others.

ALSO

Create an Internal Map from your Telephone List – which is in your imagination but should have at least an/a:

> Project Manager
> Deputy Project Manager
> Engineering Manager
> Lead Mechanical Engineer
> Lead Maritime (Hull Structure) Engineer
> Lead SubSea Engineer
> Lead Piping Engineer
> Lead Structural (Non Hull) Engineer
> Lead Electrical Engineer
> Lead Instrument Engineer
> Lead Process Engineer
> Client Document Control
> Client's Operator Document Control

for the Review of "Process" discipline Drawings the order is:

1. Lead Process Engineer
2. Lead Instrument Engineer
3. All other Leads
4. Client
5. Client's Operator
6. Lead Process Engineer

Select 10 P&ID's at Random and update the Revision to A, the Incoming Status to IFR and the Review Status to INR. Create an internal transmittal for the P&ID's to the Map.

When the transmittal is raised change the Review Status of the drawings to 1 Reviewed no Comment.

Create a company called AWTP's are us with a fake address in Brisbane and your personal (or especially made-up free email address)

Create an external distribution set for all Process drawings to both new companies.

Find the 10 P&ID's and Revise them to Rev 0 IFC / IFC

Transmit the drawings to the Distribution Set.

Create a new Company called Pump Engineers Malaysia with a fake address in Malaysia and add your personal (or especially made-up free email address)

They have been awarded a pump package and will be delivering pumps and motors. They will need

50 V Mechanical Drawing No's

250 V Electrical Drawing No's

1 IOM No

1 MDR No

250 V Instrument Drawing No's

1 VDDRL (which we will send them to complete)

We will send to them to complete approximately 50 Datasheets to complete and return. They will need to see ALL P&ID's at IFT and IFC.

The Project Name/Code is AWTP-1

F1 = AIMS Code, F2 = VDcNo

For a complete list and other settings/valid codes see Appendix 2C.

23.00 Life After Hand-Over

23.01 Management of Change

This is in operations and there are two types of Management of Change which can come in two forms, MOC's are most often initiated in the DMS or CMS applications:

23.01.1 Types

23.01.1.1 Technical

Technical MOC's affect equipment in the field used in operations. For example, we may have on our plant a pump with a 10,000 hour life. We have found out that the pump in use is now obsolete new technology has delivered a new one that is smaller, draws less power and has different fittings. Our pump is at 9500 hours – we decide to affect an MOC to change it out and carry out the necessary pipework, control system and electrical changes at 10,000 hours.

23.01.1.2 Organizational

Using the above pump example we must find out what documents that relate to it will now be superseded or made obsolete by new ones. The SOP is likely to change. The Operating Manual will change as will Parts Lists. Or where the organisation has a "standard" set of specifications for equipment that goes out with Purchase Orders an MOC can be raised to change them to meet new technology.

23.02 Forms of MOC

23.02.1.1 Planned

The two examples above are forms of planned change. We know we must change something and therefore we plan the change.

23.02.1.2 On the Fly

Using the above 10,000 hour pump life example let's say that there are two in the field and the second one is also at 9500 but it breaks down. There is no redundant stand-by pump in the system. We are forced to bring in a new pump immediately and make all the necessary field engineering changes straight away. An MOC is then raised after the work is done to ensure the changes are reported and systems/documents updated.

From a project Document Controllers perspective operations document control can be boring but it MUST be experienced.

24.00 What Else Do We Need

24.01 Hardware

To perform document control effectively we will need:

A high spec PC/Laptop preferably with 2 x 21" Monitors

Excellent Bandwidth, preferably own Server or very fast network share – note for most EEDMS applications a separate server or share on a fast server is absolutely essential

Wide format Printer with scanning capability

The difference between an MFC Scanner and a Desktop Scanner – note that most MFC's default scan to colour, black or grey scale depending on settings and only to 300 DPI resolution – some go to 600 DPI but settings have to be changed for each scan. Desktop scanners usually, not always, start at 1200 DPI. The higher the resolution the better the scan quality and the less Document Quality checking we will have to do – the most common problems are I's, J's, L's and 1's and/or O, o and 0 (zero) and/or B's and 8's looking alike. Some fine lines on drawings can disappear too.

When preparing, especially drawings, for offshore assets (FPSO, Platforms, Rigs) and for near shore assets where salt air and/or damp air is a problem we may need a laminator that can manage A1 drawings – often this is done by an out of house 3rd party provider.

24.02 Non EEDMS Software

At a software level other than the EEDMS we MUST have some form of Office applications, Word and Excel or the equivalent are MUST HAVES, Access is handy too, and either Acrobat Standard/Professional or another pdf tool with the same functionality possibly with the 3D add-in. If we are not using an EEDMS with built-in communications or a SaaS collaboration tool we may also need an FTP site for transfer of large files.

We may also require a CAD viewer tool one that will open and allow redlining for most CAD files such as DWG and DGN – that is if we are not using an EEDMS or collaboration tool with a built-in redlining/viewer tool. As an example, where there is an intention to use a Sharepoint based tool, Brava have an integration for SharePoint and it (Brava) works beautifully stand-alone.

Sharepoint alone is NOT a Document Control tool it is a file store and even that needs to be set-up correctly.

24.03 Furniture and Fittings

We need a roomy workstation we must be able to read from an A1 drawing on our left (or right if left handed) and data-bash in to a computer.

If you are responsible for planning the office layout for DC then remember we need lots of space, especially where we have to keep paper records, filing cabinets, bookcases, compactuses, plan tanks, stick file racks, plan printers and MFC's (we should have our own good to A2 size) and layout tables all eat space. We will also need space in the building for building an archive using, for example, Loeff's boxes. A simple partitioned workstation, unless we are 100% electronic, is not enough.

NOTE WELL: If you are going to deploy a compactus for paper files the floor space on which it sits must be structurally checked. A compactus itself can weigh a lot when full of paper it will be very heavy and if the floor is not designed to take that kind of weight it will buckle and buckle the compactus too making it difficult, if not impossible, to open or worse if buckling happens fast (not progressively) tip the contents on the floor or someone using it at the time!

25.00 Knowledge of a Document Control System

25.01 Understanding Databases

ALL Document Control applications along with CMS and CAD tools are driven by or have some form of database engine that you may not actually see. It is wise to take a course on, the simplest, MS Access to paint a picture of how databases work and data is entered and stored, queried and reported on.

ALL EEDMS or DC Applications are some form of a database with forms, queries, reports etc. at the front, sometimes built with MS Access and a table structure at the back in either:

MS Access

SQL Server

Oracle

Bespoke Database Application such as Visual FoxPro

.Net

ALL databases store data in tables. The "relationships" between the tables can vary depending on the way data needs to be stored.

If you would like to get a better understanding of databases and how they work it is recommended that you undertake a basic and intermediate MS Access course.

25.01.1 One to One Relationships

Some DC Database Tools have One to One relationships between different tables and fields for example one has only a One to One function for recording Tag/Equipment No's against a Document No. This is limiting.

However, someone to one relationships do exist such as Document No to Asset, Plant/System, Discipline, and Document Type.

25.01.2 One to Many Relationships

Most DC Database Applications have a One to Many relationships between Tables and Fields for example the Document No and Transmittal History.

The significant drawback could be a "Cascade" delete. If you delete a document profile ALL the data associated with it e.g. Tag/Equipment No's is deleted too – no big deal and you are VERY unlikely to delete an entire document profile unless it has zero history at all. However, you may try to delete a Doc/Tag relationship and that could delete the document profile which was not intended – does not happen in DrawCon but I have seen it happen in other tools!

25.02 Document Control Applications

Document Control applications vary greatly. NOT all are created equal.

DC Databases. DrawCon is one there are 4 others I know of and possibly more. DrawCon allows one to many relationships across a broad range of fields and has date fields for proactive document control. It can manage files stored on the network and another tool, which integrates to DrawCon, can "spy" on the network and will find files that have been moved and present the option of moving the file back or updating DrawCon. Some other DC applications only have restricted one to one relationships with items such as Tag Numbers. Despite this these applications do do what they say out of the box so careful selection is advised.

Collaboration tools are often used to send documents out for review on workflows and allows vendors direct access for document submission but do not store much data in the document profile or are not meant as document control tools but intended to integrate to one – not always true some are great DC tools others are just collaboration tools and nothing more. These are often SaaS applications and manage either one file or multiple files against one document profile. IMO avoiding those that can only store one file to a document profile should be avoided otherwise you may need to zip together at the minimum a native and pdf.

EDMS applications also vary and many do not work well in engineering without add-ons (most of which work beautifully by themselves). These manage files but might have limited data against a document profile. Some have excellent workflow tools coupled with redline/mark-up/viewer tools (e.g. Brava) which negates the need for internal transmittals but others do not and do not have a transmittal generator either. Most are records management tools and work well with and integrate to office applications but not CAD applications. Some can only manage one file against a document profile while others can manage multiple files against one profile but may create a parent (native) / child (pdf) relationship between the files and the profile.

Engineering EDMS or EEDMS applications have document profiles with all the fields we need or they are simple to add by a power user or System Administrator, have excellent workflow tools coupled with redline/mark-up/viewer tools (e.g. Brava) which negates the need for internal transmittals. They will integrate to Office and CAD applications either completely or sufficiently to allow "data mining" and management of files. These vary from off the shelf applications by software houses and fully integrated applications by CAD Software providers such as SmartPlant Foundation by Intergraph or ProjectWise by Bentley. Some are locally hosted on your own servers and others are SaaS tools.

SharePoint. All too sadly, to me at least, is becoming a weapon of choice. It has a lot of limitations not the least of which is setting a drop-dead date on workflow – in 2016 it was easy but now no. Note that searches can be slowed terribly when there are more than 5000 files and metadata fields are NOT used. If there is a SharePoint programmer inhouse speak to them you need to ask for the metadata (codes) to be added and a simple, similar to the Drawcon document profile to be added for new documents (with dropdowns) and searches. This gets around the 5000 file problem and improves search speeds and the form itself will drive where the files go.

Sharepoint, either directly or via a third party tool can be connected to email tools such as Outlook which can be very beneficial.

Note OneDrive and Teams Sharepoints are much the same as Sharepoint although some functionality may be missing. Sharepoint is also limited to, including the, path, file name and extension to 260 characters and this can be problematic and, I believe also sorted with Metadata fields.

Many DC tools, Drawcon and Teambinder are two, will link to files in Sharepoint.

Again, based on my experience, the Bentley tool ProjectWise is fantastic for CAD produced docs and drgs but is awful when it comes to non CAD files. If required to use it you may need to use a Sharepoint, set-up as above, and try to find a way to link the two.

SmartPlant foundation I am unable to comment on re DC other than to say when it is set-up properly it can be a great tool, but I do know it can be expensive to roll-out, especially on small projects and some companies have had issues with its Operations variant SmartPlant Operations. I mean no slight here either to Aveva or those that were trying to get the product(s) to work.

25.03 Software Development Models

There are a number of different software models the two most common are:

Type 1. A base product is provided and will work out of the box but may have some limitation you need changed for example a 25 character Doc No field and you need 50 (most ISO's run to 40) – note this affects not just the field in the data entry form/profile but reports etc. You may need a new field added for a particular purpose (let's say Doc SubType and/or OIMS/AIMS Code or Weight [for progress]) and that field must appear in reports etc. and the design tools to do that are not provided with the software or are just difficult to get along with and the software does not support ODBC linking to Access where we might do the job ourselves (a work-around). The software provider may, at a cost, send you a patch to do what you need straight away or within a day or so. This is a distinct advantage. The disadvantage is that your copy now becomes a non-core product and the software provider may also do some development work on the core product and release a patch for the new version which cannot be tested against your non-core version and could crash it or reverse the changes you had paid for already.

Type 2. As above except the software provider will consider the changes you require and may even poll other users and if they are happy with the proposed changes will then carry out the programming required and release a new version of the core product. The advantage is it remains core and is unlikely to crash. The disadvantage is that you could be waiting for some time for the change because the provider has a development plan and those changes will take place within the plan.

25.04 CAD Applications

CAD Applications vary a great deal too. Some are straight drawing tools with small databases and limited or no connectivity to other design tools and have no "intelligence".

Others can produce "Intelligent" drawings such as P&ID's but still have limited or no integration to other tools.

Most designers now use a fully integrated suite of design tools such as AutoDesk, Bentley, Intergraph or Aveva which all have a core database. Some of these have Calculation tools etc. or will integrate directly to those tools as well.

26.00 Finding the right DC Application for your needs

http://cad.about.com/od/CAD_Standards/a/Enigineering-Document-Management-Software.htm

Finding the right DC application for your needs is all about the questions you ask about your own infrastructure and needs and then those you need to ask of the vendors. Some are, but not limited to:

What do your systems support in terms of what Database systems are already in use?

E.g. SQL Server, Oracle Servers

> Where your IT infrastructure may not suit a possible application are you prepared to go to the expense of providing or having the vendor provide the necessary servers for that application?

Do you want to "host" your application or are you comfortable with SaaS?

> Bandwidth is a big issue across a LAN or a WAN especially where remote sites are involved. Some tools offer hybrid solutions such as, for example, ProArc which is locally hosted but has a web-based tool for remote users. Also note some companies are still very uncomfortable with having their "sensitive documents" stored on the cloud and this can, despite the fact that SaaS providers usually have more security than in-house systems, become an issue.

Do you already run a DMS application such as Documentum or FileNet?

We can find excellent add-ons for these types of tools.

Don't forget that all these tools have, in the backend, some form of database application eg. Oracle, MS Access etc.

I strongly recommend steering well away from any "system" that does not offer ODBC connectivity or a tool that allows that to happen. An example of this is applications written in Visual FoxPro (VFP). Microsoft ceased supporting it a long time ago and there are, as far as I know, no tools that permit, for example, MS Access to link to VFP in any way, shape or form. There are ways around the problems that not having ODBC can cause but, using my least favourite swear word, they are "work-arounds" such as exporting data to excel then doing any necessary data massaging and re-uploading the data from that sheet! NOT AT ALL recommended especially given some of excels, IMO, pain in the rear end weaknesses such as, eg. scrambled sorts★.

★Being a fan of using databases over spreadsheets I have found that, for example, when you do a sort in a database everything is sorted. In a spreadsheet unless you click the top right corner and highlight the entire sheet (there is another way too) then your sort will only sort the column you picked! Huge pain in.... often times when the mistake is realised its too late to hit undo that means starting all over again.

Do you want to integrate to MSOffice (with Templates – data added/mined) including Outlook?

Most applications, other than DC Databases (Drawcon can integrate to SharePoint and QDMS has some support for Sharepoint as an add-on), can integrate to various other applications. Some of the SaaS Collaboration tools might not.

If integrating to Outlook a way not to store "chatter" must be found this can, with some tools, be done with settings and allowing the user to choose whether or not to save to the DMS when the send button is pressed (post send) the user will need to complete a profile.

Do you want to integrate to CAD Applications (which)

Many applications support integration to CAD applications and some are already fully integrated because they are designed that way for example SmartPlant Foundation and ProjectWise.

Do you run Multiple projects and/or Operations?

This is especially important. If the software has to be re-installed for every project or operation then it can become cumbersome and painful to use. Some operators acquired assets from others and the coding for each asset they have could be different. Projects in this environment or an EPC environment may have different clients or classification/coding methods. If this is not something that can be done easily by a DC System Administrator then think twice about the application – having to have IT people or the vendor run configurations and set-ups is NOT optimal.

This is not uncommon and setting up a new project in some tools can be time consuming and painful while others are simple and allow import of data from core library/configuration tables such as classification codes, address books etc.

Where we are running operations will the application need to support an Operations portal?

Some applications will allow others to query them for data for a portal such as Aveva Net. Others allow the construction of a portal in the application. Portals are the most efficient and simplest way for operations to find documents in a hurry.

Do you run SAP or another CMS you might need to integrate to?

Most applications have API suites for this purpose.

Do you have or need to integrate to an Integrated Project Management System/Accounting Package/Planning Tool such as Primavera?

Many applications have some or full support for Planning tools. Some are already integrated to an IPMS e.g. CoreWorx or Omega. Where these integrations may be required or some data mining from one to the other permitted then that need must be carefully investigated.

How many documents per project

Some tools have limitations, while they may say they do not they can become terribly slow and frustrating to use when there is a lot of data stored.

Do you need Built-In Communications tools with templates for such things as TQ's?

Most of the collaboration applications and EEDMS tools offer this. Others may support, via an integration to a DMS like FileNet, the ability to build these types of forms and templates.

Do you want some kind of Web Interface and allow third party access?

Collaboration tools are usually SaaS and this is automatic and access is set-up by the system administrator but what they access, i.e. security, needs to be investigated carefully.

Collaboration Tools – Redline Mark-up

Do you need a built-in Redlining/Collaboration Tool? Most use Brava which is excellent and others use Rasterex – investigate them carefully. Note that Acrobat Standard comes with excellent mark-up functions but this is best deployed only where a "war room" squad check method is used and you plan to continue to use it.

Remote/Low Bandwidth Sites?

Remote and Low Bandwidth sites can be a huge problem especially with respect to how the data is accessed and updated. If you have bandwidth issues internally or across the WAN you will really need to carefully consider how well the tools you deploy might work. Even some of the simple SaaS tools can eat bandwidth when accessing or updating data and become slow and frustrating to use – note that when "opening" a file in a collaboration SaaS tool the file is actually (you may not see it) downloaded – a big file across a low bandwidth connection may not open or take a long time to do so.

Are you prepared to do a little in-house development?

If you are already running Sharepoint and have files stored there we may be able to develop an Access tool to add the profile data and integrate to a redlining tool such as Brava. There are other applications that will work very well with Sharepoint out of the box such as Cadac Organice.

Also note that there are some good OpenSource applications in the market place, for example Alfresco, that others have developed add-ons for. Again, some companies are very uncomfortable with OpenSource applications.

What are you currently using and will you export the data to the new tool

Most applications offer a bulk-load tool usually built in excel. This makes the transfer of files and data somewhat simpler but you may still need to export files out to Windows Explorer and then in to the new tool. We will also HAVE to do some data-quality auditing and cleansing but this is not super difficult, time consuming yes, where an excel load tool is available as we can build a conversion and/or validation sheet to populate the load tool – note some load tools do not accept data from formulae so we may need to do a copy/paste special values routine.

How much can you spend?

Some of these applications are inexpensive but you might only get what you pay for or limited functionality – (not always true), some are expensive but may not do the whole job for Engineering DC and you may not get what you expect. **Configuration is/can be key with many of these tools.**

Developing an RFP/RFQ and doing a complete needs and gap analysis can be an exhaustive process and a good RFP might run to between 55 and 100 pages.

Here is an example Other\L. RFP.pdf

with "Score Sheet" Other\Scoring-Evaluation Chart for DMS.xlsx

Unless the situation is dire the whole process can take up to 6 months pre implementation and roll-out and a trial run, called a pilot, is recommended on a FEED or other small project to identify areas that might need improvement.

In the ever growing world of "Engineering" many projects involve the "coming together" of a number of SME's and this is not always done in a Joint Venture or completely under one roof. Some of these "comings together" are necessitated by the move from government owned and controlled assets, eg. Rail, to the private sector. Good, bad or otherwise when looking at them they can appear to be a complete (circular – harder to find the way out) maze (or an outright Frankenstein's monster.

This makes having a tool or tools that permit "live" collaboration on documents ever more important. Effectively this also does away with expensive meetings especially where people have to travel to said meetings they lose a lot of time in travel to and fro.

There is a legion of collaboration tools in the market, some good, some ok, some not so good. A majority of these tools are forced, often by the unknowing, on DC's as a DC tool and a majority just are not a DC tool.

There, are in the market place now, a number, small, of great DC tools that permit "live"collaboration.

In the mind of this author a collaboration tool must have the following functionality:

If not a, proper, DC tool – integration via API's or some other suite to one.

"Live" collaboration must permit online live marking up of an "image" not the original.

> "Live" collaboration must include some kind of Instant Messaging preferably but not 100% necessarily Audit Trailed – who said what and when could become a problem if a court case evolves at some point in the future.
>
> Must allow access, which can be controlled by the project owner, to third parties all over the world. (Bandwidth could be an issue here), as can be time differences and

work week differences (eg. nations in the Muslim world where Fri and Saturday are the weekend).

Where the tool is also to be used for or is built-in to a DC tool for Reviews and Approvals there are a number of other great to haves and necessities.

Must have. Reviews on images in "layers" that all other reviewers can see – avoids duplication of comments. These individual layers must also be audit trailed and saved, and easily accessible, within the system.

Great to have. With respect to the above. The final "layer" should be for the document originator who can then copy comments from the reviewers to the final layer instead of having to do an entirely new "layer" to compile valid comments. NB many of the "viewer" packages in the market cannot do this.

Must have. System Administration that permits the appending of an electronic signature by the "Checker" and "Approver" and a list of who they are. This should be via a second password. When the "Approver" status codes a document as "Approved" then he/she is asked for a second password before his/her signature is applied to the appropriate part of a "review stamp" or the document. ALL audit trailed.

Must have. A set of, or singular, system stamp that is applied when a status code is applied to a document with the code(s) already explained and the usual "get out" clause too.

Must have. (If time is not a huge issue – good to have). A way of comparing revisions and showing what has changed. Example:

> We have received from a Vendor a drawing. We called it Rev A. We reviewed and marked it up and sent it back. Sometimes these may be recorded as A1 and A2.
>
> The vendor now sends in Rev B.
>
> The system should support – giving the option of either opening the clean, A1, or marked A2 and comparing them to B and then showing, on a separate screen, what is different between the two chosen drawings. A major time saving "device".

Without such functionality actually collaborating on, reviewing and approving documents will be a difficult and time consuming process.

Two notes here. BS1192 (soon to be replaced by an ISO) – DO NOT Follow this at all – EVER. The Rev/Versioning system is backwards and, at best, the whole risks breaking the law with respect to evidence and comment capture between Revisions and Versions. Also, the suggested numbering method for linear assets, something made even worse by a UK Road Agency, is just plain daft – we have mandatory metadata fields or can build them we do not need all that info in a Document Number at all. Not written by someone who played in the real world. The intent is great the execution lamentable.

The function of a DC will soon change. Most, if not all, nations (exclusions are China and Vietnam and I think they would also accept digitally signed documents they must already have Records Management Acts for online trading and things like WeChat wallet.

Nearly everything we do will be entirely electronic in the future. I actually miss the paper but not the filing…. We will still need all the skills and knowledge in the book but we will be system administrators for DMS applications and data bashers – filling in document profiles, enabling workflows (internal transmittals) and sending Transmittals or making sure the system has and that they are correct.

27.00 Finding an EEDMS Solution

First and foremost, you must have an experienced IT Project Manager, Prince 2 is essential, and one that will listen to ALL users – it is wise to actually appoint an IT knowledgeable Document Controller to the EEMDS project on a part then full time basis not for managing documents but for providing essential input.

When you have done some of the Needs and Gap Analysis it is also wise to have a part time project team who will attend demonstrations, ask questions and provide feedback from across the user group try to "trap" one from every possible group, IT knowledge is not essential here as we have to remember not everyone is IT skilled and ease of use for non IT skilled people is an essential part of any tool.

For those of you who have already done the Document and Correspondence Control course some of this material will be a repeat. For others it is ESSENTIAL that you have done the pre-reading and also have read at the very least Chapters 25 and 26 of this book.

27.01 Understanding the differences between Engineering DC/DM and Records Management – The most Common mistake Operating Companies Make

As we have discovered Engineering Documents, Correspondence and Records are ALL entirely different and managed differently.

http://cad.about.com/od/CAD_Standards/a/Enigineering-Document-Management-Software.htm

27.01.1 Engineering or Controlled Documents

ALL Engineering/Controlled documents in a project and/or Technical Documents used at a Corporate level or in Operations have a complex life-cycle.

They are "drafted" and a snapshot taken at certain points in the life-cycle at revisions (not versions) with a specific status such as IFR,

IFT, IFA etc. NO engineering/controlled document becomes a record in the operations sense until handed over.

Here is an example of revision/status – this is a rather complex example but not uncommon note we are not using versions and are assuming revision in the CAD/Native application takes place at every point from mark-ups.

Revision	Status	Description
A	IFR	The document has been drafted and Intra-Discipline reviewed and now require Inter-Discipline (Squad Check) Review.
B	IFR	Where comments need to be addressed and the document needs re-review
C	IFT	ALL comments addressed or exempted and the documents are sent out for Tender/RFP/RFQ
D	IFR	There is another probable back-draft where the tenderers offer new technology equipment and some design change is necessary this may then require re-review
E	IFA	ALL comments addressed or exempted and the documents may then be sent to the "client" for Approval
F	IFA	There may be some back-drafting where client comments need to be addressed and resent for approval
0	IFC	They are "Issued for Construction" or "Issued for Use" and sent to the winning bidder, client and others (distribution matrices)
1	IFR	There may be some constructability or operability issues during construction that are managed via an ECR and they may need further back-drafting and revision and review
2	IFA	Client Review/Approval of ECR driven revisions
3	IFC	The now fully revised document is re-issued for Construction or Use

		Some, not all, documents need As Built mark-ups and drafting prior to hand over
4	AD	As Delivered or Mechanically Complete revision from site mark-ups
5	AC1	As Pre/Hydro Commissioned revision from site mark-ups
6	AC2	As Commissioned revision from site mark-ups
7	AC3	As Handed Over to Operations Personnel revision from site mark-ups
8	AB	As Built

Now let's add the possible versions and are assuming revision in the CAD/Native application takes place at every point from mark-ups or the version is a scanned or "redlined" mark-up.

Revision		Status	Description
-	1	IDR	A draft sent by the Responsible Engineer for Intra-Discipline Review – usually a paper print and NOT managed by DC
A	1	IFR	The document has been drafted and Intra-Discipline reviewed and now requires Inter-Discipline (Squad Check) Review.
A	2	IDR	Comments Addressed and re Intra-Discipline Review
B	1	IFR	Where comments need to be addressed and the document needs re-review
C	1	IFT	ALL comments addressed or exempted and the documents are sent out for Tender/ RFP/RFQ
D	1	IDR	There is another probable back-draft where the tenderers offer new technology equipment and some design change is necessary this may then require Intra-discipline review
D	2	IFR	As above Inter Discipline Review

E	1	IFA	ALL comments addressed or exempted and the documents may then be sent to the "client" for Approval
F	1	IFR	There may be some back-drafting where client comments need to be addressed AND inter discipline review is necessary
F	2	IFA	There may be some back-drafting where client comments need to be addressed and resent for approval
0	A	IFC	They are "Issued for Construction" or "Issued for Use" and sent to the winning bidder, client and others (distribution matrices)
0	B	IFR	There may be some constructability or operability issues during construction that are managed via an ECR and they may need further back-drafting and revision and review
1	A	IFA	Client Review/Approval of ECR driven revisions
2	A	IFC	The now fully revised document is re-issued for Construction or Use
			Some, not all, documents need As Built mark-ups and drafting prior to hand over
2	B	AD	As Delivered or Mechanically Complete revision from site mark-ups
2	C	AC1	As Pre/Hydro Commissioned revision from site mark-ups
2	D	AC2	As Commissioned revision from site mark-ups
2	E	AC3	As Handed Over to Operations Personnel revision from site mark-ups
3	A	AB	As Built

NOTE the change in version identifiers from Numeric where Alpha Revisions are used to Alpha where Numeric revisions are used. This is best practice but not always possible in some EEDMS tools.

ALL this material will need or have to have Distribution Matrices – easily configurable by users which may also need to include a nested matrix – this is where, for example, a lead discipline engineer is really busy and wants to move his review to another member of his team or is away. We must have transmittals and/or audit trailed workflows.

27.01.2 Correspondence

Correspondence has a limited life-cycle in this example we are assuming a letter or memo has been done outside the EEDMS or the EEDMS does not manage correspondence.

Drafted by Author/Owner
Typed by Administration/PA
Reviewed/Corrected by Owner/Author
Corrected and Printed by Administration/PA
Signed by Author/Owner
Scanned by Administration/PA and added to, with the native the DMS
Sent by Administration/PA

There are NO revisions however each "stage" could have a version in an EEDMS if kept at every stage or an EEDMS is integrated to the native application E.g. Word.

27.01.3 Records

After hand over Engineering Documents become records and are managed/revised by an Management of Change process. Any signed/ sent correspondence is a record.

Other records which the system may need to be able to generate via Template forms or store with a "Standard" profile in scanned format are, for example, Maintenance Records, Leave Applications and so on.

27.01.4 Data

Data in the Document Control world is the material inside a CAD application such as AutoCAD or a Calculation tool. As Document Controllers we may not need to manage the data itself the application should do that BUT if the application does not support roll-back, in case of a mistake, we may need to store a complete native (sometimes because there is more than 1 file – E.g. 3D models) in a zip file at each revision/status at version 1 or A therefore it is ESSENTIAL that an EEDMS support one to many relationships for files between the document profile and the files themselves sometimes (not easy to follow and therefore not recommended) Parent / Child relationships where the parent is the native and the children are renditions and scans.

Note that in some cases the EEDMS can be integrated to CAD and Office tools. It is wise to develop a proactive DC database and the system should have and manage templates against each document type to which or from which data can be added or mined.

Where an integration is not possible it is a good idea for Document Control to liaise closely with the System Administrator for the CAD packages and when a lot of material is "Issued" obtain a .csv file of the metadata that makes up the document profile which can be in or manipulated into bulk-load tool format.

A Document Controllers life blood data is the metadata that makes up a document profile such as Asset, Plant/System/Area, Discipline, Document Type/SubType, Title etc. We manage this in our EEDMS or DC tool. The base data, for drop downs in our Document form, is stored in easily configurable by System Administrators or Power Users library/configuration tables.

27.02 Business Case & Situation Analysis / Nuts and Bolts / Minimum Functionality

It is critical to identify why a new EEDMS or DC application is required and what it might need to be able to do in some dot point form which can then be expanded upon fully at a later date to from an RFP/RFQ document.

How the application is to be deployed and what systems, hardware, software supported and whether the company will accept a Software as a Service, SAAS, application across the internet or some form of hybrid must also be determined.

In the pre-read information most of this is covered in .\..\EEDMS\B. nuts-bolts-web.pdf

27.03 Managing Engineering Data – CAD Applications

Refer to page 70. The best possible solution for Document Controllers is to have an application that integrates to CAD tools. Between DC, Engineers and others (they should already exist) Templates for each document type should be developed and associated with that type.

In a proactive system when the metadata for each document is added these systems add a file place-holder. If a user selects that place-holder either by clicking on it directly or by checking out the system should then select the right template and pre-populate it with the metadata. Any changes made to that metadata by the designer/user should then be automatically updated in the EEDMS when the document is checked back-in or saved with a formal revision.

A majority of CAD tools support roll-back that allows a user to go back to an earlier revision/version if a mistake has been made. Where this is not possible the designer/user should send to document control either a native file (with X-Refs bound on) or a zip file (with X-Refs or where multiple files are created such as a 3D model) with the rendition to store in the EEDMS application – this provides roll-back functionality.

It is acceptable to have multiple sheet drawings in one CAD file but it is not acceptable for each sheet to have the same Document Number – Document Numbers must be unique. It is also not acceptable to Issue to Document Control multiple sheet drawings in one rendition or scan file they must be separated.

Where integration is partial or not available to CAD packages the system administrator or power users for each package must be prepared to provide to Document Control a csv file containing base metadata for the document profiles when there is a large, say more than 5, issue of drawings for example the outputs for Piping Isometrics, Loop Diagrams and Shop Detail drawings. At a minimum document control will need:

Document No, Rev No, Title, Asset, Plant/System/Area, Discipline, Document Type/SubType. We may also need Cross References to other drawings and documents shown in the border (not X-Refs to templates such as the border itself) and Cross References to Tag/Equipment and/or Instrument No's and Cables. Especially where this data is not stored or secured in the CAD tool and/or where the association between the document and the cross reference data can easily be lost.

27.04 Managing Engineering Documents

See also pages xx to xx of this book and read the section of this book that relates to document control tasks.

ALL EEDMS applications should have two document profiles. A standard one for correspondence and records and an engineering profile. The engineering profile is to be the default for ALL Controlled Documents.

Controlled documents, at a base level, can be identified from Document Classification.xlsx

For the purposes of associating templates with, especially drawing types, see the Drg Types tab.

ANY DC application or EEDMS MUST support in an easy to use and/or update by Document Controllers format:

Internal Distribution Matrices and Workflows
External Distribution Matrices and Transmittals

NOTE that not all documents are sent out based on a matrix and it must be a simple task, with simple and saveable filters, to send any document on a workflow or transmittal at any time.

ANY DC application or EEDMS MUST have easy to edit/update/ populate configuration and/or library tables for:

> Assets
> Plant/System/Area
> Discipline
> Document Type/SubType
> Equipment Numbers
> Address Book
>> Internal (Like a phone book)
>> External
> WBS
> Cross Referenced Documents

Easy for DC's to update to, edit and update Configuration or Library Tables (Config/Lib)for simple codes such as Asset, Plant/System Area, Discipline, Document Type/ Sub Type and others may be necessary too such as WBS, Address book (internal and external), Tag Numbers, PO Numbers. Should be made MANDATORY.

NOTE that a really good DC tool will allow most functions to be done one of two ways particularly with respect to adding data to Library / Configuration tables. For example, "drop downs" in a document profile should allow the user to type in a value. If that value does not correspond to a value in the Config/Lib table the system should ask if the value needs to be added Yes and No buttons on a pop-up. Yes, opens the respective table for data entry and then returns to the record in the Document Profile form, No prompts for a correct selection from the associated "drop down". If data is being entered to something like a Tag/Equip No field in the actual Config/Lib table there should be a simple, based on a filter, method of associating the respective documents to it.

ANY DC application or EEDMS MUST be able to support a "no revision" document in To Be Drafted status we must be able to add data, with due dates, for documents that have not been drafted or do not yet exist/have files.

A DC application or EEDMS should have a bulk-load tool for files/metadata in an easy to use format such excel and it should be possible to use the tool to make mass corrections to metadata such as titles or discipline codes – for example it is easy to confuse a loop diagram with an electrical drawing and they may be entered as electrical when they are instrument drawings. It is also possible that some disciplines may be split at a later date, not entirely recommended, but mechanical can become: mechanical; mechanical services such as HVAC; materials handling such as conveyors; and rotating equipment such as the drilling equipment on a drilling rig.

The system must also be able to provide warnings at multiple levels particularly where:

A document profile, with history such as revisions and transmittals etc is being deleted e.g.

The system should ask with a Pop Up – ARE YOU SURE – YES or NO (buttons)

> When YES is selected it should ask via a Pop Up – ARE YOU REALLY SURE - YES or NO (buttons)
>
> When YES is selected a pop-up with a blank data entry field should come up saying Type the word DELETE.
>
> Only when this is done should any document profile be deleted.
>
> Anytime NO is selected or the word is not typed in to the field the system should default back to the relevant document profile.

A document number is being changed where the document has history such as revisions and transmittals e.g.

The system should ask with a Pop Up – ARE YOU SURE – YES or NO (buttons)

> When YES is selected it should ask via a Pop Up – ARE YOU REALLY SURE - YES or NO (buttons)

> When YES is selected a pop-up with a blank data entry field should come up saying Type the word RE-NUMBER.

> Only when this is done should any document number be changed.

> Anytime NO is selected or the word is not typed in to the field the system should default back to the relevant document profile.

27.05 Managing Engineering Correspondence

Engineering correspondence entails, usually form based, correspondence such as Technical Queries, Requests for Information, Engineering Change Requests, Variation Requests, Variation Orders, Site Instructions and so on.

These documents all have a lifecycle and associated matrix they must be stored and versioned at every addition/change.

With respect to Technical Queries we are only interested in the document when each major field has been added to. We are NOT interested in the "chatter" that may lead to the information being added to that field. This is also true of RFI's, ECR's, Variation Requests.

It MUST be simple for any user to open the system, select Engineering Correspondence, and find the right template type for the action they need to open. This is true for both internal and external users. Where the system does not support communications or forms the document has to be scanned in by DC on receipt and final reply.

Any DC tool or EEDMS should support personal working directories for all users and also allow DC's and others to scan direct from an MFC to the working directory.

Any DC tool or EEDMS should support or have OCR functionality and a vectorising function for scanned drawings should also be considered.

For a complete needs analysis we must consider ALL the questions on page 62 to 64 of this document and ask of ourselves if the needs identified in this RFP document .\..\EEDMS\L. RFP.pdf are all necessary for our tool some of which we have covered above.

The Project Manager for the EEDMS project must be prepared to ask hundreds of questions of every possible group of users and chair needs meetings then ask each group to assign a delegate to the "project team" for the early life of the project itself mostly part time but it is wise to have an IT knowledgeable DC full time.

27.06 Gap analysis

In a majority of situations, it is likely some form of control exists over Controllable Documents and Correspondence we need to determine what this is and if it is possible to build upon it or if it will be kept on for old material and new added to any new system or if a complete export import from old to new, with DQ auditing done is necessary.

> Why do we need a new system – is this a matter of poor training practices where new users lack some knowledge of the system and confidence in it has been lost? For example:
>
> In Western Australia a major miner had built a complex Iron briquetting plant (it's been demolished). Prior to it going operational they installed a very powerful CMS called MIMS, not sure it exists anymore, they took the right step of correctly training all the users that were going to the site and installed a completely clean system. The problem is that this training did not apply

to users arriving onsite to replace others or fill a gap. They effectively became data-bashers they knew how to open the system, add data and run some reports but that was all. It was a complex application and takes some getting to know. Those who are not properly trained find it difficult and/or frustrating to use and are unable to actually get the best out of its functionality and all confidence in the system, most certainly trust, was lost.

If the existing system only fails on certain levels E.g. Manages Files well but not associated data can we fix with an add-on specifically for Eng DC? For example:

The company may be running Sharepoint which users have gotten used to but it does not manage data well and has no integration for viewing/redlining CAD files. The users like the file management capabilities and structures but not the lack of data/metadata and missing viewer. In this case it is possible to explore what systems are in the marketplace that can be integrated directly to Sharepoint. At a minimum we may be able to quickly integrate an already built MS Access database DC tool and Brava/Rasterex as viewers or simply make sure that all files are also stored in PDF rendition format and have Acrobat Standard available on all user PC's.

27.07 EDM Requirements for Engineering (Including Operators) - where it often goes wrong

27.07.1 Engineering Vs Office (Eng DC/DM vs RM)

Unless they have already had exposure to Engineering DC or attended this or another course on Engineering DC most IT people understand records management but NOT engineering document management. This is also true of Engineers, Accountants and other non-Document Control people. If they have no exposure to it at all they will not understand our needs.

This is where a huge mistake can be made. It has been in the past. One major Perth based Operator did a full needs analysis during which Projects DC's were consulted. They determined that the application being offered to them by the vendor of another application they had for the purpose in-house met 80% of the requirements.

The problem was the 20% that was not there was the 20% that Document Controllers rely on on a daily basis and well over 80% of the material stored in the system was Engineering and Projects documentation.

The new tool had some great functionality but the mission critical, for DC's, tools such as Transmittals, Workflows and Distribution matrices just was not there. This caused enormous issues with project IMC's regularly butting heads with Corporate RM/IMC's/IT and at least two, in some part integrated to the DMS, Access based applications sprang in to life but in the main documents were double handled – added to a DC database tool then added to the DMS massive extra cost in terms of both time and manpower and should have been completely unnecessary.

The other massive mistake made was that they knew there were a lot of errors in the existing system instead of implementing a project to DQ then cleanse the data they just imported it. Problem there is fixing it later, because the hard to use bulk-load tool was not immediately available (data was imported via ODBC linking) and did not support Validation or bulk updates, takes a lot more time and effort – the data is still being fixed many years later.

Two other operating companies have spent millions on two applications a DMS with an integrated DC solution the problem is the RM/IT people dictated the specification on the DC tool and effectively gutted it. In one case when rolled out on the pilot project, a live project, numerous problems that needed to be addressed were identified by DC's and Design users – they were very unhappy but IT/RM, lacking understanding and/or unable to listen did not understand/take action and the end result was the add-on got junked and another non-integrated solution (which will mean double handling) was found – huge costs involved not to say the least of the user disenchantment along the way.

27.08 The Return on Investment

We could be spending a lot of money not just on an application but selecting one and then implementing it with configuration, data export/import/DQ and full roll-out and user training. We must get a lot of "bang for our buck" i.e. great return on investment.

Any system chosen has to score highly and give us at least 100% of must haves and over 60% of nice to haves. Beware of the word Work-Around these are OK in the short term (<3 months) but are a serious pain in the longer term and should be avoided at all costs. If the issue causing the work-around cannot be addressed and quickly what you are looking at is not a great solution. To me Work-Around is a swear word.

..\..\EEDMS\M. document-management-return-on-investment-analysis.pdf be aware this may not be Engineering DC compliant but goes a long way to explaining what must considered when looking at Return on Investment – note though that often these tools are score and dollar focused and there is no way to value user satisfaction particularly among Document Controllers, Designers and Operators.

27.08.1 Rules-of -Thumb.

DMS applications have great functionality but most are NOT engineering DC tools and will not work without expensive add-ons many of which can manage files and work perfectly well as an individual tool.

ALL operating assets are engineered and those documents associated with the asset, although records at handover, will at some time, E.g. MoC or brownfields expansion/upgrade projects, need to be revised and that is an Engineering process and the documents managed in a correct manner.

27.08.2 Top 10 Reasons Why SharePoint is NOT an EDM Solution

In the main the later versions of SharePoint are excellent file management tools is lacking in workflows especially assigning drop dead dates, does not do transmittals, or cannot open/view/redline CAD natives etc.

All is not lost with an add-on, some integration and/or develop with integratable tools SharePoint can be made to work for you.

Also be aware that the author has seen reports that only 6% of companies that rolled out Sharepoint in some form or another are happy with it, it's likely that that, without add-ons at least, drops to less than 6% for engineering companies.

For better and a more detailed explanation please read (also in the appendices here) information:

..\..\EEDMS\Top 10 Reasons Why SharePoint is NOT an EDM Solution.pdf

27.09 RFP/RFQ & Scoring

Work Through This (use your imagination on some of the answers)

http://www.technologyevaluation.com/register.aspx?redirectURL= http://itadvisor.technologyevaluation.com/SurveyStart.aspx?AreaModel Id%3d464%26SessionLanguageId%3d0%26StartQuestion%3d2734932

NOTE that not all software providers submit their products to this site for evaluation.

and update this Other\L. RFP.pdf and this Other\Scoring-Evaluation Chart for DMS.xlsx

Again, it is essential that we ask a lot of questions of ourselves, identify what we have, and our needs and then work out what we must have in a new system and the nice to haves.

This is a long process.

27.10 The Request for Quotation / Proposed Solution / Tender Process

We have to do a lot of research about what tools are in the marketplace that might suit our needs. Without going to a major "blast" or "saturation" we should send our RFQ/RFP document out to at the very least 6 to 10 solution providers.

What we did here will give us some providers/probable solutions but not all providers have been accessed or submitted to this site for assessment their tools:

http://www.technologyevaluation.com/register.aspx?redirectURL =http://itadvisor.technologyevaluation.com/SurveyStart.aspx?Area ModelId%3d464%26SessionLanguageId%3d0%26StartQuestion%3d2 734932

Using our fully developed excel score sheet we must narrow this to two very likely solution providers and two that come very close.

Depending on ultimate needs and potential integrations at the very minimum the RFP/RFQ document should go to:

Idox	- McLaren FusionLive (note Enterprise is not recommended)
Software Innovations	- ProArc
Coreworx	- Coreworx
Bentley	- ProjectWise with full Bentley CAD suite
Intergraph	- SmartPlant with Foundation (not SPOperations)
Blue Cielo	- Meridian Enterprise
Synergis	- Adept with full AutoDesk CAD suite or SolidWorks
Aveva	- Aveva Data & Documents with full Aveva design suite and Aveva Net
EMC2	- Documentum with EPFM/D2
Assai	- Assai – 2 possible solutions
Aconex	- Aconex
ACS Software	- AutoEDMS
Autodesk	- Vault Collaboration – with full AutoDesk CAD suite
Cadac	- Organice

Asite	- Asite
4Projects	- 4Projects
Conject	- ConjectPM (Formerly BIW)
Omega.no	- PIMS
OpenText	- LiveLink
Alfresco	- Alfresco (NASA use it!)
Comnia	- Comnia (RIB software)
iTWOcx	- iTWOcx (RIB software)
kinetix.com.hk	- PowerDoc2
Itaz	- Globodox
ShareCat	- ShareCat
Gnaros Software	- DocBoss (http://docboss.com/) Includes an MDR/VDB function
M-Files	- http://www.documentmanagementsoftware.com.au/

Others in the mix

QA Software	- Teambinder with QDMS integration between them FIXED ESSENTIAL
Rollosoftware	- DrawCon (Integrate to Sharepoint/Brava)
DocumentCorp	- DrawBridge Enterpise

The post RFP/RFQ/Tender process must entail product demonstrations with a number of pre-provided, by us, situations/processes to test. The team must comprise the PM, an IT knowledgeable DC, and a user from every possible user group. The product demonstrations must be done on your premises however, in the initial instance web "meetings" and demonstrations are acceptable.

> For the demonstration also have a fixed list of questions from the vendors RFP reply. Develop other questions and make notes of them as you go along you may wish to ask other vendors the same questions.

Be absolutely certain of your minimum requirements –
the must haves

Be prepared to add other needs along the way

After the product demonstrations, or during, keep a score sheet and poll all the team for their views on each product demonstrated and what they would ultimately select for their needs.

Some negotiations can then be entered in to with the top two particularly with respect to implementation data import/export/DQ, configuration, user training – a little "back scratching" can go a very long way. Some flexibility too – must haves are rigid but nice to haves are not.

27.11 Award

The award should not be based on price alone unless your budget is limited.

The MUST HAVE's – especially those of Engineering Document Control and Operations must be met

The ideal is to also meet better than 60% of nice to haves.

As mentioned above be prepared to make trade-offs.

NEVER accept "Work-Arounds" like a short-cut a work-around is the longest distance between two points and can mean double handling. If a work-around is proposed to solve a must have DO NOT accept the application the system must either have what you need developed into it or to be issued as a development, core, patch within a short time frame.

27.12 Implementation Planning

ALL the vendors have experts at doing this it is ok to "Project Manage" yourselves - unless you have expert staff on-board or are prepared to hire them, even for the short term, it is best not to attempt the implementation of any EEDMS or DC application on your own!

Work very very closely with the Vendor with respect to Implementation, Population, User (all levels) Training and roll-out to users.

27.13 Information Architecture / System Architecture

A copy from earlier pages but worth repeating!
What "Database" Applications do you already run?

Oracle, SQL Server, other Bespoke systems

Do you have Sharepoint?

What CAD applications and Office Applications are in use? Which must you integrate with or out-rightly replace (e.g. Outlook)

Will the application need its own dedicated server or will it work from a dedicated share?

Will your current system run Citrix for remote operations and support your CAD applications over the link?

What OS are your servers running on?

What OS are your desktops and laptops running on?

ALL these questions must be answered before the RFP/RFQ process begins or as a part of that process you may need to make some early enquiries of vendors in case they are running on systems that are not compatible with your own especially where the company will not spend money on another server either directly or through the EEDMS vendor for the applications under consideration.

Where your infrastructure may not suit a possible application are you prepared to go to the expense of providing or having the vendor provide the necessary servers for that application?

Do you want to "host" your application or are you comfortable with SaaS

> Bandwidth is a big issue across a LAN or a WAN especially where remote sites are involved. Some tools offer hybrid solutions such as ProArc which is locally hosted but has a web based tool for remote users.

Do you already run a DMS application such as Documentum or FileNet?

We can find excellent add-ons for these types of tools.

Do you want to integrate to MSOffice (with Templates – data added/mined) including Outlook

> Note that most applications, other than DC Databases (Drawcon can integrate to SharePoint and QDMS has some support for Sharepoint as an add-on), can integrate to various other applications. Some of the SaaS Collaboration tools might or could be limited in what they will integrate with and how.

27.13.1 What kind of Deployment do you need?

27.13.1.1 Client Workstation

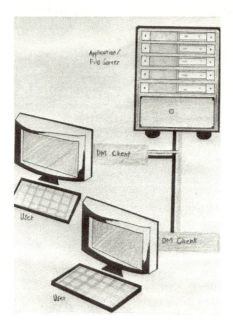

27.13.1.2 Network Client

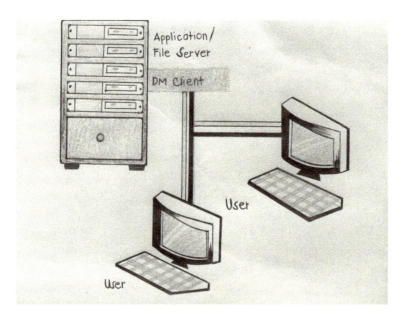

27.13.1.3 Client Browser Deployment (SaaS or In-house)

Bandwidth can and will be an issue

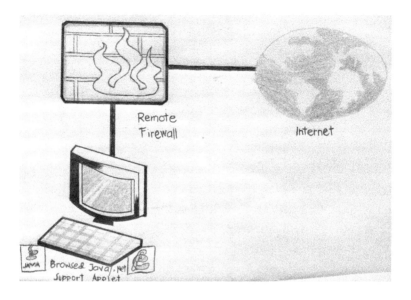

27.14 Remote Operations

Bandwidth −carefully check what bandwidth you have and if it can be upgraded and what you might need. NOTE well that some CAD applications and EEDMS applications will not, in my experience anyway, run or not run very well across a Citrix or Terminal Server set-up.

How best to Disseminate Up To Date Information to Remote Operations − if bandwidth is an issue

Live "Mirror" Servers

Differential Updates during low bandwidth times such as late at night

Using a SaaS or Web Browser based application − some, not all, SaaS applications use a lot of bandwidth because, unseen, when documents are opened they are downloaded to a temporary directory or cache for that purpose, uploading revised information can be slow too. Low bandwidth and "speed" issues create frustration and dissatisfaction among users. Some EEDMS applications and collaboration tools do not support browsers such as Google Chrome and Firefox!

Work very closely and carefully with the vendor to ensure the best possible outcome for remote sites and low bandwidth areas.

As an example of this, yes I do know modern technology may, operative word, have addressed this, at one time I worked in a rural town with good facilities. However, the sites were on a satellite based phone system. As a part of my role it was necessary to fax assay results to the sites for grade control/mine planning.

What was found out, the hard way, was the "baud" rate between the machines (due to the 'phone" system on site was resulting in the site receiving nothing but a black page! Ultimately, using trial and error, and the odd discussion with the system provider it was found that anything above 400 baud from the sending machine just could not be handled by the "phone system" in use. Therefore we had to remember to slow the baud rate of every send. It was also incredibly slow even with a single page fax!

27.15 Retention Requirements and Backwards Compatibility

Let's revisit our Document Types spread-sheet, <u>Document Classification.xlsx</u> and look at our retention requirements.

Can the system to be deployed support document retention over such long periods?

Is the system ISO 15489 "Backward Compatibility" compliant – A MUST HAVE otherwise when CAD or Office tools are updated we may have to plan a project to open all the old material and convert them up to the new application format – time consuming and expensive. Where the actual native application is compliant the EEDMS itself may not be.

I have also seen systems that "break" intelligence in documents such as ToC's and if the document has hyperlinks to others those documents, if they are not already there, will also have to be added and the actual links changed to links that map to the documents inside the EEDMS itself.

27.16 Folder structure – Real or Virtual and are they really worth the effort?

Most, if not all, PC users are very familiar with Windows Explorer file structures and while an EEDMS may place much tighter controls over who can create, move or access each one, they can still become very unruly therefore if users MUST see a file structure it must be clearly defined.

In many cases these are virtual and the documents are actually in one big "dump" bucket.

Personal and "Group" Working Folders are a MUST HAVE. Be careful in some applications I have seen deleting a file that is in a personal or working folder also deletes it in the main file structure – THIS MUST NOT HAPPEN.

The major issue with explorer file structures is that it tends to encourage users to search down/drill down the structure. This is much slower than using a search filter tool and often they do not find something where they might expect to see it and instead of running a search tool ring DC and get abusive. There is no real problem with having a structure but as soon as a user starts drilling down one a Pop-up asking if they need search help should be automatically activated.

What must also be very closely checked is if a document is created in a Working Folder, recommended, and then moved by DC to an actual folder when "issued" if a link is kept in the Working Folder and is then deleted does it cascade delete the document in the actual folder structure – I have seen this happen!

27.17 Defining Attributes/ Metadata

What metadata MUST we capture against a document profile? – Page xx to yy of this document.

What metadata SHOULD we also capture against a document profile? – Pages zz and aa of this document.

Is it possible to relate One document profile to many files e.g. PDF Rendition, PDF Scan, Native(s)

Two document profiles are recommended – Standard for letters etc. and Engineering for Controlled Documents NOTE our DrawCon examples are ALL Engineering Profile.

27.18 Revisions vs Versions

See also pages xx through yy of this document.

NOTE WELL some DMS applications do not support revisions they do however have versions. Both are a MUST HAVE.

In the main Controlled Documents do not have versions but this is becoming far more common place with the advent of DMS tools and the Revision is the critical information for a document controller.

27.19 Transmittals/Workflows

Any document that is "Issued" or otherwise sent to any internal party (usually for review or approval) or external party (for any reason) is sent either on a transmittal or workflow. Most commonly documents issued Externally are sent on Transmittals and documents issued Internally are issued on Workflows. An example of an external and an internal transmittal is in the appendices.

EEDMS applications usually 100% audit trail workflows i.e. anytime anyone does something to the document(s) on a workflow the system records some kind of base level information E.g. Opened/Viewed, Marked-Up/Redlined, Saved/Closed, Who, Date/Time.

Transmittals are often also tracked electronically – Delivered to recipients Mail Server, Read Receipt/Acknowledgement, Documents Downloaded/Accessed.

At a minimum Transmittals – Internal and External with some user configurability are MUST haves. Workflows do make things simpler but are a VERY NICE to have.

27.20 Search and retrieval

- Searches should be based on data found in the document profile and available via a simple filter form that can be saved by the user
- Where a keyword search is used the system must search within the profile, especially Title, and in the case of Native Documents E.g. Word Files search the content too and this MUST include searching inside files that have been zipped/rar'd before being uploaded (e.g. a 3D model file has more than one associated native file and those are zipped/rar'd before being loaded).
- Searches must be fast – "google like"
- Drilling down a File Structure is NOT recommended or should enable a pop-up that asks the user if they need help linked to the simple filter

27.21 Integrations

27.21.1 CAD Applications

It is best to select a tool, depending on your budget, that will integrate with your CAD tools particularly for "data population/ mining".

> *Remember some CAD applications do not work very well over Citrix and Terminal Servers and can be frustratingly slow. It is possible that this problem has been addressed in recent times – something you need to check.*

CAD Templates pre-populate or "Data Mine"

We should be able to define/build a set of templates for Drawing Types and associate them with the Drawing Types configuration/library table. When a drawing that has not been commenced is opened or checked-out from the system the system should open the right template and pre-populate most fields such as Title and Drawing Number.

When checked-in the system should be able to mine data from the title, drawing number and cross reference fields and populate the appropriate fields and tables against the document profile including any that may have changed after check-out.

When documents are checked-in by users other than document control a pop-up form with work instructions for document control should open and be populated by the user that is then sent to document control by the system via a workflow or email for action.

Drawing X-Refs supported?

CAD drawings often have cross references not to each other but other small files kept in various locations with bits and pieces of data, including the actual border, the system should be able to maintain the integrity of those X-Ref's without the need for the designers to bind them on or provide document control with a zip file with the native and all the X-Ref's. If budget causes issues with this then the planning must be to have a strict procedure to ensure the integrity is not lost especially if the CAD system does not have roll-back functionality.

27.21.2 Office Applications

Integration to Office tools is a MUST have for Word and Excel. Nice to have for others. Should an Office integration includE Outlook?

Yes, where the application itself does not support communications. The issue becomes how we manage Outlook emails - especially "chatter".

Fixed Template – pre-populate or "Data Mine"

As above for CAD applications all Controllable document types should have a template associated with them and data population and mining between the system and the native file should be possible.

27.22 Setting up / Configuration

27.22.1 Max Attack vs Relaxed Integrations

Do we have to save everything done in an integrated application into the system. For example, one company in Australia deployed DocsOpen – it was a good system but the set-up/configuration forced ALL users to save everything they did especially Word and Excel. This became very problematic and time consuming as the users had to populate the Profile form and in a lot of cases for something that was personal, being done at lunchtime for example, or did not need to be kept – for example an address label for a courier.

The simplest method of stopping this is to have templates associated to document types and for the documents to be opened or checked-out from the system itself. Checking-in a document that is not in the system should only be done by document controllers.

Also, some configuration should be possible on the fly by the Document Control System Administrator and Power User. DC should NOT need to go to IT to have new Asset, Plant/System, Discipline, Document Type/SubType and Status codes added. We should also be able to amend or create new reports simply and easily.

27.23 Document Capturing

Does the application support a bulk upload tool built-in/provided E.g. Excel A MUST HAVE

Can a bulk-load tool be used to make mass corrections? For example loop diagrams and some other instrument drawings are easily confused with electrical drawings. If a load was done where Instrument Drawings were coded as Electrical can we export the data to load-sheet format, correct it and re-load?

Can the application support creating blocks of Document Numbers internally? Similar to: WE MUST have a simple method of block generating document numbers without risking duplications or having load-sheets fail validation or uploads fail due to duplicated numbers.

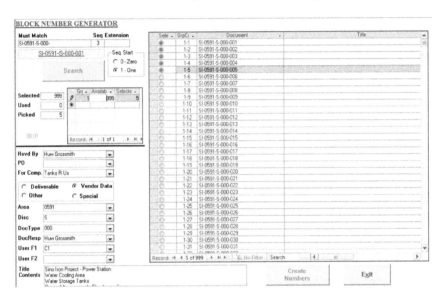

27.24 Form development for "Records"

Is it possible for a "Super User" or "System Administrator" to develop specific templates or forms for E.g. Leave Applications, Maintenance Records and can these forms be "mined" for data that may need to go to, for example, the payroll database?

It is best if these forms can be developed in-house early, pre-configuration, but we should be able to do this work ourselves and not have to rely on IT specialists or System "Specialists" from the vendor to do them for us.

27.25 Form Development for Communications

Is it possible to have pre-set forms or templates in the system for such things as Letters and Memo's, have the system provide unique numbers and track/audit trail send and expedite replies where indicated one is necessary?

It is best if these forms can be developed in-house early, pre-configuration, but we should be able to do this work ourselves and not have to rely on IT specialists or System "Specialists" from the vendor to do them for us.

27.26 Form Development for TQ's, RFI's, ECR's

Is it possible to build communications type templates and workflows etc. for Engineering Communications Documents such as TQ's, RFI'S and ECR's and have them fully audit trailed and expedited.

It is best if these forms can be developed in-house early, pre-configuration, but we should be able to do this work ourselves and not have to rely on IT specialists or System "Specialists" from the vendor to do them for us.

27.27 Expediting

Other than where already outlined above the system must be able to support expediting overdue new and revised documents from internal sources and external sources.

Where we have a proactive DC register can the system automate the production of and automatically send to (a fixed matrix):

Internal Expediting Reports such as a Yellow / Red Card system for both overdue reviews and documents due from Engineers and Designers

An early warning at say 1 working day prior to the due date sent via email/internal communications system to any designer/responsible person who has not checked-in/delivered documents now due for IFR, IFT etc. or off review.

On the due date another polite warning message sent to the designer/responsible person.

A yellow card will be sent based on some data in a library/configuration table or Due Dates from the document profile and/or Transmittals and workflows at 3 working days overdue and copied to the respective Lead Engineer or Engineering Manager and the card data sent to a permanent stats table that can be reported on.

A red A yellow card will be sent based on some data in a library/configuration table or Due Dates from the document profile and/or Transmittals and workflows at 5 working days overdue and copied to the respective Lead Engineer or Engineering Manager and Project Manager the card data sent to a permanent stats table that can be reported on.

External Expediting Reports at, say, 4 levels

Level 1 - documents due in the next 3 working days – a friendly reminder sent only to the Vendor/Third Party and any project Expeditor/Contracts Administrator

Level 2 – documents due in that day – a friendly reminder sent only to the Vendor/Third Party and any project Expeditor/Contracts Administrator – internally where a project expeditor exists this should trigger phone calls or visits.

Level 3 - documents overdue by 5 working days – a reminder that delays can cost money and further delay might trigger with holding of progress payments of having Liquidated Damages allowances deducted from progress payments – sent via the Engineering Manager or Project Manager (for their approval) to the Vendor/ Third Party and to and any project Expeditor/Contracts Administrator - Administrator – internally where a project expeditor exists this should trigger a visit.

Level 4 – documents overdue by 10 working days – progress payments to be stopped or have liquidated damages deducted until further notice or until overdue documents are delivered sent via the Engineering Manager or Project Manager and/or Legal (for their approval) to the Vendor/Third Party and to and any project Expeditor/Contracts Administrator - Administrator – internally where a project expeditor exists this should trigger a visit to collect the data.

It should be a simple matter for Document Controllers and Expeditors to print from a reports system a list of overdue data with some filters permitted such as Vendor/Purchase Order No.

27.28 Scanning and OCR

Is it possible to send a scan or OCR scan from an MFC to a personal working directory/folder in the system?

Does the System have its own OCR capability?

Is the system, where an image file is provided, able to vector scan the drawing or document?

27.29 Audit trails

Will the system fully Audit Trail all documents from Inception including metadata profiles with no document files?

Is it simple to print an audit trail based on a simple, saveable, query form for a specific document and revision or all revisions – especially useful if legal problems ensue – Evidence Act (Best Evidence)

27.30 Population and transfer of existing data

NEVER IMPORT MISTAKES FROM A PREVIOUS SYSTEM OR SYSTEMS

You must do a full audit of all the data before you export/import to a new system. Some excel or access whizkids can write files to do this for you. Just sucking everything for an old system to a new one without doing this will allow these errors to breed or the new system may reject the upload completely (all of it or, rarely, part of it) without, sometimes at least, providing a report – e.g in excel format, of what was rejected. This can result in a shedload of work to find and fix the error before uploading again.

An example, a bit wild I know, of this could be that in the old system anything mechanical had the code ME but in the new system this has been split into, eg ME1 – Rotating equipment, ME2 – fixed plant and so on. I've seen this go as far as ME6 where consideration was not given to using other codes or correct titling to sort the issue.

Careful checking of drawings, in particular, for the correct discipline may also be needed. I've mentioned the example of conveyor drawings being lumped under one discipline! In the modern era the way "loop" diagrams are done has changed. Instead of multiple pages in a report like format with just the loop shown it is now common to show the loop(s) on the Instrument Layout GA which can very easily be mistaken for an electrical drawing.

27.30.1 Data Quality Auditing/Data Cleansing

Audit all Data from other systems to ensure it is correct and conforms to all the Metadata requirements for the new system.

Does the bulk-load tool support data validation pre-load or will it try to load and then reject some or all of the documents on the list and where some will it clearly report which documents did not load and what the problem(s) are in a simple to follow report format that can be exported to another workbook, if excel, in the tool?

Some bulk-load tools do this but it is wise to do as much as possible before copying to a bulk-load tool unless a conversion sheet or tool is used beforehand. Fix it first, fixing it later takes a lot of time.

27.31 Other possible essential requirements

Does the system support BIM (ISO/TS 12911:2012) – especially for EPC/EPCM/EPIC/Constructors.

Does the system support the creation of and/or integrity of Smart Manuals/MDR's. Where to be created the Document Profile will need two addition checkboxes and (fields) – For Manual (Section) and For MDR (Section) - especially for PMC/EPC/EPCM/EPIC/Constructors/Vendors

Does the system support DCS/PLC feedback/input and integrity especially where it relates to errors coming back through the system and finding the error in a correctly associated manual and opening the page on the operators desktop.

27.32 User Training

For the best possible outcomes the initial training for all users should be done via the software vendor. For company training at a later date the vendor must be prepared to provide manuals and video and/or desktop training via the PC – any PC training should be followed by some form of competency exam and where the user gets a question wrong – the system is to record which question and take them back to that section of the training and repeat until they pass. 3 fails means no further log-in and a report sent to their superior and trainer for further action.

27.32.1 User Training for "System Administrators"

SYSTEM ADMINISTRATORS MUST UNDERSTAND HOW THE SYSTEM WORKS AND HAVE A BASIC KNOWLEDGE OF TABLE STRUCTURES ETC

A number of System Administrators must be trained and this must include at least one person each from Document Control Corporate and Projects.

They must be able to provide third level support, form building, add/remove data to library or configuration tables, add/change security settings, add new users and directory structures, open new projects and transfer data from projects to operations based on specific criteria plus some new user training.

27.32.2 User Training for Document Controllers [Power Users]

ALL DOCUMENT CONTROLLERS MUST HAVE SOME LEVEL OF UNDERSTANDING HOW THE SYSTEM WORKS

ALL Document Controllers, not trained to System Administrator level, must be trained to Power User level and be able to:

Provide second level support, add/remove data to library or configuration tables, add/change security settings, add new users and directory structures, open new projects and transfer data from projects to operations based on specific criteria plus some new user training.

27.32.3 User Training for Desktop Users (Designers/Engineers/Admin Staff)

ALL users must be able to find, where permitted access/read or check-out and in documents.

It is wise for the company to ensure new user training is mandatory and part of an induction process and it must be passed see above.

27.33 Ongoing Training

When new versions of the software are released they should be released with training material that explains what has changed and revised course material for the entire application.

It is wise to have a System Admin or Trained EEDMS trainer in-house.

While users, such as DC's, doing a hand-over can provide some coal face training they may NOT cover everything and that means, with staff turn-over that in 2 to 5 years that the company will have a lot of part trained users and lose confidence in the system.

Induction training is strongly recommended at the basic level before being granted access for anything but training.

New hire document controllers or IT/RM people MUST pass training to their respective level before being granted further access.

AFTER WORD(S) AND UPDATES

Engineering Document Control for ALL

Dec 2012 Update (possibly already incl above)

This update is intended for or relates directly to Page 161 – Collaboration Tools.

In the ever-growing world of "Engineering" many projects involve the "coming together" of a number of SME's and this is not always done in a Joint Venture or completely under one roof. Some of these "comings together" are necessitated by the move from government owned and controlled assets, eg. Rail, to the private sector. Good, bad or otherwise when looking at them they can appear to be a complete (circular – harder to find the way out) maze (or an outright Frankenstein's monster.

This makes having a tool or tools that permit "live" collaboration on documents ever more important. Effectively this also does away with expensive meetings especially where people have to travel to said meetings they lose a lot of time in travel to and fro.

There is a legion of collaboration tools in the market, some good, some ok, some not so good. A majority of these tools are forced, often by the unknowing, on DC's as a DC tool and a majority just are not a DC tool.

There, are in the market place now, a number, small, of great DC tools that permit "live"collaboration.

In the mind of this author a collaboration tool must have the following functionality:

If not a, proper, DC tool – integration via API's or some other suite to one.

"Live" collaboration must permit online live marking up of an "image"

> "Live" collaboration must include some kind of IM (preferably but not 100% necessarily Audit Trailed – who said what and when could become a problem if a court case evolves at some point in the future.

> Must allow access, which can be controlled by the project owner, to third parties all over the world. (Bandwidth could be an issue here).

> Where the tool is also to be used for or is built-in to a DC tool for Reviews and Approvals there are a number of other great to haves and necessities.

>> Must have. Reviews on images in "layers" that all other reviewers can see – avoids duplication of comments. These individual layers must also be audit trailed and saved, and easily accessible, within the system.

>> Great to have. With respect to the above. The final "layer" should be for the document originator who can then copy comments from the reviewers to the final layer instead of having to do an entirely new "layer" to compile valid comments. NB many of the "viewer" packages in the market cannot do this.

Must have. System Administration that permits the appending of an electronic signature by the "Checker" and "Approver" and a list of who they are. This should be via a second password. When the "Approver" status codes a document as "Approved" the he/she is asked for a second password before his/her signature is applied to the appropriate part of a "review stamp" or the document. ALL audit trailed.

Must have. A set of, or singular, system stamp that is applied when a status code is applied to a document with the code(s) already explained and the usual "get out" clause too.

Must have. (If time is not a huge issue – good to have). A way of comparing revisions and showing what has changed. Example:

We have received from a Vendor a drawing. We called it Rev A. We reviewed and marked it up and sent it back. Sometimes these may be recorded as A1 and A2.

The vendor now sends in Rev B.

The system should support – giving the option of either opening the clean, A1, or marked A2 and comparing them to B and then showing, on a separate screen, what is different between the two chosen drawings. A major time saving "device".

Without such functionality actually collaborating on, reviewing and approving documents will be a difficult and time consuming process.

Jan 2017 Update

My daughter is no longer the youngest Grosso – by the time this hits the market I will have become/was a "Grand Uncle" twice or thrice or, possibly a bigger number, more!

The world of Engineering evolves at an astounding pace. I've updated some of the pages in the book with respect to some of the "fundamentals" particularly with respect to "collaboration" which is becoming ever more essential – especially "live" collaboration with organisations and SME's (Subject Matter Experts) potentially being anywhere on the planet.

What I did not mention with respect to collaboration is that in some places, let's say somewhere in the Middle East that observes either Fri/Sat or Thur/Fri as the weekend, time zone differences and actual holiday dates and weekend days can work both for and against you with a bit of careful planning "live" collaboration may not be needed – something needing urgent comment or update by a third party elsewhere could be sent before CoB Wednesday and it could well be back on Sunday because they have Thur/Fri to work on it – your weekend. Time differences can be handy where, for example, your part of the organisation may be short of, say, CAD licences – if you are in Aussie your CAD guys can borrow licences from an US based office or at least until the US guys turn up to work. Time differences and the observance of different holidays and weekend days are something you may have to keep in mind.

It can be easy to forget time zone differences but even easier, when in head down/tail up mode, to forget working day differences – for example you are in a Sat to Wed workday nation (KSA is/was) and on Sat you fire off an email, in your EEDMS or Outlook with Read Receipt on and you flag for follow up, to Perth - Australia (Mon to Fri) and then wonder on Sunday why you've not got a Read Receipt or Reply! You feel a bit silly when you remember working day difference. The time zone difference can be handy though if you fire off something CoB your time Monday because you may well have a reply or Read

Receipt waiting for you Tuesday morning because they are 5 hours in front but could, for a while, leave you cussing if it was sent to say Houston – USA some 9 hours behind.

The number of "Standards" that we may need to comply with or be mindful of either as DC's and/or the IT/Soft Systems people and/or the business as a whole grows ever more. To be frank if we tried to follow the entire suite – even read it all – we'd probably go nuts….. Note there is not one for DC. Others have tried and there was interest but in the end it went almost nowhere.

ISO 9001 has also changed. Based on what I have been able to get hold of thus far with respect to DC it is both a little more loose than it originally was (if that is possible) and somewhat tighter too. One notable "exclusion" is it says nothing now about "Obsolete" (Cancelled or Superseded) documents at all and tends to allude more to records.

It is on the subject of records where things get a little messy…..

Please remember that in the traditional sense of the word that current Engineering Documents ARE NOT or are unlikely to become records until after hand-over and subjected to MoC. That said, superseded and any cancelled (if they existed) documents/revisions become records.*

Example

Rev/Ver**	Reason for Issue	Status	Notes
A1	Issued for Review	IFR	Unmarked copy – A RECORD
A2	Issued for Review	Code 2	Compiled Signed Mark-Up*** - A RECORD
B	Issued for Tender	IFT	A RECORD
C1	Back Draft - IFR	IFR	Unmarked copy – A RECORD****
C2	IFR	Code 1	Signed Coded – A RECORD
D	Issued for Approval	Code 1	Signed Coded – A RECORD
0	Issued for Construction	IFC	Signed - LIVE
**			May only appear in DC Tool (ie on Document as A, B, C)

★★★			In a collaboration tool that allows mark-ups in layers it should retain each layer too.
★★★★			Sometimes back drafting is necessary as the vendors may have new kit or propose something that might be better suited to purpose.

If you use a Hard Copy or Windows Explorer type file structure then in an A3 file in a wallet the filing order top down would be:

> 0 on top of D (Stamped S/S), on top of C2 (Stamped S/S), on top of C1 (Stamped S/S), on top of B (Stamped S/S), on top of A2 (Stamped S/S), on top of A1 (Stamped S/S). OR

> Two files – Master and Superseded. Personally, in a Master file I would still keep C1, C2 and D below 0 (helps back tracking) – otherwise 0 in the master and the rest in the Superseded file latest S/S Rev to oldest S/S Rev.

It is on the subject of records where the number of Standards is somewhat large. While not all affect us directly as DC's it is wise to understand what some say must be done particularly with reference to MetaData and how it must be recorded.

The list (there could be more – I also hope that this is top down):

> ISO 15489 (parts -1 AND -2) – Note the bit about Backward Compatibility has not changed

> ISO 23081 Metadata for Records (parts -1, -2 and -3)

> ISO 26122 Work Process Analysis for Records

> ISO TR 13028 Implementation Guidelines for Digitization of Records – If this does not say anything

about making Scans from, let's say, Wet Signed originals or PDF Renditions from Natives I'll be very surprised and upset. It may also NOT state anything about Vectorising Drawings for which you only have prints.

ISO 13008 Digital Records Conversion and Migration Process – as above (might also pick up on something I say in the book – don't export/import or otherwise migrate errors)

ISO 16175 Principles and Functional Requirements for Records in the Electronic Office (Parts -1, -2 and -3)

ISO 30300 Management System for Records – Fundamentals and Vocabulary

ISO 30301 Management System for Records – Requirements – I have done a quick Index Check and the words/acronyms CAD or Computer Aided Design do NOT appear.

ISO 30303 Management System for Records – Requirements for bodies Providing Audit and Certification

ISO 30302 Management System for Records – Guidelines for Implementation

ISO 30304 Management System for Records – Assessment Guide (Note mine is NOT built on this – it is built on best practice as I know/knew of it and years of experience and "borrowed" [ie freely available on the internet])

Others that are of importance/relevance to Engineering DC/Data are (but not restricted to)

ISO 29481 (Parts 1 and 2) – Building Information Models

ISO 16757 (Parts 1 and 2) - Data structures for electronic product catalogues for building services

BS1192:2007+A2:2016 - Collaborative production of architectural, engineering and construction information. Code of practice★★★

Of less relevance to us, unless involved in some form of QA on CAD produced material★★

http://www.iso.org/iso/home/search.htm?qt=CAD&sort=rel&type=simple&published=on Way too many/specialized to list here.

Frightening isn't it!

★As I have mentioned during the life of a project we must keep track of all this information and, these days, the electronic files that make them up. On hand-over, or well before, we need to find out what the clients requirements are. Some clients insist on everything (all records) being kept for life of plant plus x years. In this case I'd send them the lot but keep an electronic copy (including the soft system they are in – where backward compatibility kicks-in) for, say, five years as potential evidence should litigation occur for any reason – after 5 years someone in the organisation you work for should then make a decision on if it should be kept or "archived off" permanently or destroyed.

★★ Quite often this will be a problem for a CAD person but not always. Many "clients" and others have tools through which CAD material, especially drawings, can be run for compliance to their/other standards.

★★★ Well intended but should never be followed from a DC perspective.

Just recently I have found some issues with nomenclature in some applications that we may use on a day to day basis for Document Control.

Most Commonly Used	Could also be called	Notes
Document Profile	"Template" or "Form"	The GUI "Form" you complete for each Deliverable Document. The word "form" comes from, eg. MS Access, when designing a program each GUI is, most often, a form (but could be a table).
Template	"Profile" or "Form"	An, eg. MS Office Template OR CAD Template file (.dotx etc)
Form	"Document Profile" or "Template"	Forms are most commonly used in EDMS and collaboration or DC tools for specific purposes such as eg's. RFI's, TQ's, Variations, Issues (or other) Logs **and/or** (using common parlance for DB's – a GUI that needs the user to provide data such as a Document Profile). This could also be an eg. An, eg. MS Office Template used for a specific purpose – usually, not always, printed. Where not built-in to the EDMS/DC Tool being used.

This is one area I would really like to see ISO, after consultation with Engineering DC's, address. The nomenclature really does need to be standardised. The most commonly used nomenclature, among others, above is how I would like to see it done.

AFTER WORD(S) [YES MORE]

As I said before the pace of change in many sectors is both frantic and, on the surface, slow. New technology arrives every day. Revised and new methods of working come in to being every day but are often slow to be accepted, released to the consumer or acknowledged. Examples of this are in the keeping of entirely electronic records. While many nations moved quite some time ago to accept electronic signatures others still have not (often requiring multiple wet signed and stamped/ chopped originals) and among those that allowed e-signing the uptake was slow to take a hold. I still sometimes like to hang a sign, among others, in my DC area – Welcome to the Dead Tree Society, along with "The impossible – done immediately, Miracles – longer.

Taking documentation entirely electronic has been slow to say the least. I vividly recall, when IBM Compatible XT 10Mhz (at the time 2+ times as fast and the standard 4.77 Mhz) / 1 mB RAM (hard to do/get and expensive) / (huge) 20mB HDD's hit desks and really basic networks came to fruition in the mid 80's, having an argument with someone that said that these things will reduce the amount of paper we use. My reasoning was that with these machines and software like, eg. W4W and Lotus 123, we could manipulate words and data so much more quickly and produce so much more, we otherwise may not have considered, eg. For the Monthly reports that we'd use ever more paper just in a different way. Using the Monthly report example we moved from an, often, type written report with a few graphs done on graph paper of say around 20 pages to a huge 100 plus page report that, most likely only 20 pages of which were read. At the time I was not wrong.

We have thankfully moved on from there, albeit really slowly, and the report mentioned in the example is now often circulated only in electronic format although many, especially of my age group, despite what technology might offer, will still print stuff off to read it. I've been there and recall being frustrated that having sorted a 42" plasma (top line thing at the time) screen capable of clearly displaying an A1 (most common format) drawing that reviewers still wanted prints to review...

CAD has come a long way too. Drawing board to 2D design tools to 3D design too. 3D design still has some small fallibilities. At one time many could not manage Pipework under 100 mm OD then it was 50mm OD and last I heard it's down to 5mm OD which still means at the very least some 2D CAD work or, worse for those having to do them, piping Iso's for the small stuff being drawn by hand on graph paper!

The total amount of 2D drawings produced on projects has reduced significantly and often, not always, constructors and others are now sent bits of 3D models (and possibly Shoppies) and that, apart from Specs, Datasheets and the like, is all they get. That said the speed at which drawings such as Loop Diagrams and Piping Iso's can be produced, especially if you are working in a reactive environment, can leave you wishing you'd not gone to work that day! When this, 3D model files only, was being pushed in early to mid 00's it confused the heck out of a lot of them – "where's all the drawings" – but now appears to be common practice.

Cloud solutions and "live" collaboration has almost, not entirely, permitted us to work from home – a discipline all its own!

BIM – Building Information Management has also sprung up and been leapt upon in many places and, in the main, been built into some of the better Eng EDMS / DC tools. I mentioned in the book about DC's collecting data they may not otherwise collect and where it might be used such as CMMS tools and Operations Portals. Ops Portals are something that, particularly in Western Australia, has been done for some time. To my way of thinking BIM is, more or less, exactly the same thing – hand over enough data to operate, efficiently, the asset that is being/has been developed – ie. an Ops Portal.

On page 76 I have outlined some of the "other data" we might need to, be asked for, or we should consider collecting Document to Equip/Tag Relationships. It is also wise, where time permits, to collect against the drawings, where possible, such relationships as Cable No, Piping Line No and (if you have not worked it out already) Instrument Numbers.

If it is at all possible, with the right permissions and PPE et al go out in to the plant, if you know it well enough or with, say, a commissioning person, take the relevant P&ID's and a filtered Equipment List for that part of the plant (add extra fields), take with you a Digital Camera (preferably with a GPS "stamp" or if not a GPS, find the kit and take a photo of the ID Plate and record the following information on your Equipment List:

Serial Number (of the kit) ★
GPS Location

And when you get back to the office and have uploaded your pics map to them.

★Equipment Numbers / Instrument Numbers rarely change – they do if the bit of kit is replaced with a new one. Serial numbers can and do change for example an instrument might stop working and is replaced like for like the serial number will change.

ALL this information is useful to the eventual CMMS and/or an operations portal.

It can also be rewarding – hey you had something to do with this – more or less – end result. I have, in the past, even worked on a Gold Producing plant where I could follow the PFD's and P&ID's one end to the other and even got to handle (all the way to the airport with an armed security guard next to me) bars of gold! I've had the privilege of seeing briquetted iron coming from one plant, briquetted Nickel and Cobalt from another and seen other stuff too – even watched ore trains leaving a plant I was an LDC on during design/construction.

The pace of change in, for example, the resource and other sectors is often aimed at greater efficiency and driving operating / cost to recover costs down. Yet other sectors appear to be somewhat slow, or very guarded, about developments – alternative energy and propulsion (well I/C Type) spring to mind. We yet do not appear to have developed any form of "long distance" propulsion that does not have to rely on Oxygen being present somewhere. It's sort of mind blowing when we stop and think that in '68 Man Walked on the Moon yet we still have not sent a man to Mars – which at present constitutes a 7 year one way trip - nor have we come up with SciFi to SciFact Stasis (Red Dwarf springs to mind here) without which (until we find a way of not having to use Oxygen in propulsion) would aid inter planetary and inter stellar travel.

My home nation appears to have completely missed the boat when it comes to the development of solar power a nation the majority of which has excellent amounts of sunshine! I can only applaud the work that people like Elon Musk are doing with this, sadly, in other parts of the world. Even Abu Dhabi, plenty of sunshine and money there too, has started construction of a "sustainable" city, Masdar, and where is Australia in all this – nowhere really – plans or suggestions for solar cities have fallen over many times. I will freely admit here that, at present, the manufacture of solar cells is a somewhat dirty industry, and Lithium mining (for the batteries) and processing is far from clean either but at least we could attempt to make an effort to perhaps do something about that too.

It is probable that the affects of the resource sector "collapse" (2012) – to my mind a deliberate action for more reasons than one (it's happened before) - will either be an increase in the pace of change with a view to cost cutting and efficiency or a total slow down – no money around to spend on R&D.

It does bother me that awesome amounts of money is always being spent on the machinations of war. Sure, some of the technology makes it to "civvie" street – GPS for one – but it is incredibly rare it manages to go the other way.

It is, as I said before, this pace of change that keeps me in the "game". Although I will freely admit that at times the "game" is not what I would call soulful and I will head off and teach English O/S which I do find soulful.

Oct 2022 Update

A lot of things have changed since I last did any form of update sheet for this book.

At last count I am now a grand uncle 5x over. My daughter is now far from the youngest "Grosso".

Firsttrace and Kinnosa appear to have disappeared and I am unable to find out if another party is supporting those who have Kinnosa.

In the relatively recent past Aconex has been acquired by Oracle and TeamBinder (not including QDMS) by InEight. Teambinder since this acquisition has come on in leaps and bounds.

I've also come across two newish Standards. BS1192 - Collaborative production of architectural, engineering and construction information. Code of practice. While I understand why it was released my experience with it – not great – the Rev numbering method in it is non-sensical. Sadly, I have not yet had any access to the ISO19650 Suite (-1:2019, -2:2018, -3:2020, -4:2022 and -5:2021)

There appears to now be a DC Standard: SA/SNZ 168:2017, until I have access to it or a copy, I am unable to comment on what the content is and how relevant it might be.

Many CAD Tools have progressed to the point where, sadly, Engineers are able to produce drawings!

My Experience with some of the drawings that appear not to have had qualified draftsperson input is that they are awful and if in a position to do so I'd review them very carefully, add loads of redline comments and send them back. I'm also sad to say the use of a Cross Reference box in drawing titles appears to have gone too and this is just wrong.

Oh, while I think of it…. IFC is now also a drawing type (3D) and it can be confusing when talking to a designer and being at crossed purposes i.e. you thinking Issued for Construction and they the drawing type!

This book will, eventually, be accompanied by a website on which more info and links to White Papers can be found. Possibly, sometime in the future, video of myself or others running training courses too. Online training for DC is not yet 100% possible but it is none too far away either.

I hope that this book has provided you with not only the tools to do the job but the Why's – one of the most FAQ's I get (after How do I…). Go out there and enjoy your career!

Work Smart, Play Hard
Huw

LIST OF APPENDICES

Appendix No	Content
1	Definitions
2	DrawCon Installation Instructions
3	Setting up a DrawCon Project – 3 Day Seminar
4	Drawings
5	Transmittals
6	Paper Aeroplane
7	Mind Maps/Flowcharts – Links/Examples
8A	Classifications (Mining)
8B	Classifications (Oil/Gas)
8C	Classifications (Civil)
9	How To Use the DrawCon Block Number Generator
10	Worked Practicals for Download – On Memory Stick Only
11	Pre-Read Material – EEDMS – Index – Docs On Memory Stick Only
12	Tests
13	Course Slides

APPENDIX 1

Definitions

Engineering Document Control – Definitions

Engineering Document Control itself is the management of drawings and documents that relate to the design and operation (not necessarily maintenance records) of assets such as, for example, (at the vendor level) a pump right through to (at the Operator level) an Oil/Gas Rig, mine plant, mineral/oil-gas refinery. We do NOT usually manage correspondence although Technical Queries, RFI's and ECR's are sometimes called correspondence – they are NOT.

Not all of the material that will be controlled by Document Controllers during a Green or Brown field project is deliverable to Operations/Operators.

Engineering Data Management is the management of ALL data that makes up the deliverable documents and other information such as Tag to Document relationships, 3D models, calculations etc. which may not be printed or frozen at specific points in time. A majority of this data must either be retained or delivered to Operations/Operators.

Green Field Project a new project on bare earth or where there is no pre-existing infrastructure such as subsea wells, rigs etc.

Brown Field Project a project where work is being undertaken on an existing asset to update, modify, expand or demolish it in part or full.

Deliverable Documents such as Datasheets, Calculations, Manuals etc. that are deliverable to a client organisation during life of a project or to Operations/Operators at project end.

Asset an item of value that is maintained by an operator for the purpose of producing income - such as, for example, (at the vendor level) a pump right through to (at the Operator level) an Oil/Gas Rig, mine plant, mineral/oil-gas refinery.

Plant Area Code a logical breakdown of a large asset such as a mine plant in to correlated "chunks" or areas for example:

001 - Mine
100 - Administration Area
200 - Workshops and Warehousing
300 - Run of Mine Pad, Grizzly and Chute

Work Breakdown Structure – something DC's are becoming more commonly exposed to - WBS) A division of a project into tasks and subtasks. The tasks are numbered to indicate their relationship to each other. WBSs are indispensable for project planning, particularly when estimating time and resource requirements. Some industries use established work breakdown structure systems for billing and reporting purposes. Note these structures are similar to but not always the same as those used to formulate controlled document numbers for DC purposes.

Discipline – an Engineering, sometimes business, activity such as, for example, Mechanical, Instrumentation or Scheduling/Project Controls and HSE

Document Type – groups documents in to particular correlated types e.g. Datasheets, Drawings, Calculations

Document Sub Type - (not recommended but often used) – A coding method that classifies specific document types in to subtypes where a discipline code may not provide enough data with the document type code for an accurate classification e.g. Noise Calculation, P&ID, Instrument Loop Diagram, Piping Isometric.

★★Sometimes Document Types and SubTypes do not adequately define a document for Operations needs or they are coded incorrectly (along with Discipline) and operations will have their own coding system, which they either assign or audit against. These are often called either AIMS or OIMS Codes. (Asset Information Management Standard or Operations Information Management Standard). When that system is mature it is often a concatenation of a Document SubType and Document Type e.g. PID for P&ID, MYK (where K denotes a Datasheet and MY is "Noise" or IYK (Datasheet, Instrument, Valve).

Incoming Status The status of a document when it is received in DC (usually from an external party) e.g. Issued for Review. Issued for Approval

Review Status The status of a document that was sent in for Review or Approval after review/squad check by a team or the lead/package/ nominated Engineer e.g. Proceed, Proceed except as Noted – Revise and Resubmit.

CTR – Cost Time Resource Similar to WBS but used more by Oil/ Gas Companies than any others.

Tag or Equipment Number A reference number used for identifying individual pieces of equipment, instruments etc. in a plant. It is usually comprised of the plant area code (often numeric), an alpha code which is an abbreviation for the equipment type and a sequence number. E.g. 301-GRZ-001 (301 being the plant area code for the Grizzly – GRZ being the alpha code for a Grizzly and 001 is the sequence number).

Piping/Pipe Line Number Identifies pipe(s) running through each section of the plant or as a whole. The numbering methods vary but generally include:

Line No – Generally just 1, 2, 3 and so on

Material/Fluid – an abbreviation of the type of material being carried by the pipe. E.g. PWA (Process Water)

Area in Plant – Usually the Plant Area Code e.g. 501 (Cyclones)

Line Size – Internal Diameter (ID) of the pipe. E.g. 300 (300mm)

Material of Construction. The material the pipe itself is constructed from. E.g. CS for Carbon Steel

Insulation. Pipes are often insulated to prevent heat loss or gain. Usually H – Hot or C – Cold

Phase. Usually S – Solids, L – Liquids, G – Gas

Other. Sometimes used to denote Jacketing or Coating

On a Piping Iso Drawing all of the above and a sheet number E.g. -001, -002 and so on the title should show the number of sheets e.g. 1 of 10.

Instrument Number Often an abbreviated form of a Tag Number shown above – due to the small nature of the symbols used and a lack of space on drawings these are often an alpha code for an instrument type and sequence number for that area of the plant with no dashes. E.g. PSV001

Squad Check - Documents issued either internally or from external contractors/vendors often require Review (IFR) the team that completes the review is a "squad" and the review is commonly called a Squad Check and may be done in a "War Room" – reviews are usually done on paper or electronically on a transmittal or workflow.

Also known as an **Inter-discipline Review IDR or even Inter-discipline Check IDC** – where the document(s) is to be reviewed by team members of more than one discipline.

On rare occasions DC's may be responsible for creating transmittals or workflows for an **Intra-discipline review** where the document(s) are to be reviewed by team members within one discipline only – generally this is done by the discipline lead and on a no revision document print and is rarely seen in DC.

Transmittal A document that is used to "formally" send controlled documents to either Internal (Internal Transmittal) or External recipients in paper or electronic format.

Workflow Some DC applications and collaboration tools have replaced transmittals with Workflows.

Distribution Matrices

Internal – A list of recipients for specific types of documents usually discipline or package (Vendor P/O) based. E.g. Mechanical Documents requiring review Mechanical Engineer, Piping Engineer, Structural Engineer, Electrical Engineer, Instrument Engineer, Process Engineer back to Mechanical Engineer

External – A list of recipients for specific types of documents, usually in "Packages" based on either a package of work to be carried out by a Vendor or Constructor. These usually evolve starting with a list of Tenderers. Once awarded the "losing tenderers" are "deactivated and others such as site DC and construction contractors (where a vendor package) are added.

Other Terminology in Use

A -- <u>AEC</u>, <u>Action Items</u>, <u>Annotations</u>, <u>Approval Codes</u>, <u>Approval Process</u>, <u>Arbitration</u>, <u>As-Built</u>, <u>Authoring Application</u>, <u>Approved for Construction</u>, <u>Archive</u>

B -- <u>Basic Engineering Documents</u>, <u>Batch Production Process</u>, <u>Brownfield</u>, <u>Building Information Modelling</u>, <u>Bill of Quantity(BoQ) / Bill of Materials (BoM)</u>, <u>Bill of Lading</u>

C – <u>Check-in/Check-out</u>, <u>Claim</u>, <u>Clarification Request</u>, <u>Comment Resolution Sheet</u>, <u>Commercial Evaluation of Bids</u>, <u>Commissioning</u>, <u>Commit</u>, <u>Controlled Document</u>, <u>Correspondence</u>, <u>Correspondence Reference</u>, CAD – Computer Aided Design

D -- <u>Daily Progress Report</u>, <u>Design Change Note</u>, <u>Detailed Engineering</u>, <u>Deviation Request</u>, <u>Document Control Index</u>, <u>Document Control Process</u>, <u>Document Control Software</u>, <u>Document Number Methods</u>, <u>Document Transmittal Note</u>, <u>Document Redlining Software</u>, <u>Document Management Software</u>, <u>Drawing Register</u>, <u>Document Types</u>, <u>Decision Codes</u>

E -- <u>Electronic Transmittal</u>, <u>Engineering Coordination Procedure</u>, <u>Engineering Change Request</u>

F-- <u>Field Assessment Test</u>, <u>Field Design Change Note</u>, <u>Field Quality Assurance Plan</u>, <u>Factory Acceptance Tests (FAT)</u>

G -- <u>Guideline</u>, <u>Geotechnical Report</u>, <u>General Correspondence</u>

H – HSE/HSEQ

I -- <u>Input Document</u>, <u>Inspection Call</u>, <u>Inspection Release Note</u>, <u>Inter-disciplinary</u>, <u>Invoice</u>, <u>Inspection Certificate</u>, <u>Issued for Construction</u>, <u>Issued For Approval</u>, <u>Issued For Information</u>, <u>Issued For Quotation</u>, <u>Issued for Tender</u>, <u>Issued for Review</u> and as above a 3D drawing type .IFC

J—I've seen used as the Dsicipline Code for Instruments!

K --

L --Legal Validity of Email, Lock, Look Ahead Report

M-- Master Document List, Material Dispatch Clearance Certificate, Monthly Progress Report

N-- Non-Acceptance Note, Non Conformance Report, NTP - Notice to Proceed

O --Overdue Report

P -- Package, Pre-Dispatch Inspection, Progress Monitoring, Progress Report, Punch List

Q -- Quality Check/Quality Assurance, Quality Assurance Plan (QAP)

R -- Redlining, Release for construction, Release for fabrication, Request for Information (RFI)

S -- Scope Change Order, Submission Codes, Superseding Documents, Supplier Document Register, Site Instructions (SI)

T --Technical Evaluation, Technical Query, Transmittal

U -- Un-controlled Documents

V -- Vendor Engineering, Vendor Document Register, Version Control, Variation Order Request

W -- Weekly Progress Report, Work Flow, Work Breakdown Structure

X --

Y --

Z --

Also NOT a definitive List

APPENDIX 2

Drawcon Installation Instructions

– (DrawCon is available for download with a 60 day licence)

Installing DrawCon to a personal Laptop or Computer

MS Access IS NOT installed:

Download and Install

http://download.cnet.com/Microsoft-Access-2010-Runtime-32-bit/3000-10254_4-75452791.html

Make a Directory on c:\ as Drawcon

Make a Directory on c:\Drawcon as Library files

Make a Directory on c:\Drawcon as Manual

Copy the file drawcon10.mde to c:\drawcon

Copy the files in drawcon\library to c:\drawcon\library files

Copy the files in drawcon\manual to c:\drawcon\manual

NOTE the Library Files are usually installed on a network share

Right click on c:\drawcon\drawcon10.mde and create a shortcut drag it to your desktop

Double click on the shortcut

Access / DrawCon may give some form of security error in the yellow bar at the top click OK or Continue

There may also be a number of security warnings when DrawCon tries to load files keep clicking ok. It may also not find one or more files – it will ask where they are browse to c:\drawcon\library files and click on the file it is looking for. DrawCon might, after all this, appear to crash. Fear not. Double click on your shortcut.

Click File
Click Options
Click Trust Center

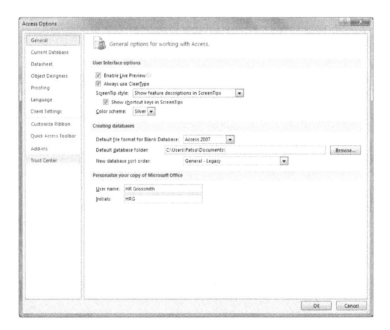

Click Trust Center Settings

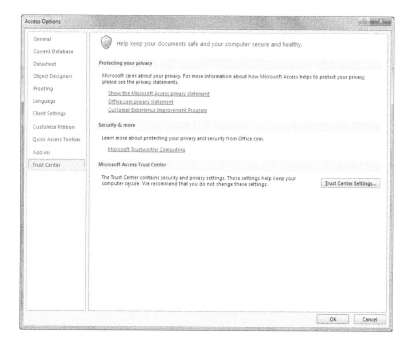

Click Trusted Locations

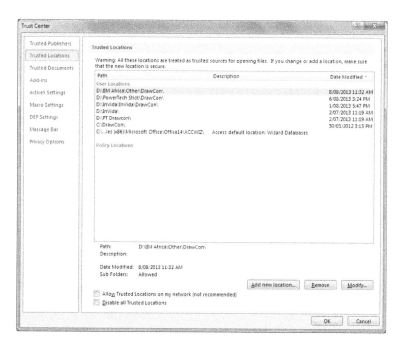

Click Add New Location

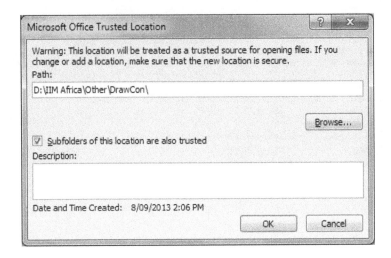

Browse to C:\DrawCon and make sure the Subfolders of this location are also trusted is checked

Click OK, OK, OK this should resolve the security issues.

MS Access IS installed:

Make a Directory on c:\ as Drawcon

Make a Directory on c:\Drawcon as Library files

Make a Directory on c:\Drawcon as Manual

Copy the file drawcon10.mde to c:\drawcon

Copy the files in drawcon\library to c:\drawcon\library files

Copy the files in drawcon\manual to c:\drawcon\manual

NOTE the Library Files are usually installed on a network share

Right click on c:\drawcon\drawcon10.mde and create a shortcut drag it to your desktop

Open MS Access NOT DrawCon

Click File

Click Options

Click Trust Center

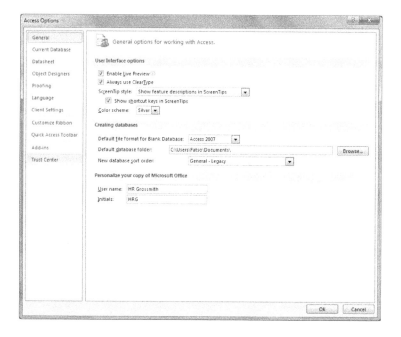

Click Trust Center Settings

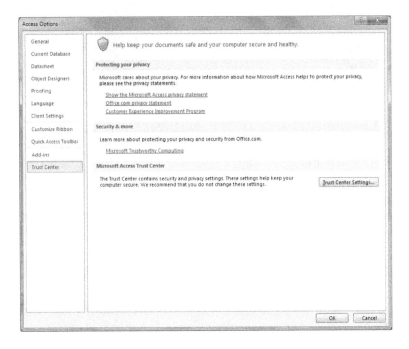

Click Trusted Locations

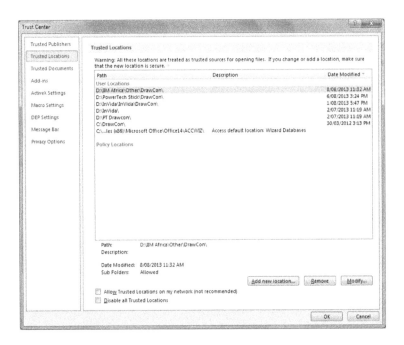

Click Add New Location

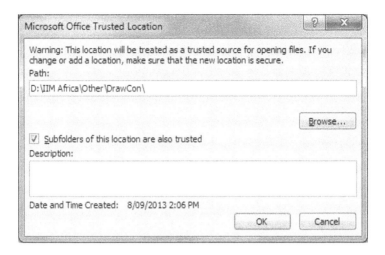

Browse to C:\DrawCon and make sure the Subfolders of this location are also trusted is checked

Click OK, OK, OK this should resolve the security issues.

Click on your shortcut to Open Drawcon. It may ask where some files are – browse to c:\drawcon\library files and select the file it asks for.

NOTE the manual is for an older version but is still largely relevant.

Possible Error

If you see this message:

The database cannot be opened because the VBA project contained in it cannot be read. The database can be opened only if the VBA project is first deleted. Deleting the VBA project removes all code from modules, forms and reports. You should back up your database before attempting to open the database and delete the VBA project.

There is a problem with MS Access not DrawCon. The resolutions on the MS Website do not work, especially the solution where you have to run the CMD or DOS box and one of the others requires re-installing Access 2010 with no update SP1 decompiling the project (which I will not give out) and then re-installing 2010 SP1 and recompiling the project - the application (Access) itself is also not ISO15489 compliant with respect to backward compatibility.

In the DrawCon directory for download are two VBE7*.dll files.

On your PC open Windows explorer and do a search VBE7*.DLL – rename the two files VBE7*dll by adding –Backup before .DLL and copy the two files from the download in to the same directories you found the files you renamed in. This is a slight downgrade but has never caused any problems on my Laptops or PC's if you do experience problems delete the files and change the names of the renamed files back. You may need to find or download Access 2007 and ask me for compatible files.

Note this may have been addressed with SP2 which I have downloaded and run and DrawCon still runs too but the VBE7 files may not have been updated with this patch.

APPENDIX 3

Creating a DrawCon Project

Open Drawcon

Follow the DrawCon installation instructions in Appendix 2.

NOTE WELL DrawCon is a Database with very limited exceptions it is not necessary to click Save each time data is entered.

From the Main Menu under Processes click C – Projects then

Click

This opens a new form complete it as below

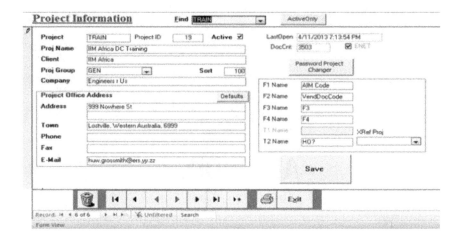

E-mail must be your own email address and a valid one for returning this assessment to.

Click Save to create a project – this is quick you may not see it happen. We will accept all the default values it imports for the time being.

Click exit.

Then from the Main Menu Click 0 Valid Code Menu

Under System Codes Click C Transfer Codes

Select from the Drop Down

   Get From Project - FEG

Select from the Drop Down

   Transfer Table - tArea

Leave the check boxes as they are and click Transfer

Then repeat for all Transfer Tables except tTranConf

When complete click Exit

Click Main Menu

This process imports all the data already set up in that project under the Valid Code Menu.

Which excludes our Internal "Telephone List" – See Chapter 22A on Pages 117 and 118

Now we are going to cheat big time.

Press F11 this displays the table structure.

Find tDocResp and Double Click it will open.

Go to Windows Explorer and find your c:\Drawcon\Library Files\ directory

Find DCFEG.MDB

Hold down the Shift Key and Double Click DCFEG.MDB you must keep the Shift Key Held down until it opens which may take a minute or two.

Find the table tDocResp

It looks like this:

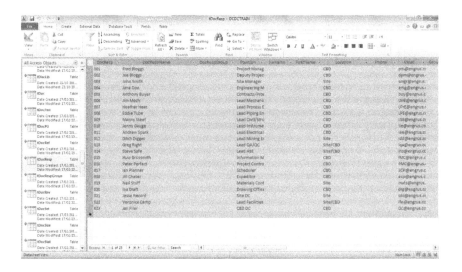

Click in the Grey Area in the top right corner – this will highlight all the fields.

Press Ctrl and C

Go back to your DCTrain database.

Put your cursor in the grey area on the first blank line it should go black

Press Ctrl and V

This will paste in your Internal Recipients

Click the White (Close Window) X NOT the Red and White X

To check what we did worked click 0 Valid Code Menu

Under Transmittal Codes click E Internal Recipients (Doc Resp)

All your Internal Recipients should now be there

We have just created a DrawCon project and populated a number of fields for use in our day to day work.

APPENDIX 4

Drawings

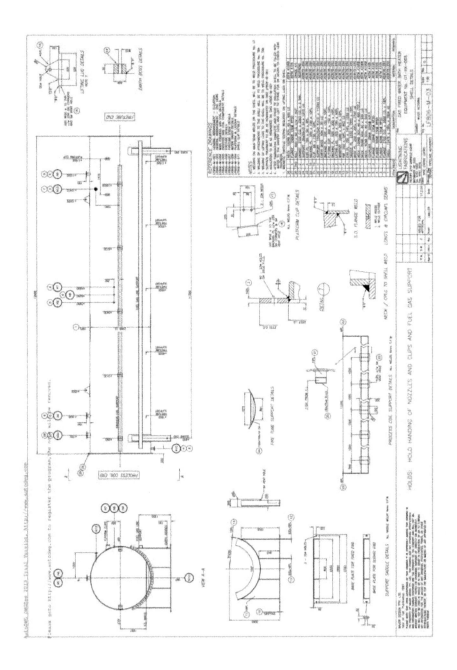

AutoCAD SHX Text 2013 Trial Version. http://www.cadsofttools.com

Please goto http://www.cadsofttools.com to register the programs.The trial version has some restrictions.

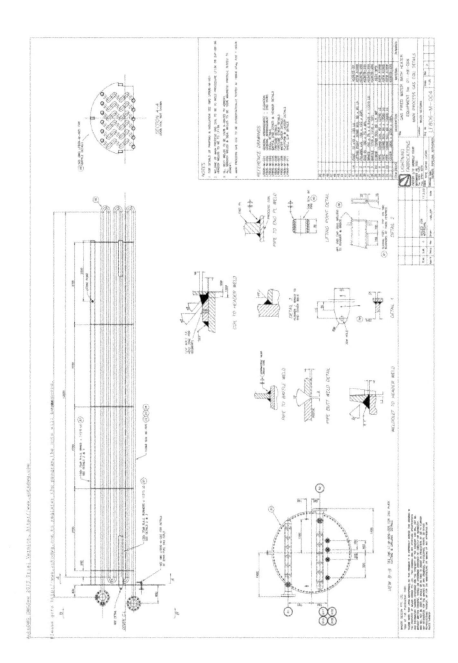

Please note: http://www.orlinkdwg.com to register the program, the note will become active.

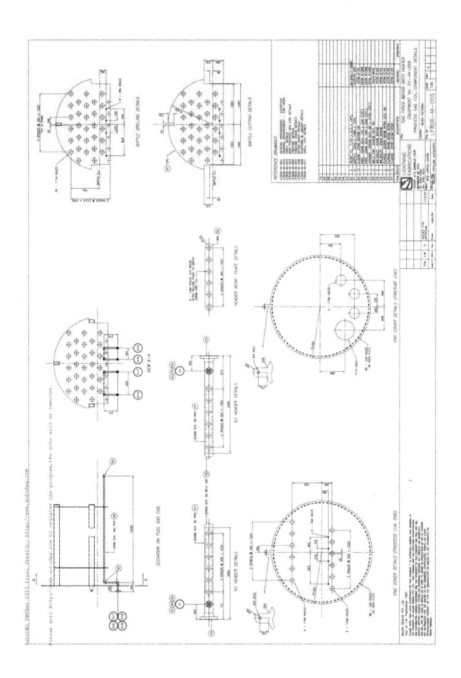

Autodesk Designer 2013 Trial Version. http://www.autodesk.com

Please goto http://www.autodesk.com to register the program. The note will be removed.

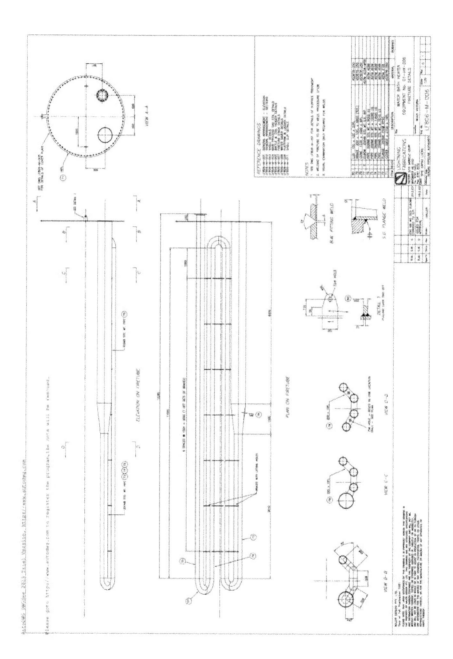

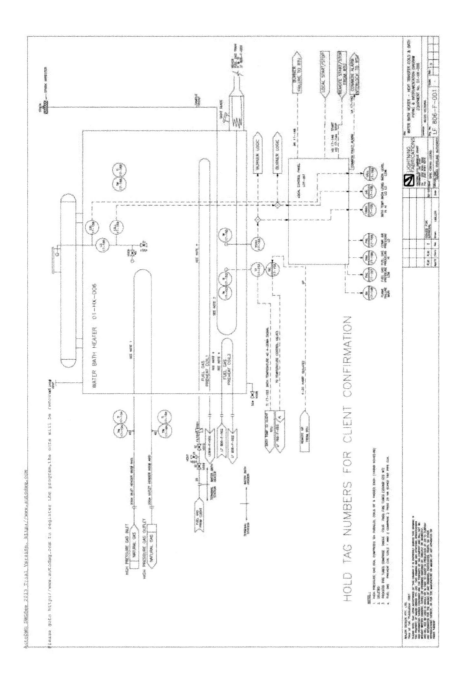

HOLD TAG NUMBERS FOR CLIENT CONFIRMATION

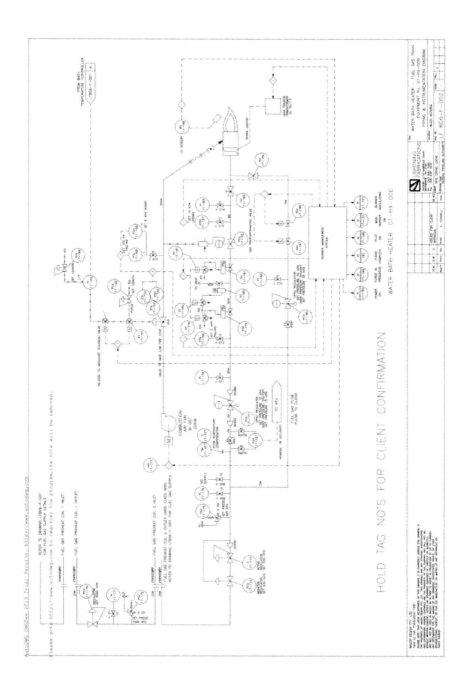

HOLD TAG NO'S FOR CLIENT CONFIRMATION

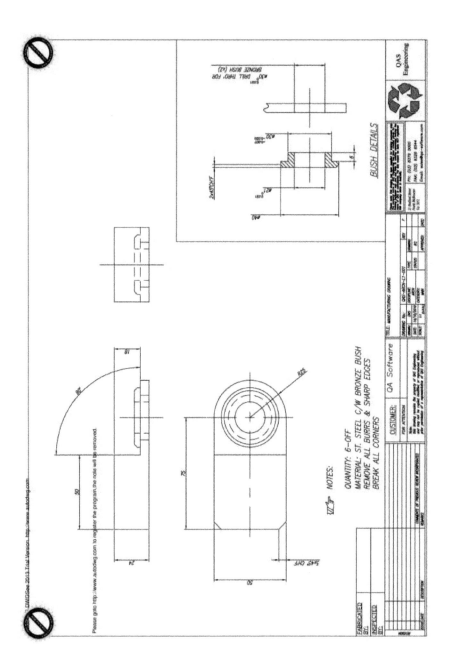

NOTES:
QUANTITY: 6-OFF
MATERIAL: ST. STEEL C/W BRONZE BUSH
REMOVE ALL BURRS & SHARP EDGES
BREAK ALL CORNERS

BUSH DETAILS

DWGSee 2013 Trial Version. http://www.autodwg.com

Please goto http://www.autodwg.com to register the program, the note will be removed.

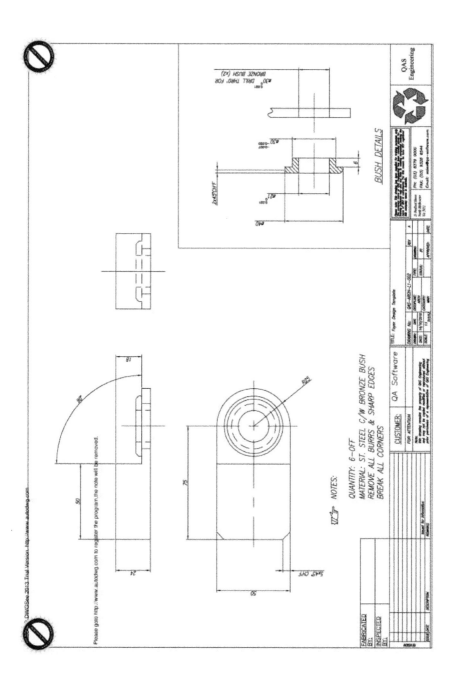

NOTES:

QUANTITY: 6-OFF
MATERIAL: ST. STEEL C/W BRONZE BUSH
REMOVE ALL BURRS & SHARP EDGES
BREAK ALL CORNERS

BUSH DETAILS

ø30° DRILL THRO' FOR
BRONZE BUSH (x2)

DWGSee 2013 Trial Version. http://www.autodwg.com

Please goto http://www.autodwg.com to register the program.,the note will be removed.

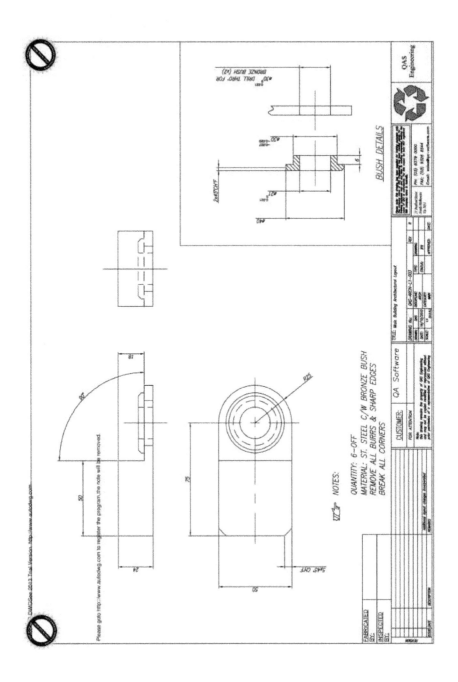

BUSH DETAILS

ø30° DRILL THRO' FOR
BRONZE BUSH (x2)

NOTES:

QUANTITY: 6-OFF
MATERIAL: ST. STEEL C/W BRONZE BUSH
REMOVE ALL BURRS & SHARP EDGES
BREAK ALL CORNERS

DWGSee 2013 Trial Version. http://www.autodwg.com

Please goto http://www.autodwg.com to register the program,the note will be removed.

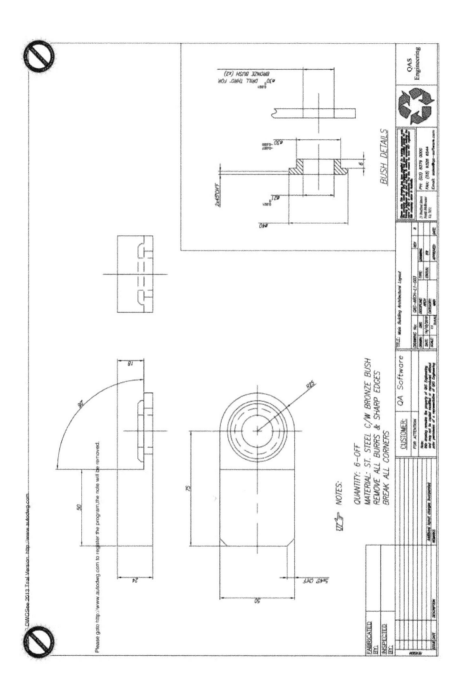

NOTES:

QUANTITY: 6-OFF
MATERIAL: ST. STEEL C/W BRONZE BUSH
REMOVE ALL BURRS & SHARP EDGES
BREAK ALL CORNERS

BUSH DETAILS

Ø30 DRILL THRO' FOR
BRONZE BUSH (x2)

2xØ5YPT

Please goto http://www.autodwg.com to register the program, the note will be removed.

DWGSee 2013 Trial Version http://www.autodwg.com

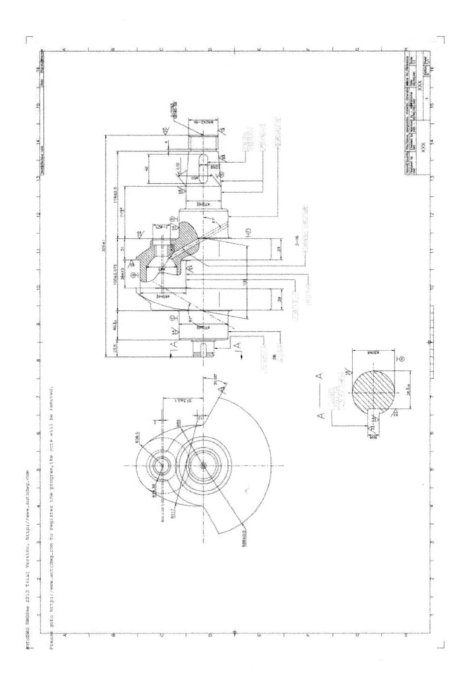

AutoCAD DWGSee 2013 Trial Version. http://www.dwgsee.com

Please goto http://www.autodwg.com to register the program,the note will be removed.

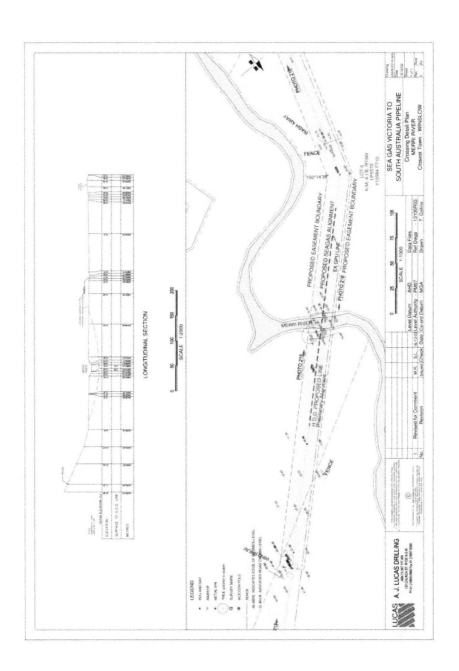

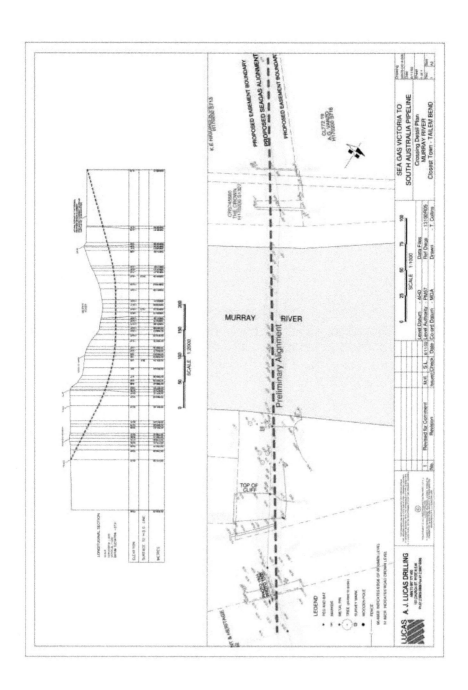

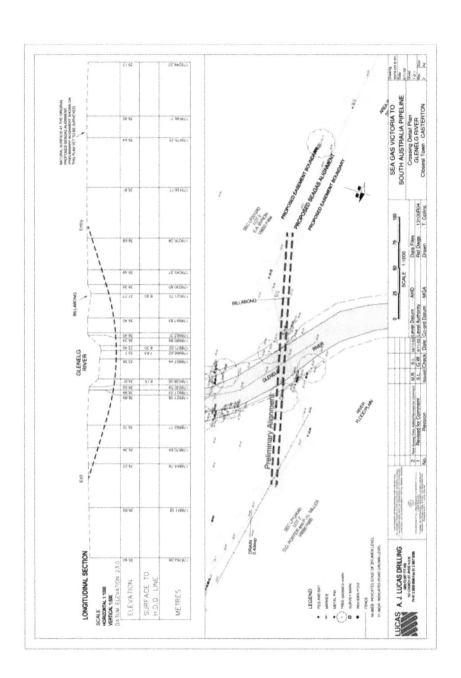

LONGITUDINAL SECTION

SCALE
HORIZONTAL 1:1000
VERTICAL 1:500

DATUM ELEVATION 23.0

ELEVATION

SURFACE TO
H.D.D. LINE

METRES

GLENELG RIVER

BILLABONG

LEGEND

PEG AND BAT
MARKER PIN
METAL PIN
TREE (species to north)
SURVEY MAIN
WOODEN POLE
FENCE

INDICATES EDGE OF BITUMEN LEVEL
INCH INDICATES ROAD CROWN LEVEL

A. J. LUCAS DRILLING

SEA GAS VICTORIA TO
SOUTH AUSTRALIA PIPELINE

Crossing Detail Plan
GLENELG RIVER
Closest Town - CASTERTON

SCALE 1:1000

PROPOSED EASEMENT BOUNDARY
PROPOSED SEAGAS ALIGNMENT
PROPOSED EASEMENT BOUNDARY

BILLABONG

GLENELG RIVER

RIVER FLOODPLAIN

Preliminary Alignment

DRAIN

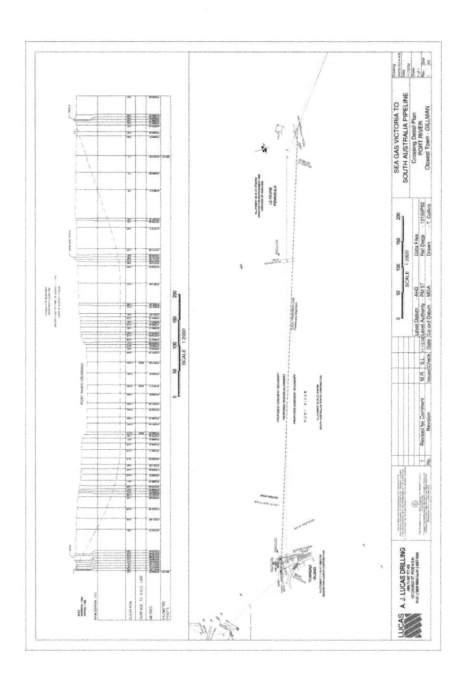

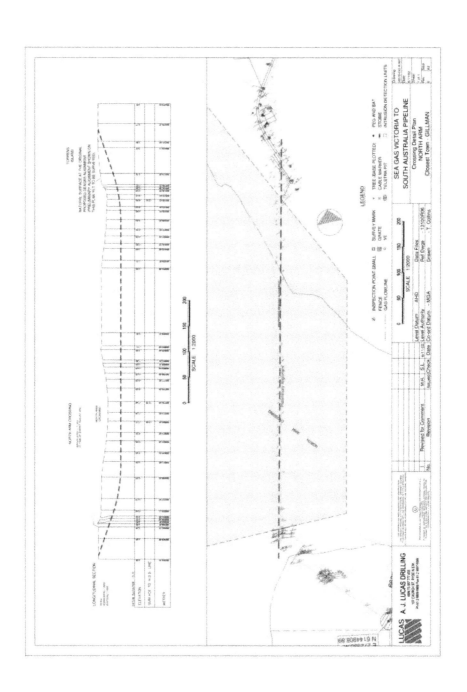

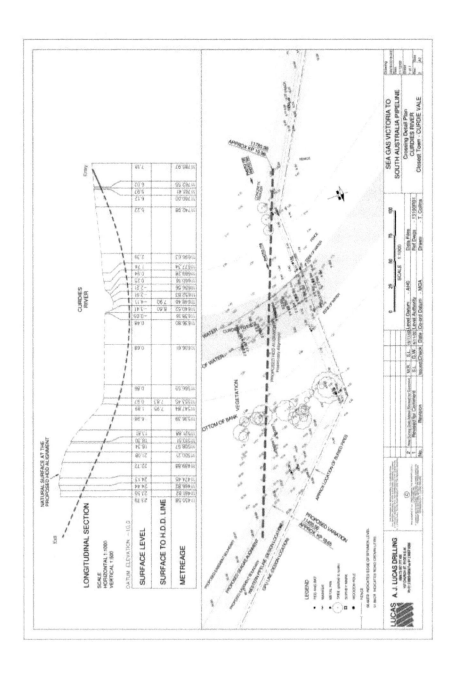

LONGITUDINAL SECTION

SCALE
HORIZONTAL 1:1000
VERTICAL 1:500

DATUM ELEVATION −10.0

SURFACE LEVEL

SURFACE TO H.D.D. LINE

METREAGE

CURDIES RIVER

NATURAL SURFACE AT THE
PROPOSED HDD ALIGNMENT

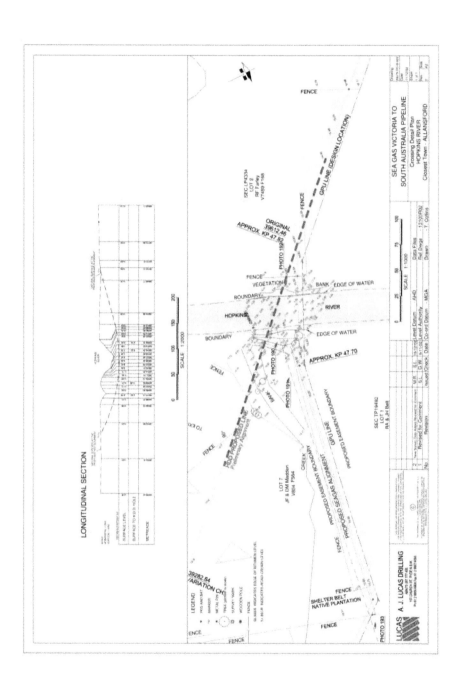

LONGITUDINAL SECTION

SCALE 1:2000

SEA GAS VICTORIA TO
SOUTH AUSTRALIA PIPELINE
Crossing Detail Plan
HOPKINS RIVER
Closest Town - ALLANSFORD

A. J. LUCAS DRILLING

SCALE 1:1000

FENCE

GPL LINE (DESIGN LOCATION)

SEC LP4334
LOT 2
RF Fanley
V7459 F168

ORIGINAL
APPROX. KP 47.82
396 12.46

PHOTO 192

FENCE

VEGETATION   BANK   EDGE OF WATER
BOUNDARY

HOPKINS   RIVER

BOUNDARY   EDGE OF WATER

APPROX. KP 47.70

PHOTO 190

PHOTO 191

FENCE

PROPOSED SEA GAS LINE
Preliminary Alignment

TO EXIT

CREEK

LOT 7
JF & DM Maddison
V803A F564

GPL LINE
PROPOSED EASEMENT BOUNDARY
PROPOSED SEAGAS ALIGNMENT
PROPOSED EASEMENT BOUNDARY

SEC TP19492
LOT 1
RA & JH Bell

FENCE
SHELTER BELT
NATIVE PLANTATION

FENCE

PHOTO 193

39282.84
/ARIATION CH

LEGEND

FENCE

FENCE

APPENDIX 5

Transmittals

Document Circulation Form / Internal Transmittal Example from DrawCon in Word Format:

Iron Khan

Document Circulation Form : SC-0002

TranDate: **12-Sep-13**
Originator:

DOCUMENTS			
Document	**Rev**	**Status**	**Title**
FEG-170-AA-GAR-0001	A	IFR	IRON MONARCHY - IRON KHAN AIRPORT Reserved Number: PO CON-002 - Airport Experts Created: 31-Aug-13 / Huw Grossmith

DOCUMENTS

Document	Rev	Status	Title
FEG-170-AA-GAR-0002	A	IFR	IRON MONARCHY - IRON KHAN AIRPORT Reserved Number: PO CON-002 - Airport Experts Created: 31-Aug-13 / Huw Grossmith
FEG-170-AA-GAR-0003	A	IFR	IRON MONARCHY - IRON KHAN AIRPORT Reserved Number: PO CON-002 - Airport Experts Created: 31-Aug-13 / Huw Grossmith
FEG-170-AA-GAR-0004	A	IFR	IRON MONARCHY - IRON KHAN AIRPORT Reserved Number: PO CON-002 - Airport Experts Created: 31-Aug-13 / Huw Grossmith
FEG-170-AA-GAR-0005	A	IFR	IRON MONARCHY - IRON KHAN AIRPORT Reserved Number: PO CON-002 - Airport Experts Created: 31-Aug-13 / Huw Grossmith

DISTRIBUTION

Name	Position	Reason for Issue
Action Required		
Andrew Spark	Lead Electrical Engineer	Issued for Review
Eddie Tube	Lead Piping Engineer	Issued for Review
Heather Heat	Lead Process Engineer	Issued for Review
Ina Draft	Drawing Office Manager	Issued for Review
Jane Doe	Engineering Manager	Issued for Review
Jenny Gauge	Lead Instrument Engineer	Issued for Review
Jim Mech	Lead Mechanical Engineer	Issued for Review
Manny Steel	Lead Civil/Structural Engineer	Issued for Review
Veronica Camp	Lead Facilities Engineer	Issued for Review

Incoming Status Codes			
IFR – Issued for Review	IFT – Issued for Tender	IFA – Issued for Approval	IFU – Issued for Use
IFC – Issued for Construction	IFP – Issued for Procurement	ASB – As-Built	IFI – Issued for Information
CAN – Cancelled	RES – Reserved	SS – Superseded	

Please acknowledge receipt of transmittal. Please confirm completion of required actions by 19–Sep–13

Generated by DrawCon10

Document Circulation Form / Internal Transmittal Example from DrawCon in Outlook (msg) Format:

Page 1

From:	
To:	lee@engrus.com.zz
	LPE@engrus.com.zz
	LPrE@engrus.com.zz
	drg@engrus.com.zz
	emg@engrus.com.zz
	lie@engrus.com.zz
	LME@engrus.com.zz
	LSE@engrus.com.zz
	lfe@engrus.com.zz
Date:	30/12/1899 4:00:00 PM
Subject:	Document Circulation Form : SC-0002

Iron Khan
Document Circulation Form : SC-0002

TranDate: 12-Sep-13

Originator:

DOCUMENTS

Document	Rev	Status	Title
FEG-170-AA-GAR-0001	A	IFR	IRON MONARCHY - IRON KHAN AIRPORT Reserved Number: PO CON-002 - Airport Experts Created: 31-Aug-13 / Huw Grossmith
FEG-170-AA-GAR-0002	A	IFR	IRON MONARCHY - IRON KHAN AIRPORT Reserved Number: PO CON-002 - Airport Experts Created: 31-Aug-13 / Huw Grossmith
FEG-170-AA-GAR-0003	A	IFR	IRON MONARCHY - IRON KHAN AIRPORT Reserved Number: PO CON-002 - Airport Experts Created: 31-Aug-13 / Huw Grossmith
FEG-170-AA-GAR-0004	A	IFR	IRON MONARCHY - IRON KHAN AIRPORT Reserved Number: PO CON-002 - Airport Experts Created: 31-Aug-13 / Huw Grossmith
FEG-170-AA-GAR-0005	A	IFR	IRON MONARCHY - IRON KHAN AIRPORT Reserved Number: PO CON-002 - Airport Experts Created: 31-Aug-13 / Huw Grossmith

DISTRIBUTION

Name	Position	Reason for Issue
Action Required		
Andrew Spark	Lead Electrical Engineer	Issued for Review
Eddie Tube	Lead Piping Engineer	Issued for Review
Heather Heat	Lead Process Engineer	Issued for Review
Ina Draft	Drawing Office Manager	Issued for Review
Jane Doe	Engineering Manager	Issued for Review
Jenny Gauge	Lead Instrument Engineer	Issued for Review
Jim Mech	Lead Mechanical Engineer	Issued for Review
Manny Steel	Lead Civil/Structural Engineer	Issued for Review
Veronica Camp	Lead Facilities Engineer	Issued for Review

Incoming Status Codes

IFR - Issued for Review	IFT - Issued for Tender	IFA - Issued for Approval	IFU - Issued for Use
IFC - Issued for Construction	IFP - Issued for Procurement	ASB - As-Built	IFI - Issued for Information
CAN - Cancelled	RES - Reserved	SS - Superseded	

Please acknowledge receipt of transmittal. Please confirm completion of required actions by 19-Sep-13

Generated by DrawCon10

25_11_2013

External Transmittal from DrawCon in Word Format:

Engineers r Us - Iron Khan
Document Transmittal TR-0001

TranDate: **12-Sep-13**
Originator:

DOCUMENTS			
Document	Rev	Status	Title
FEG-120-AA-GAR-0001	A	10	IRON MONARCHY - IRON KHAN CONSTRUCTION CAMP Reserved Number: Created: 31-Aug-13 / Huw Grossmith
FEG-120-AA-GAR-0002	A	10	IRON MONARCHY - IRON KHAN CONSTRUCTION CAMP Reserved Number: Created: 31-Aug-13 / Huw Grossmith
FEG-120-AA-GAR-0003	A	10	IRON MONARCHY - IRON KHAN CONSTRUCTION CAMP Reserved Number: Created: 31-Aug-13 / Huw Grossmith
FEG-120-AA-GAR-0004	A	10	IRON MONARCHY - IRON KHAN CONSTRUCTION CAMP Reserved Number: Created: 31-Aug-13 / Huw Grossmith
FEG-120-AA-GAR-0005	A	10	IRON MONARCHY - IRON KHAN CONSTRUCTION CAMP Reserved Number: Created: 31-Aug-13 / Huw Grossmith
FEG-120-AA-GAR-0006	A	10	IRON MONARCHY - IRON KHAN CONSTRUCTION CAMP Reserved Number: Created: 31-Aug-13 / Huw Grossmith
FEG-120-AA-GAR-0007	A	10	IRON MONARCHY - IRON KHAN CONSTRUCTION CAMP Reserved Number: Created: 31-Aug-13 / Huw Grossmith

DOCUMENTS

Document	Rev	Status	Title
FEG-120-AA-GAR-0008	A	10	IRON MONARCHY - IRON KHAN CONSTRUCTION CAMP Reserved Number: Created: 31-Aug-13 / Huw Grossmith
FEG-120-AA-GAR-0009	A	10	IRON MONARCHY - IRON KHAN CONSTRUCTION CAMP Reserved Number: Created: 31-Aug-13 / Huw Grossmith
FEG-120-AA-GAR-0010	A	10	IRON MONARCHY - IRON KHAN CONSTRUCTION CAMP Reserved Number: Created: 31-Aug-13 / Huw Grossmith
FEG-130-AA-GAR-0001	A	10	IRON MONARCHY - IRON KHAN PERMANENT CAMP Reserved Number: Created: 31-Aug-13 / Huw Grossmith
FEG-130-AA-GAR-0002	A	10	IRON MONARCHY - IRON KHAN PERMANENT CAMP Reserved Number: Created: 31-Aug-13 / Huw Grossmith
FEG-130-AA-GAR-0003	A	10	IRON MONARCHY - IRON KHAN PERMANENT CAMP Reserved Number: Created: 31-Aug-13 / Huw Grossmith
FEG-130-AA-GAR-0004	A	10	IRON MONARCHY - IRON KHAN PERMANENT CAMP Reserved Number: Created: 31-Aug-13 / Huw Grossmith
FEG-130-AA-GAR-0005	A	10	IRON MONARCHY - IRON KHAN PERMANENT CAMP Reserved Number: Created: 31-Aug-13 / Huw Grossmith
FEG-130-AA-GAR-0006	A	10	IRON MONARCHY - IRON KHAN PERMANENT CAMP Reserved Number: Created: 31-Aug-13 / Huw Grossmith
FEG-130-AA-GAR-0007	A	10	IRON MONARCHY - IRON KHAN PERMANENT CAMP Reserved Number: Created: 31-Aug-13 / Huw Grossmith
FEG-130-AA-GAR-0008	A	10	IRON MONARCHY - IRON KHAN PERMANENT CAMP Reserved Number: Created: 31-Aug-13 / Huw Grossmith

DOCUMENTS

Document	Rev	Status	Title
FEG-130-AA-GAR-0009	A	10	IRON MONARCHY - IRON KHAN PERMANENT CAMP Reserved Number: Created: 31-Aug-13 / Huw Grossmith
FEG-130-AA-GAR-0010	A	10	IRON MONARCHY - IRON KHAN PERMANENT CAMP Reserved Number: Created: 31-Aug-13 / Huw Grossmith

DISTRIBUTION

Company Name	Contact Name	Reason for Issue
Camps and Messing	Doc Control	Reviewed no Comment (Submit IFC/CF)

Document Status Codes

10 - Reviewed No Comment

Please acknowledge receipt of transmittal. Please confirm completion of required actions by 19-Sep-13

External Transmittal from DrawCon in Outlook (msg) Format:

Engineers r Us - Iron Khan
Document Transmittal TR-0001

TranDate: **12-Sep-13**
Originator:

DOCUMENTS			
Document	Rev	Status	Title
FEG-120-AA-GAR-0001	A	10	IRON MONARCHY - IRON KHAN CONSTRUCTION CAMP Reserved Number: Created: 31-Aug-13 / Huw Grossmith
FEG-120-AA-GAR-0002	A	10	IRON MONARCHY - IRON KHAN CONSTRUCTION CAMP Reserved Number: Created: 31-Aug-13 / Huw Grossmith
FEG-120-AA-GAR-0003	A	10	IRON MONARCHY - IRON KHAN CONSTRUCTION CAMP Reserved Number: Created: 31-Aug-13 / Huw Grossmith
FEG-120-AA-GAR-0004	A	10	IRON MONARCHY - IRON KHAN CONSTRUCTION CAMP Reserved Number: Created: 31-Aug-13 / Huw Grossmith
FEG-120-AA-GAR-0005	A	10	IRON MONARCHY - IRON KHAN CONSTRUCTION CAMP Reserved Number: Created: 31-Aug-13 / Huw Grossmith
FEG-120-AA-GAR-0006	A	10	IRON MONARCHY - IRON KHAN CONSTRUCTION CAMP Reserved Number: Created: 31-Aug-13 / Huw Grossmith
FEG-120-AA-GAR-0007	A	10	IRON MONARCHY - IRON KHAN CONSTRUCTION CAMP Reserved Number: Created: 31-Aug-13 / Huw Grossmith

DOCUMENTS

Document	Rev	Status	Title
FEG-120-AA-GAR-0008	A	10	IRON MONARCHY - IRON KHAN CONSTRUCTION CAMP Reserved Number: Created: 31-Aug-13 / Huw Grossmith
FEG-120-AA-GAR-0009	A	10	IRON MONARCHY - IRON KHAN CONSTRUCTION CAMP Reserved Number: Created: 31-Aug-13 / Huw Grossmith
FEG-120-AA-GAR-0010	A	10	IRON MONARCHY - IRON KHAN CONSTRUCTION CAMP Reserved Number: Created: 31-Aug-13 / Huw Grossmith
FEG-130-AA-GAR-0001	A	10	IRON MONARCHY - IRON KHAN PERMANENT CAMP Reserved Number: Created: 31-Aug-13 / Huw Grossmith
FEG-130-AA-GAR-0002	A	10	IRON MONARCHY - IRON KHAN PERMANENT CAMP Reserved Number: Created: 31-Aug-13 / Huw Grossmith
FEG-130-AA-GAR-0003	A	10	IRON MONARCHY - IRON KHAN PERMANENT CAMP Reserved Number: Created: 31-Aug-13 / Huw Grossmith
FEG-130-AA-GAR-0004	A	10	IRON MONARCHY - IRON KHAN PERMANENT CAMP Reserved Number: Created: 31-Aug-13 / Huw Grossmith
FEG-130-AA-GAR-0005	A	10	IRON MONARCHY - IRON KHAN PERMANENT CAMP Reserved Number: Created: 31-Aug-13 / Huw Grossmith
FEG-130-AA-GAR-0006	A	10	IRON MONARCHY - IRON KHAN PERMANENT CAMP Reserved Number: Created: 31-Aug-13 / Huw Grossmith

DOCUMENTS

Document	Rev	Status	Title
FEG-130-AA-GAR-0007	A	10	IRON MONARCHY - IRON KHAN PERMANENT CAMP Reserved Number: Created: 31-Aug-13 / Huw Grossmith
FEG-130-AA-GAR-0008	A	10	IRON MONARCHY - IRON KHAN PERMANENT CAMP Reserved Number: Created: 31-Aug-13 / Huw Grossmith
FEG-130-AA-GAR-0009	A	10	IRON MONARCHY - IRON KHAN PERMANENT CAMP Reserved Number: Created: 31-Aug-13 / Huw Grossmith
FEG-130-AA-GAR-0010	A	10	IRON MONARCHY - IRON KHAN PERMANENT CAMP Reserved Number: Created: 31-Aug-13 / Huw Grossmith

DISTRIBUTION

Company Name	Contact Name	Reason for Issue
Camps and Messing	Doc Control	Reviewed no Comment (Submit IFC/CF)

Document Status Codes

10 - Reviewed No Comment

Please acknowledge receipt of transmittal. Please confirm completion of required actions by 19-Sep-13

APPENDIX 6

The Paper Aeroplane

F-16 Falcon Paper Airplane
Folding Instructions Type A-1

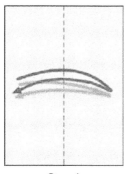

Step 1
Start with a 8 1/2"x11"
paper. Fold paper in
half vertically and
unfold.

Step 2
Next fold the top
corners inward to the
center crease.

Step 1   Step 2

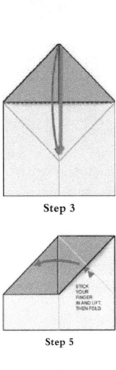

Step 3

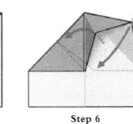

Step 4

Step 3
Fold the top point downward as shown.

Step 4
Fold the top corners inward to the center crease and then unfold the right side corner.

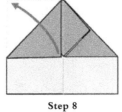

Step 5

Step 6

Step 5
Put your index finger under the flap and lift the flap towards the left.

Step 6
Flip the flap to the left side.

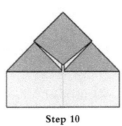

Step 7

Step 8

Step 7
Fold the new triangle flap to the left side.

Step 8
Unfold the left side flap.

Step 9

Step 10

Step 9
Repeat steps 5, 6 and 7 for the left side.

Step 10
The fold should looks like this.

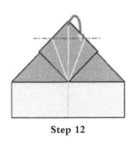

Step 11

Step 12

Step 11
Fold the both side flaps toward the center line and unfold.

Step 12
Make a mountain fold at the top corner section.

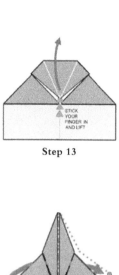

Step 13

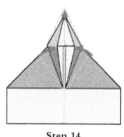

Step 14

Step 13
Put your index finger under the flap as shown with the green arrow. Pull up the top flap corner while pressing the base part with your index finger.

Step 14
Pull up the tip. This part becomes airplane's nose.

Step 15
Fold the model in half. Use a mountain fold.

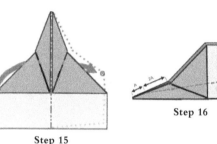

Step 15

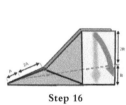

Step 16

Step 16
Fold the wing downward. Repeat on the other. The model should look like the picture shown in 17.

Step 17
Add a rudder as shown in this diagram. It should be 3/4 inches height, and should be parallel with the body of the airplane. Repeat for the other wing.

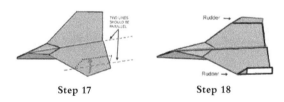

Step 17

Step 18

Step 18
The F-16 Falcon jet is complete. Bend the trailing edge of the wings slightly upwards. This will compensate for the airplane's tendency to nose dive.

NOTE THE COPYRIGHT OF PAGES 226, 227 AND 228 belongs to others.

APPENDIX 7

Mind Mapping and Flowcharting

Useful Websites

http://www.mind-mapping.org/Visual-Thinking-Center-image-map.html
http://www.informationtamers.com/WikIT/index.php?title=Main_Page
http://mlswift.me/2013/09/14/how-to-build-a-basic-mind-map/
http://creately.com/blog/diagrams/flowchart-guide-flowchart-tutorial/
http://www.edrawsoft.com/flowchart-examples.php

Flowchart Examples

To efficiently create the flowchart, it is best to start work from the flowchart examples. Now we will present some flowchart examples on flowcharting for proper understanding of this technique.

Flow Chart Example 1

Draw a flowchart to find the sum of first 50 natural numbers.
Answer: The required flowchart is given in Fig. 1.

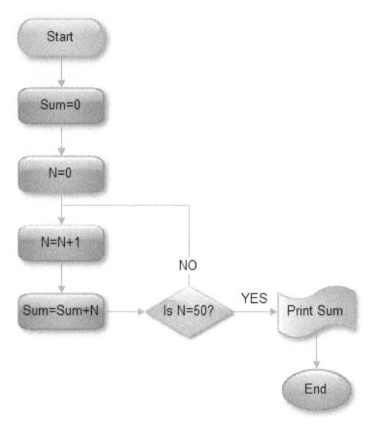

Fig. 1 Flowchart for sum of first 50 natural numbers

Flow Chart Example 2

Draw a flowchart to find the largest of three numbers A, B, and C.
Answer: The required flowchart is shown in Fig 2

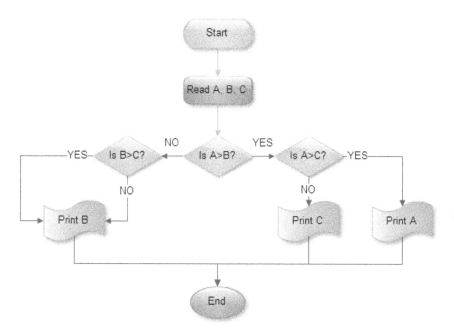

Fig 2 Flowchart for finding out the largest of three number

Flowchart Example 3

Draw a flowchart for computing factorial N (N!)
Where N! = 1?2?3?....N .
The required flowchart has been shown in fig 3
Answer:

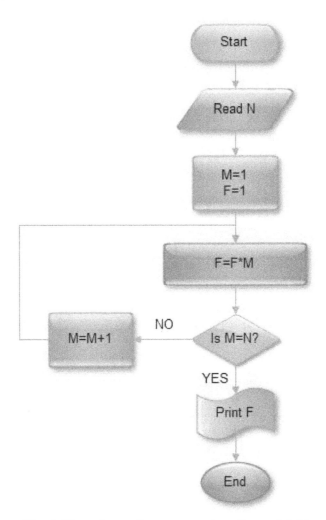

Fig 3 Flowchart for computing factorial N

Flowchart Example 4

A product assembly team in a gaming machine manufacturer were looking for ways of building the product more efficiently. They broke down the assembly process into a set of Flowcharts, showing how sub-assemblies were made and then built into the final product. Analysis of the reel assembly process revealed two improvements:

1. The kit of parts was already checked by the kit assembly line, who were sometimes careless, as they knew the kit would be rechecked. The assembly line process was improved so the check here could be removed. This saved over two minutes per reel in checking, and up to fifteen minutes when the kit was faulty.
2. Fitting the reel band after the reel had been attached to the base was awkward. Fitting the band before the reel was attached to the base was more comfortable and saved about a minute per reel.

The process Flowcharts, before and after improvement, are shown in Fig. 4.

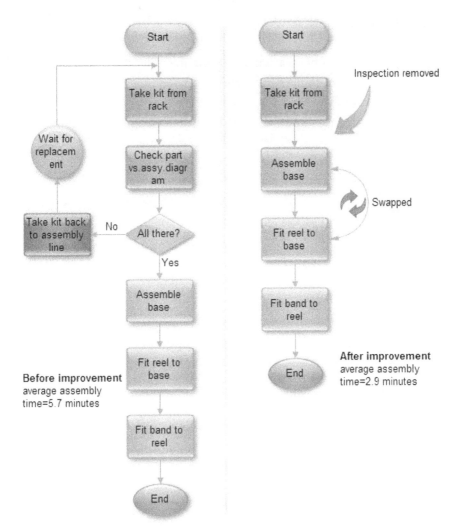

Fig 4 Flowchart for gaming machine manufacturer

The following flowchart examples can be edited and modified with our flowchart software.

Free Download Flowchart Software and View All Examples

APPENDIX 8A (MINING)

Classifications

NOTE: Asset and Area/Systems Codes for Oil/Gas refer Appendix 2B and for Civil Appendix 2C

Site or Asset Code

> FEK - Iron King
> FEP - Iron Prince
> FED - Iron Duke
> FEG - Iron Khan (after Genghis/Chinggis)
> FEE - Iron Pharaoh
> FES - Iron Sultan
> FEQ - Iron Queen

The site we are going to develop is FEG.

Plant Areas

001	Mine
099	Mine Site Wide
100	Administration Area
120	Construction Camp

130	Permanent Camp
170	Airport
200	Workshops and Warehousing
300	Run of Mine Pad
301	Grizzly
302	Chute
400	Plate Feeder
500	Crushing and Screening
600	Stockpile Conveyors and Stackers
700	Load-out
701	Load-Out System – Chute 01
702	Load-Out System – Chute 02
703	Load-Out System – Chute 03
704	Load-Out System – Chute 04
750	Load-out Tunnel
775	Load-Out Clam Shell Gate – 01
776	Load-Out Clam Shell Gate – 02
777	Load-Out Clam Shell Gate – 03
778	Load-Out Clam Shell Gate – 04
800	Port Rail System
900	Reclaim and Ship Loading

We may as we go break these down further.

Disciplines are Engineering or Non-Technical. For our purposes they will be:

AA	Architectural
CI	Civil
CO	Communications
EL	Electrical
FS	Fire Safety
GE	Geology/Geotechnical
GN	General

HS	Health, Safety & Environment
HV	High Volume Air-conditioning
HY	Hydraulic
IN	Instrumentation
ME	Mechanical
MI	Mining
PI	Piping
PR	Process
QA	Quality
ST	Structural

Some design houses use numbers for discipline codes e.g., 10 – Civil, 15 – Structural and so on. Also note that often these disciplines have a single letter code such as C – Civil and so on.

Document Types

Documents are often classified in to Types. Some of the documents in the list below as DC's we generally do not deal with for example Payment Claims but sometimes we do.

These include subtypes for certain drawings which the author generally does not recommend see Titles.

ACC	Drawing - Accommodation
AUD	Audit
BLD	Drawing - Building
BLK	Drawing - Block Diagram
BOM	Drawing - Bill of Materials
CAL	Calculation / Analysis
CAR	Corrective Action Request
CEF	Cause and Effect
D3D	3D Model(s)
DAS	Data Sheet
DTL	Drawing - Detail

ELV	Drawing – Elevation
ESH	Drawing – Emergency Shutdown
EST	Estimate
EVA	Evaluation / Review / Assessment
FOR	Forecast
FRM	Form Template
GAR	Drawing – General Arrangement
GND	Drawing – Grounding
HAZ	Drawing – Hazardous Area Classification
HVC	Drawing – Heating Ventilating Air Conditioning
IAF	Interface Agreement
INT	Drawing – Interconnection
ISO	Drawing – Isometric
LAY	Drawing – Layout
LET	Letter
LGN	Drawing – Legend
LOG	Drawing – Logic Diagram
LOP	Drawing – Loop Diagram
LST	List / Register / Index
LVL	Drawing – Level Diagram
MAN	Manual
MAP	Map
MEM	Memorandum
MOC	Management of Change Request
MOM	Minutes of Meeting
MTS	Drawing – Material Selection
PDG	Drawing – Protection Diagram
PFD	Drawing – Process Flow Diagram
PHC	Drawing – Pneumatic / Hydraulic Connection
PHL	Philosophy / Basis
PHO	Photograph
PID	Drawing – Piping and Instrument Diagram
PLN	Plan
PLT	Drawing – Location Plot Plan

PND	Drawing - Panel Junction Box Diagram
POL	Policy
PRO	Procedure
PRS	Presentation
PSC	Drawing - Panel Schedule
PSU	Drawing - Piping Support
REC	Record
REG	Regulation
RFI	Request for Information
RPT	Report
SAF	Drawing - SAFE Chart
SCH	Schedule
SCM	Drawing - Schematic Diagram
SFD	Drawing - Safety Analysis Flow Diagram
SFM	Safety Moments
SHF	Drawing - Shop Fabrication
SKT	Sketch
SLN	Drawing - Single Line Diagram
SOW	Scope of Work
SPC	Specification
STD	Standard / Codes
SUR	Survey
TPD	Drawing - Topology Diagram
TRM	Drawing - Termination Diagram
TRN	Transmittal Sheet
UFD	Drawing - Utility Flow Diagram
VDL	Vendor Document/Data List/Schedule
WRD	Drawing - Wiring Diagram

Document Title Convention

For Drawing and Document Titles we will be insisting on the standard 4 line format - like:

Iron Monarchy – Iron Khan

Run of Mine
Chute
General Arrangement and Details

OR

Iron Monarchy – Iron Khan
Plate Feeder
Over-speed Detector – 400-OSD-0001
Datasheet

Incoming Status Codes

IFR	Issued for Review	TRUE	14.00	TRUE	1.00
IFT	Issued for Tender	TRUE	14.00	TRUE	2.00
IFA	Issued for Approval	TRUE	14.00	TRUE	3.00
IFU	Issued for Use	TRUE	14.00	TRUE	4.00
IFC	Issued for Construction	TRUE	14.00	TRUE	5.00
IFP	Issued for Procurement	TRUE	14.00	TRUE	6.00
ASB	As-Built	FALSE	0.00	TRUE	7.00
IFI	Issued for Information	FALSE	0.00	TRUE	8.00
CAN	Cancelled	FALSE	0.00	TRUE	100.00
RES	Reserved	TRUE	14.00	TRUE	100.00
SS	Superseded	FALSE	0.00	TRUE	100.00

Review Status Codes

0 – Deliverables

Doc Stat Code	DocStatName	fDocStatSub2											
		Originator Log	Originator Lag	Ext Review Log	Ext Review Lag	Client Log	Client Lag	Prog Val	Mile Stone	Log Approved	Log Final	Doc StatTag	Doc StatSort
01	Reserved/In Preparation	0	14.00	0		0	0.00	0.00%		0	0	-1	1.00
02	Issued for Review	-1	0.00	0	0.00	0	0.00	60.00%		-1	0	-1	100.00
03	Issued For Tender	0	14.00	0		0	0.00	80.00%		-1	0	-1	4.00
04	Issued for Approval	-1	0.00	0	14.00	-1	14.00	85.00%		-1	-1	-1	100.00
05	Issued for Construction / Use	-1	14.00	0	0.00	0	0.00	95.00%		0	-1	-1	100.00
06	Issued for Procurement (Vendor to Complete)	-1	0.00	0	0.00	0	0.00			-1	-1	-1	100.00
07	As Built	-1	0.00	0	0.00	0	0.00	100.00%		0	-1	-1	100.00
10	Reviewed No Comment	-1	0.00	0	0.00	0	0.00	80.00%		0	0	-1	3.00
11	Reviewed with Comment (Proceed as Noted)	-1	0.00	0	0.00	0	0.00	60.00%		0	0	-1	5.00
12	Not Approved (Do Not Proceed)	-1	0.00	0	0.00	0	0.00	50.00%		0	0	-1	6.00
13	Accepted as IFC/CF	-1	0.00	0	0.00	0	0.00	95.00%		-1	0	-1	7.00
14	Accepted as As Built	-1	0.00	0	0.00	0	0.00	100.00%		0	-1	-1	100.00
15	Issued For Information	0	14.00	0		0	0.00	0.00%		0	0	-1	9.00
20	Under Review	-1	0.00	0	0.00	0	0.00	60.00%		0	0	-1	100.00
99	Superseded / Cancelled	0	14.00	0		0	0.00	0.00%		0	0	-1	99.00

1 – Vendor Docs

01	Reviewed – No comments – Submit "Certified Final/IFC"	TRUE	14.00	FALSE	0.00	FALSE	0.00	85.00%		FALSE	FALSE	TRUE	2.00
02	Reviewed – Revised as noted and submit "Certified Final/IFC". Work may proceed.	TRUE	14.00	FALSE	0.00	FALSE	0.00	70.00%		FALSE	FALSE	TRUE	3.00
03	Not Approved – Revise as noted and resubmit for review. Work Will Not Proceed.	TRUE	14.00	FALSE	0.00	FALSE	0.00	50.00%		FALSE	FALSE	TRUE	4.00
04	Accepted as "Certified Final/IFC" (Submit As Built)	TRUE	14.00	FALSE	0.00	FALSE	0.00	95.00%		TRUE	FALSE	TRUE	5.00
05	Accepted as As Built	FALSE	0.00	FALSE	0.00	FALSE	0.00	100.00%		FALSE	FALSE	TRUE	100.00
06	Information Only.	FALSE	14.00	FALSE	0.00	FALSE	0.00	0.00%		FALSE	FALSE	TRUE	6.00
20	On Review/Squad Check	FALSE	14.00	FALSE	0.00	FALSE	0.00	60.00%		FALSE	FALSE	TRUE	1.00
99	Superseded/Cancelled	FALSE	14.00	FALSE	0.00	FALSE	0.00	0.00%		FALSE	FALSE	TRUE	7.00

2 – Other Docs and 3 – Special Docs – NOT USED

Revisions and Versions

This is the ideal, rarely happens, there is often a 2nd review and, where the client/operations, are not in the review process, changes made after the IFA is issued so we can go all the way up to Rev D or E before we get sign off. It also happens that when the constructor gets to site he finds a problem with the Rev 0 and makes mark-ups and fires it back in and changes are made again how the Revisions are handled varies some just go 1, 2, 3 and so on but others may go 0A, 0B etc. until sign off then to 1 and the As Built would then be Rev 2 or even later.

Revision	Status	Notes
A	Issued for Review★ [IFR]	(In DrawCon the review teams are called Maps but the reviews are done in print (they could be done electronically if everyone had Acrobat Pro or something similar such as Brava Viewer) – in newer DMS applications they are called Review Teams and Reviews are on a workflow which is "activated" by DC and the application includes a reviewing tool built-in.
B	Issued for Tender	Issued out to Tenderers
C	Issued for Approval	Issued to the Client for Approval (Usually after some back-drafting when Tender Drgs/Docs are in)
0 [Zero]	Issued for Construction or Issued for Use	Signed by all those that have too and sent externally to Vendors or Constructors usually identical to B.
1	As Built	Rev 0 is often marked-up on site by the constructors and commissioning team and then sent in for the CAD guys to amend the drawing to As Built

The most common system of Revisions (a revision is applied at a certain point in the life of a document e.g. IFR) followed is: A, B, C, D and so on with no I, J or O used for obvious reasons then IFC Rev 0 and post IFC revisions 1, 2, and so on.

There are lots of variations to this. One employer used P1, P2 and so on til Rev 0. Another, post IFC used 0A, 0B and so on until 1 – As Built (not recommended if drawing need not be As Built).

The method used is often dictated by the client. Some clients, because it is how (by default) databases sort, like numeric then alpha so 1, 2, 3, A, B, C

Some now, use a Revision and a Version similar to the above 0A or something like A-1, 0-A,0-1 – most often this is applied when a document has come in from a vendor or designer is stamped, reviewed and given a return status – i.e. the incoming Revision is A but after status it may become A-1. NOT recommended practice. Some DMS applications do this automatically but the Transmittal they generate do not show the Version just the revision.

Revision/ Version	Status	Notes
A	Issued for Review* [IFR]	(In DrawCon the review teams are called Maps but the reviews are done in print (they could be done electronically if everyone had Acrobat Pro or something similar such as Brava Viewer) – in newer DMS applications they are called Review Teams and Reviews are on a workflow which is "activated" by DC and the application includes a reviewing tool built-in.
A-01	2	Reviewed as Noted, Revise and Resubmit
B	Issued for Tender	Issued out to Tenderers
C	Issued for Approval	Issued to the Client for Approval (Usually after some back-drafting when Tender Drgs/Docs are in)
0 [Zero]	Issued for Construction or Issued for Use	Signed by all those that have too and sent externally to Vendors or Constructors usually identical to B.
0-A	IFR	ECR No 999 Changes and Noted by Diamonds – IFA
1	IFC	ECR No 999 Changes and Noted by Diamonds - IFC
1-A	As Constructed	Site mark-up of Rev 1 post Construction
1-B	As Commissioned	Site mark-up of Rev 1-A post commissioning
1-C	As Handed Over	Site mark-up of Rev 1-B post hand over to Operations
2	As Built	All site mark-ups incorporated

For our practical we will NOT be using Versions.

Values for F1 – AIMS

AIMS Code	Description
ABC	Asset ABC Categorisation
AGA	Drawings - Alignment Data
AMP	Plan – Asset Management
AOA	Analysis - Alarm Objectives
APL	Layout - Area Protection
ARP	Plan – Asset Reference
ASI	Assembly Instructions (If NOT in IOM/VEM)
ASR	Master Equipment List
ATS	Schedule – Alarm & Trip
BDS	Basis For Design – Structural
BED	Diagrams - Cable Block (Electrical)
BFD	BOD Database – Structural
BID	Diagrams - Cable Block (Instrument)
BMA	PM Assembly
BOM	Bill of Material
CAL	Layout - Underground Cable (Instrument)
CBF	Diagrams - Civil Foundations (Structural)
CBS	Contamination Baseline Survey
CCP	Plan – Corrosion Control Philosophy
CDK	Datasheets – Communications
CEG	Control Engineering Guide
CEK	Calculations – Telecommunications
CFA	Manual – Certification
CGS	Performance Standards - Facility Specific
CIL	Cable Schedule – Instrument
CLK	Layout – Communications Equipment
CML	Manual – Crane
CMR	Competency Reports
CNK	Diagrams – Communications Interconnection
COL	Contamination Register
COP	Procedure – Commissioning

AIMS Code	Description
COR	Report – Commissioning
CPK	Performance Curve – Communications
CQK	Cable Schedule – Communications
CRL	Cylinders Register
CSD	Drawing - Cross-Sectional Details – Rotating Equipment
CSE	Cable Schedule – Electrical
CSK	Sketches – Communications
CSP	Construction Specification
CSR	Report - Control Systems
CTR	Test Records – Commissioning
CXD	Diagrams - Civil Drainage
CZD	Diagrams - Civil Underground
DBS	Basis For Design
DDC	Calculations – Deluge System
DEC	Calculations – Design
DID	Diagrams - Ducting & Instrumentation (HVAC)
DLC	Report – DCS Loading Calculations
DNS	Safeguarding Narrative
DRL	Document Register
DRP	Design Review
DSC	Dossier - Structural & Civil
DSR	Design Report
DVS	Integrity Envelope Monitoring Requirements
EAL	Layout - Earthing
EAR	Environmental Aspect Register
ECL	Layout - Cable Tray (Electrical)
EDB	Electrical – Database
EDC	EDC Coding
EDL	Load List
EEC	Calculations – Electrical
EEL	Layout – Electrical Equipment
ELD	Layout – Multi-discipline Equipment

AIMS Code	Description
ELI	Equipment List – Mechanical
ELM	Layout – Mechanical Equipment
ELR	Layout – Rotating Equipment
EMP	Plan – Energy Management
ENM	Manual – Design
EPE	Performance Curve – Electrical
EPL	Layout - Facility
ERP	Plan – Emergency Response
ESK	Sketches – Electrical Equipment
ESP	Equipment Specification (Split out by Disc)
ESR	Report - Engineering Shutdown
ETL	Equipment Tracking
EVP	Plan – Environmental Plan
EXN	SAP M4 History Notifications for EX Devices
EYK	Datasheets – Electrical
EZV	3D Model – Electrical
FES	Equipment Schedule – Fire & Gas
FGL	Layout - Equipment – Fire & Gas
FGS	Sketches – Fire & Gas Equipment
FIL	Diagrams - Logic – Fire & Gas
FLD	Layout - Field
FLH	Functional Location Hierarchy
FMD	Flow Metering Dossier
FMR	FMCA Study Reports
FOP	Drawing - Fire Protection – Structural
FPA	Plan – Flare
FPP	Plot Plan – Platform Safety
FPR	Report - Fixed Fire Protection
FSP	Philosophy – Flow Assurance
FWR	Fire Water Report
FZL	Layouts – Fire Zone
GAR	General Arrangement – Mechanical Seals
GAS	General Arrangement – Structural

AIMS Code	Description
GMP	Plan – Greenhouse Gas Management
GPL	Layout - Power Cable (Above Ground)
HDB	Process Model – Database
HDC	Simulations – Process (Dynamic)
HHR	Hydraulic Hose Register
HOR	Hazard & Operability Review
HSY	Simulations – Process (Steady State)
IBL	Layout - Instrument & Marshalling Box
ICC	Calculations – Instrument
ICL	Layout - Cable Tray (Instrument)
IDB	Instrumentation – Database
IDD	Diagrams – Electrical Interconnection
IEK	Integrity Envelope
IFR	Schedule – Input/Output (F)
IIX	Instrument List
IKD	Sketches – Instrumentation Equipment
ILR	IO Schedules: PCS
INR	Installation Reports – Structural
IOM	Manual – Installation and Operation (IOM)
IPC	Performance Curve – Instrument
IPR	Safety Requirements Specification
IQL	Layout – Instrumentation Equipment
ISO	Isometric – Piping
ISS	IO Schedules: SIS
ITD	Diagrams - Instrument Line
ITS	Reports - Inspection Services Report (ISR)
IWD	Diagrams - Wiring & Termination (Instrumentation)
IXD	Diagrams – Instrumentation Interconnection
IYK	Datasheets – Instrumentation
IZV	3D Model – Instrument
JTA	Drawings – Arrangement
KLC	Heat Loading Calcs (CCR / FAR)
LCD	Diagrams – Logic (Electrical)

AIMS Code	Description
LDR	Dossier – Level
LFU	Certificates – Lifting Equipment
LGD	Diagrams – Logic (Control)
LIC	Licenses
LID	Lifting Equipment Register / Dossier
LIR	Dossier – Lifting Load Certificates and Manuals
LLQ	Line List – Piping
LMT	LOTO Matrix
LOD	Diagrams - Loop
LPL	Layouts - Lighting & Small Power
LSP	LONG Term Storage Procedure
LUS	Schedule – Lubrication
MAC	Certificates – Materials
MCF	Material / Mill Test Certificates
MDR	Report – Manufacturer's Data
MEC	Calculations – Mechanical
MHD	Layouts - Fixed Mechanical Handling Device
MMF	ERP (SAP) Configuration Design Document
MMQ	Maintenance Costing Structure
MPC	Performance Curve – Mechanical
MPI	Maintenance Plans/Items
MPL	Measuring Points
MPR	Maintenance and Spares Preservation Job Routines
MPS	Strategy – Maintenance & Inspection
MPT	Maintenance Task Lists
MRP	Plan – Maintenance Reference
MSD	Database – Material Safety
MSF	Mapping Study - Fire & Gas
MSM	Manual – Material Safety
MSP	Plan – Material Selection
MSS	Sketches – Mechanical Equipment
MYK	Datasheets – Mechanical
MYR	Datasheets – Rotating Equipment

AIMS Code	Description
MYV	Datasheets – Relief Valves
NCR	Non-Conformance Report
NDT	Non Destructive Testing - Procedures, Reports, Qualifications, Test Records
NED	Schematics - Instrument Hook-Up & Flow
OAH	Organisational Hierarchy
OMP	Manual – Operating Procedure
OPM	Manual – Operating Procedure
OSP	Plan – Oil Spill Contingency
PAP	Drawing - Pipe Support Location Plan
PCT	Test Records – Pre-Commissioning
PDB	Piping – Database
PDP	Preservation Dossier
PFD	Diagrams - Process Flow (PFD)
PGA	General Arrangement – Piping
PHD	Drawing - Installation
PID	Diagrams & Schemes
PJD	Plans – Piping Sections & Details
PLD	Layout – Platform
PMP	Plan – Pipeline Management
PMQ	PSV Dossier
PNL	Special Items List – Piping
POL	Policy
PPP	Philosophy – Process
PQL	Support List – Pipe Schedule
PRS	Report - Protection Relay Setting
PRT	Maintenance Procedures
PSF	Drawings – Process Safeguarding Flow Scheme (PSFS)
PUL	Punch-list
PWD	Drawings - Pipe Support
PXC	Calculations – Process
PYK	Datasheets – Process

AIMS Code	Description
PZV	3D Model – Piping
RES	Rotating Equipment Specifications
RMR	Model – SPARC
RSA	Database – Risk & Reliability Maintenance
SBE	Schedule – Distribution Board
SCF	Seismic Certification
SCH	Schedule - Planning, Manpower, Production, Shipping
SCM	Manual – Safety
SCS	Study – Safety Case (and associated studies)
SDD	Shop Detail Drawing
SER	Structural Engineering Report
SES	Drawings – Steelwork
SGS	Sketches – Structural & Civil
SLD	Diagrams – Single Line
SLS	Schematics - Lube & Seal Oil
SNL	Electrical Equipment & Distribution List
SOD	Schematics – Electrical Equipment
SPR	Spare Parts Interchange-ability Records (SPIRS) OR Database - ESPIR
SQR	Report – SOREL
SRL	Special Tools and Equipment List
SSC	Specifications - Structural & Civil
SSL	Drawing – Safety Signs
STS	Drawings - Pipe Supports
SVS	Report - Structural Survey
SWV	Structural – Database
SXC	Calculations – Structural
SYD	Layout – Lifting Equipment
SZV	3D Model – Structural
TBI	Termination Schedule – Instrument
TCD	Drawings – Communication Systems
TDR	Technical Deviations

AIMS Code	Description
TED	Drawing – Transit Frame (Electrical)
TJD	Drawing – Transit Frame (Instrument)
TLK	Equipment Schedule
TOP	Procedure – Temporary Operating (TOP)
TRM	Manual – Training
TSE	Termination Schedule – Electrical
TTK	Diagrams – Wiring & Termination (Communications)
TVL	Layout – CCTV Equipment
UCL	Layout – Electrical Cables (Underground)
UPD	Plan – Piping
UYD	Datasheets – Umbilical
VCA	Vendor Catalogue (Not to be Submitted in Place of IOM)
VDB	Manual – Valve Data Book
VDD	Drawings – Valves
VEM	Manual – Vendor Equipment
VGA	General Arrangement – Pressure Vessel
VIM	Manual – Vendor Information
VPS	Verification Schedule
VRP	Pressure Vessel Register
VVD	General Arrangement – Relief Valves
VWP	Procedures – Engineering Management System
WAP	Plan – Waste Management
WCD	Weight Control Database
WLD	Warranty List
WMP	Philosophy – Water Management
WOC	Work Centres - Capacities, Cost Centres, Activity Types
WPQ	Welding Procedures, Specifications, Qualification Records, Inspection Records
WRD	Diagrams – Wiring & Termination (Electrical)
ZUR	Certificates – Relief Valves

Values for F2 – VdocCode

tVendDocCodes	
Vendor Doc Code	**Description**
A01	VENDOR DOCUMENT SCHEDULE
A02	FABRICATION/PRODUCTION SCHEDULE
A03	PROGRESS REPORTS
A04	BOUGHT OUT ITEMS LIST
A05	TABLE OF CONTENTS (All Manuals / MDR)
B01	GENERAL ARRANGEMENT DRAWINGS
B02	ACCEPTABLE NOZZLE LOADS
B03	INTERFACE AND CONNECTION SCHEDULE
B04	FOUNDATION LOADING DIAGRAM AND SUPPORT DETAILS
B98	GA OF FLAME FRONT GENERATOR
B99	SPECIAL – GA FLARE CONTROL PANEL
C01	PIPING AND INSTRUMENT DIAGRAMS (P & ID's)
C02	ONE LINE ELECTRICAL DIAGRAMS
C03	SCHEMATIC DIAGRAMS
C04	UTILITIES SCHEDULE
C05	WEIGHT DATA SHEETS
C06	EQUIPMENT DATA SHEETS
C07	NOISE LEVEL DATA SHEETS
C08	SCHEDULE OF EX CERTIFIED EQUIPMENT
C09	DETAILED DESCRIPTION OF OPERATION
C10	HVAC DUCTING AND INSTRUMENT DIAGRAMS AND FLOW DIAGRAMS
C11	Process Flow Diagrams, HEAT AND MASS BALANCE
C12	ELECTRICAL POWER SUPPLIES DATA SHEET
C13	ENCLOSURE VENTILATION REQUIREMENTS
C14	INSTRUMENT INDEX
C15	INSTRUMENT DATA SHEETS
C16	CAUSE AND EFFECT CHARTS

tVendDocCodes	
Vendor Doc Code	**Description**
C17	INSTRUMENT/ELECTRICAL LOGIC DIAGRAM
C18	VDU SCREEN DISPLAY GRAPHICS(D2)
C19	BLOCK WIRING SCHEMATIC
C20	SIL VERIFICATION, AND MAINTENANCE DOCUMENTATION
C21	COMPLETED DATA SHEETS
C22	MANUFACTURERS DATA SHEETS
C23	COMPLETED PURCHASER TECHNICAL QUESTIONNAIRES
C24	CONTROL NARRATIVES / SYSTEM DESCRIPTIONS
D01	CROSS SECTION DRAWING / EXPLODED VIEW DIAGRAM WITH PARTS LIST
D02	MECHANICAL SEAL DRAWINGS
D03	SHAFT ALIGNMENT DRAWINGS
D04	NAME PLATE FORMAT DRAWINGS
D05	SUB ASSEMBLY ARRANGEMENTS
D06	DETAILED FABRICATION DRAWINGS
D07	ARRANGEMENT AND CONNECTION DRAWINGS
D08	CIVIL GENERAL ARRANGEMENT DRAWINGS
D09	CIVIL EQUIPMENT FOUNDATION DRAWINGS
D10	BURIED SERVICES DRAWINGS
D96	AS BUILT DRAWINGS
D97	SUPPORT STRUCTURE DETAIL DRAWINGS
D98	DETAILED DRAWINGS - PILOTS
D99	DETAILED DRAWINGS - FLARE TIP
E01	ELECTRICAL CONNECTION DIAGRAM
E02	INSTRUMENT/ELECTRICAL PANEL/ SWITCHBOARD DETAIL DRAWINGS
E03	TERMINATION DIAGRAMS

tVendDocCodes	
Vendor Doc Code	**Description**
E04	CABLE SCHEDULE
E05	INSTRUMENT TERMINATION AND HOOK UP DETAILS
E06	INSTRUMENT LOOP OR SEGMENT DIAGRAMS
E07	INSTRUMENT PLC DATA COMMUNICATION PROTOCOL
E08	TRANSFORMER DETAILS
E09	PLC RACK LAYOUT AND CONFIGURATION DRAWING
E10	CONTROL SYSTEM INPUTS AND OUTPUTS
E11	ELECTRICAL INSTALLATION DRAWINGS
E99	ALARM AND TRIP SCHEDULE
F01	PRESSURE VESSEL/TANK MECHANICAL CALCULATIONS
F02	PROCESS/UTILITY CALCULATIONS
F03	STRUCTURAL STEEL CALCULATIONS
F04	FOUNDATION SUPPORT CALCULATIONS
F05	SYSTEM HEAD LOSS CALCULATIONS
F06	LATERAL CRITICAL SPEED CALCULATIONS
F07	TORSIONAL CRITICAL SPEED CALCULATIONS
F08	BEARING LIFE CALCULATIONS
F09	THRUST BEARING SIZING CALCULATIONS
F10	HEAT EMISSION CALCULATIONS
F11	ACOUSTIC ANALYSIS FOR RECIPROCATING COMPRESSORS
F12	HYDRAULIC CALCULATIONS
F13	EXCHANGER THERMAL RATING CALCULATIONS
F14	INSTRUMENT CALCULATIONS
F15	ENCLOSURE VENTILATION SYSTEM CALCULATIONS

tVendDocCodes	
Vendor Doc Code	**Description**
F16	EXHAUST DUCT CALCULATIONS
F17	COUPLING SELECTION CALCULATIONS
F18	LUBE AND SEAL OIL SYSTEM SIZING CALCULATIONS
F19	ANTI SURGE VALVE SIZING
F20	PULSATION DAMPER DESIGN CALCULATIONS
F21	ROTOR/SHAFT SYSTEM UNBALANCED RESPONSE ANALYSIS
F22	PIPING STRESS ANALYSIS
F23	CRANE FAILURE MODE ANALYSIS
F24	ESD VALVE
F25	RELIEF VALVE AND BURSTING DISC CALCULATIONS
F26	ELECTRICAL PROTECTION STUDY
F27	CURRENT AND POTENTIAL (CT/VT) TRANSFORMER CURVES
F28	MOTOR PERFORMANCE CURVES
F29	COMBUSTION GAS TURBINE PERFORMANCE CURVES
F30	CENTRIFUGAL PUMP PERFORMANCE CURVES
F31	ROTARY PUMP CURVES
F32	CENTRIFUGAL COMPRESSOR PERFORMANCE CURVES
F33	FAN PERFORMANCE CURVES
F34	ENGINE PERFORMANCE CURVES
F35	GENERAL PERFORMANCE DATA
F36	SPEED/TORQUE STARTING CURVES
F37	RECIPROCATING PUMP PERFORMANCE CURVES
F38	LIGHTING PERFORMANCE DATA

tVendDocCodes	
Vendor Doc Code	**Description**
F39	BATTERY CHARGE/DISCHARGE CALCULATIONS
F40	POWER SYSTEM ANALYSIS DATA
F41	RELIABILITY/AVAILABILITY DATA AND CALCULATIONS
F42	PERFORMANCE GUARANTEE
F43	SHORT CIRCUIT CALCULATIONS
F44	INTRINSIC SAFETY CALCULATIONS
F45	INCREASED SAFETY MOTOR CALCULATIONS
F46	ELECTRICAL GENERATION STABILITY STUDY
F99	MISCELLANEOUS CALCULATIONS
G01	ERECTION, & INSTALLATION PROCEDURE
G02	UNPACKING AND PRESERVATION PROCEDURE
G03	HANDLING AND SHIPPING PROCEDURES
G04	PRE-COMMISSIONING/COMMISSIONING PROCEDURE
G05	ERECTION FASTENERS SUMMARY LIST
G06	SLINGING/LIFTING ARRANGEMENT
G99	TRANSPORT ARRANGEMENT
H01	QUALITY MANAGEMENT SYSTEM CERTIFICATE
H02	QUALITY PLAN
H03	INSPECTION AND TEST PLAN
H04	PRESSURE TEST PROCEDURES
H05	PERFORMANCE TESTING AND ACCEPTANCE TEST PROCEDURES
H06	SOFTWARE QUALITY SYSTEM
H07	WEIGHING PROCEDURE
H08	HEALTH SAFETY MANAGEMENT SYSTEM
H09	HEALTH SAFETY MANAGEMENT PLAN

tVendDocCodes	
Vendor Doc Code	**Description**
H10	PROPOSED SOFTWARE LISTING
H11	COMPANY ENVIRONMENT MANAGEMENT SYSTEM
H12	PROJECT ENVIRONMENT MANAGEMENT SYSTEM
J01	LUBE OIL AND OPERATING FLUIDS SCHEDULE
J02	RECOMMENDED START-UP AND COMMISSIONING SPARES LIST
J03	RECOMMENDED SPARES FOR TWO YEAR'S OPERATION
J04	SPECIALIST TOOLS
K01	PERFORMANCE TEST REPORT / RESULTS
K02	FACTORY ACCEPTANCE TEST REPORT (FAT)
K03	VIBRATION REPORT
K04	NOISE REPORT
K05	WEIGHING REPORT AND CERTIFICATE
K06	DIMENSIONAL REPORT
K07	FIRE TEST REPORTS/CERTIFICATES
K08	EQUIPMENT HAZARDOUS AREA CERTIFICATES
K09	HAZOP REPORTS
K10	REGISTER OF SAFETY RELATED DEVICES
K13	HAZARDOUS AREA CLASSIFICATION
L01	MATERIAL TEST CERTIFICATE
L02	WELDER PERFORMANCE QUALIFICATION CERTIFICATES
L03	NDE OPERATOR QUALIFICATIONS
L04	PRODUCTION TEST RESULTS (INCLUDING WELDING)
L05	NDE RECORDS
L06	HEAT TREATMENT RECORDS

tVendDocCodes	
Vendor Doc Code	**Description**
L07	MATERIAL TRACEABILITY RECORDS
L08	NAME PLATE RUBBING / PHOTO'S
L09	ELECTRICAL MACHINERY TYPE TESTS
L10	ROUTINE TEST CERTIFICATE - ELECTRICAL MACHINERY
L11	MEASUREMENT OF RESISTANCE
L12	PAINTING/INSULATION INSPECTION REPORT
L13	POSITIVE MATERIAL IDENTIFICATION (PMI) RECORDS
L14	ELECTRICAL SWITCHBOARD TYPE TESTS
L15	TRANSFORMER TYPE TESTS
L16	TRANSFORMER ROUTINE TESTS
L17	HAZARDOUS AREA INSPECTION
L18	HYDROSTATIC TEST REPORT
N01	PRESSURE TEST CERTIFICATES
N02	INSTRUMENT TEST AND CALIBRATION CERTIFICATE
N03	LIFTING EQUIPMENT TEST CERTIFICATES
N04	INSULATION RESISTANCE TEST
N05	VESSEL & EXCHANGER CODE DATA REPORTS
N06	CERTIFICATE OF COMPLIANCE
N07	RELEASE NOTES
N08	INDEPENDANT INSPECTION AUTHORITY RELEASE NOTE/WAIVERS
N09	CONCESSION RECORDS (Deviation Decision Requests)
N10	MATERIAL SAFETY DATA SHEETS (MSDS)
N11	CERTIFICATE OF CONFORMITY
P01	WELD PROCEDURE SPECIFICATIONS (WPS) AND QUALIFICATIONS (WPQ) RECORDS

tVendDocCodes	
Vendor Doc Code	**Description**
P02	NON-DESTRUCTIVE EXAMINATION PROCEDURES (NDE)
P03	MANUFACTURING PROCEDURES INCLUDING HEAT TREATMENT
P04	SURFACE PREPARATION AND PAINTING PROCEDURE
Q01	MATERIAL CERTIFICATES - Bulk Items
Q02	MATERIAL CERTIFICATES - Package Welded interfaces
Q99	ISO 9001 CERTIFICATES FOR ALL MILLS SUPPLYING PRESSURE RETAINING COMPONENTS
R01	DESPATCH DOSSIER
R02	INSTALLATION AND OPERATING MANUAL
R03	MAINTENANCE MANUAL
R04	MANUFACTURING DATA RECORDS - (MDR)
R05	REQUISITION COMPLIANCE STATEMENT
R06	HAZARDOUS AREA VERIFICATION DOSSIER
R07	CONTROL SYSTEM CONFIGURATION
R08	PROJECT CONSTRUCTION PLAN
R09	PROJECT COMMISSIONING PLAN
R10	LABOUR HISTOGRAM
R11	POWER STATION TRAINING PLAN

NOTE WELL. Where a mature Document Type or AIM/OIM Code system exists for document the author does not support the idea of having a totally separate code system for Vendor Documents.

APPENDIX 8B (OIL/GAS)

Classifications

Site or Asset Code

FPSO1 - Oil Marquis (Ship/Hull Name)

Plant /System Area Codes

We may as we go break these down further.

System/Area Code	Description
001	Well Head - 001
002	Well Head - 002
003	Well Head - 003
004	Well Head - 004
005	Well Head - 005
006	Well Head - 006
007	Well Head - 007
008	Well Head - 008
009	Well Head - 009
010	Well Head - 010
050	Subsea Lateral Pipeline - 001

051	Subsea Lateral Pipeline - 002
052	Subsea Lateral Pipeline - 003
053	Subsea Lateral Pipeline - 004
054	Subsea Lateral Pipeline - 005
055	Subsea Lateral Pipeline - 006
056	Subsea Lateral Pipeline - 007
057	Subsea Lateral Pipeline - 008
058	Subsea Lateral Pipeline - 009
059	Subsea Lateral Pipeline - 010
080	Subsea Main Pump Facility
090	Subsea Main Pipeline
095	Riser
100	Turret
200	Water Separation
220	Water Treatment and Return
300	Filtration
400	Condensate Separation
450	Condensate Storage
475	Condensate Offtake
485	Flare System/Tower
500	Oil Treatment
550	Oil Storage
575	Oil Offtake
600	Hull
625	Anchor
650	Helipad
675	Cranes and Gantries
700	Bridge
750	Accommodation and Mess
800	Control Systems
850	Fire Prevention / Control Systems
900	Cathodic Protection Systems

For ALL other codes and information refer Appendix 2A

APPENDIX 8C (CIVIL)

Classifications

Site or Asset Code

AWTP-1 (Loosely based on http://www.watersecure.com.au/pub/virtualtours/bundamba/)

Plant /System Area Codes

We may as we go break these down further.

System/ Area Code	Description
001	Pumps in Existing Sewage Treatment Plant (Connection)
050	Pipeline from Existing Sewage Treatment Plant
100	Main Tank including Clarifiers
200	Micro-Filtration – Train 1
210	Micro-Filtration – Train 2
220	Micro-Filtration – Train 3
230	Micro-Filtration – Train 4
250	Reverse Osmosis – Train 1
260	Reverse Osmosis – Train 2

270	Reverse Osmosis – Train 3
280	Reverse Osmosis – Train 4
300	UV Advanced Oxidation – Train 1
310	UV Advanced Oxidation – Train 2
320	UV Advanced Oxidation – Train 3
330	UV Advanced Oxidation – Train 4
350	Water Quality Analysis – Train 1
360	Water Quality Analysis – Train 2
370	Water Quality Analysis – Train 3
380	Water Quality Analysis – Train 4
400	Remineralisation – Train 1
410	Remineralisation – Train 2
420	Remineralisation – Train 3
430	Remineralisation – Train 4
500	Pure Water Storage Tank
550	Pure Water Pipeline (to Dam/Power Stations)
600	Nitrogen Removal – Train 1
610	Nitrogen Removal – Train 2
650	Residuals Treatment – Train 1
660	Residuals Treatment – Train 2
700	Concentrate Water Release/Pipeline
750	Sludge Removal
800	Admin Building
810	Mess/Lunchroom
820	Covered Rec Area
850	Car Park
880	Control Room
900	Wetland Treatment Trial Area

For ALL other codes and information refer Appendix 2A

APPENDIX 9

How to Use the Block Number Generator in DrawCon

How to use the Block Number Generator in Drawcon

In this example we are going to pretend that you will NOT be using the numbers that appear on Piping Isometric drawings and need to set aside numbers for them.

Open DrawCon DCTrain Project

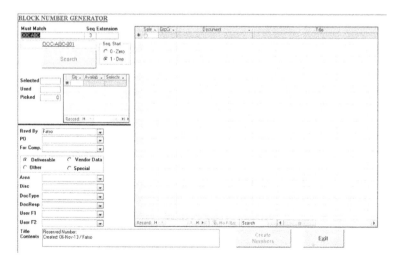

From the Main Menu select 7 Block Generator

Let's say you need 1000 Piping Iso's for area 550 Cyclones.

In the must match field type FEK-560-PI-ISO

In the Seq Field change the number from 3 to 4

NO extension

Select the Piping Engineer in Rsvd By

In Area select 550 – Cyclones

In Disc Select PI

in DocType Select ISO

In DocResp select the Piping Engineer

In F1 select ISO

In Title Contents

IRON MONARCHY - IRON KING

CYCLONES

RESERVED - 06/11/2013 BY HRG

PIPING ISOMETRIC

NOTE to drop lines in the Title Content field you must use Ctrl and Enter at the same time.

Click Search

In Selected type 1000

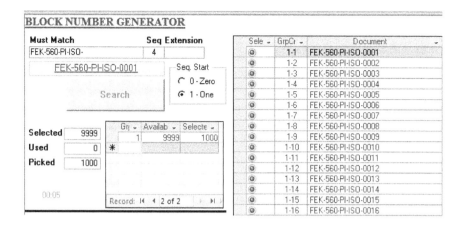

The radio buttons on the right should go blue. The Create Numbers button at the bottom should go Red.

Click Create Numbers (It may take some time to run)

When Create Numbers has run check Used it should show 1000 and the radio buttons will be blank again.

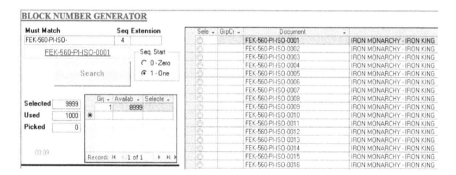

Click Exit

Open your Document Form and Click Filter Form

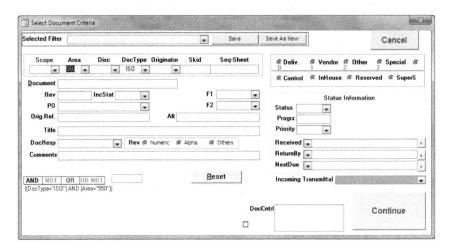

Click Continue

At the bottom of your document form it should show the number of records for the filter applied

ALL DONE.

NOTE the Generator does not currently, working on it, add data to the IncStat/DocStat/Rev No and Date (when they are added too) fields.

To add these.

Exit the Document Form

Click 8 Report Menu and 0 Query Builder then Click New

Step 1

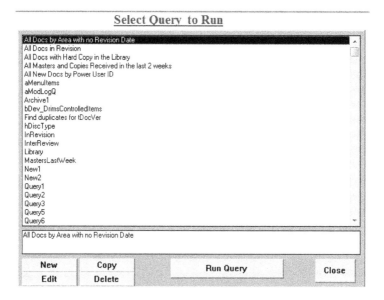

Select Simple Query Wizard and OK

Step 2

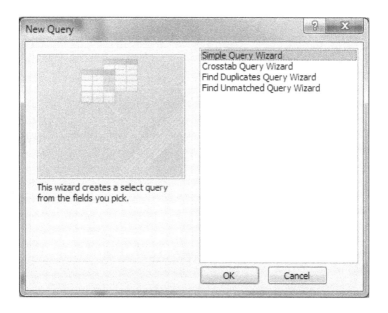

In the Drop Down select Table: tDoc and the fields as shown below

Step 3

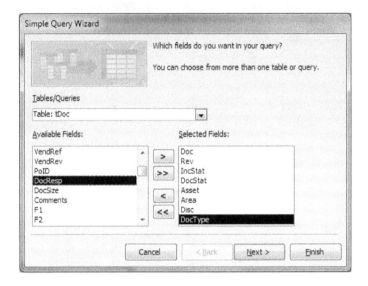

Select Next then modify the pop-up as below

Step 4

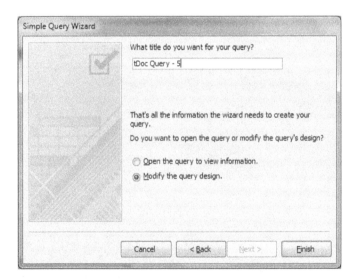

Select Finish

Step 5

In Criteria under DocType type ISO

NOTE if you have ISO's in more than one Area you will need to add 550 in the Criteria under Area

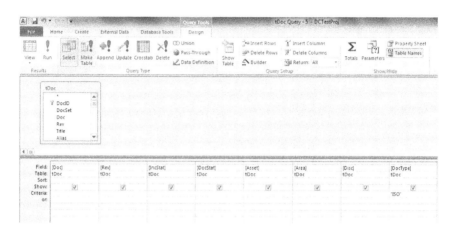

Select the ! Run Button to run the query to see if it has applied the filters correctly – there should be 1000 records.

Click the View Design Button.

Step 6

Click the Update Button

I Update

In the UpDate To line type:

Under Rev -

Under IncStat type RES

Under DocStat type 0-20

Click the ! Run Button

Click Yes

Exit the Query and Close the Form. Return to the Main Menu and Select the Document Form. Apply the same filter.

NOTE that the Revision subform has NOT updated but the fields have.

Exit the Document Form

Click 8 Report Menu then 0 Query Builder. Follow Steps 1 to 5 as above NOTE in Step 3 you also need DocID and RecDate

Step 6

Select the View Design Button

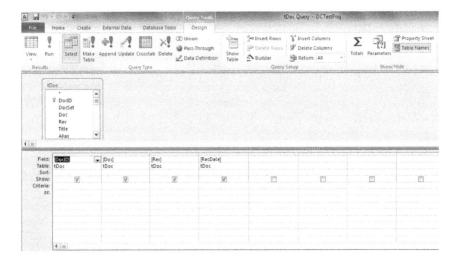

Click Update and Update the RecDate to Today's Date

then Click Append

Append

Append to tDocRev

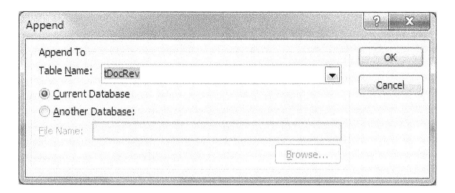

Click OK

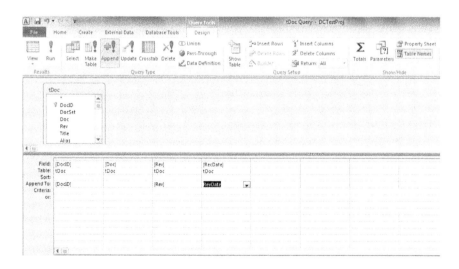

Under the field RecDate use the drop down to select RevDate

Click ! RUN button

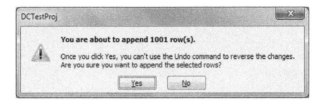

You will get an error similar to this

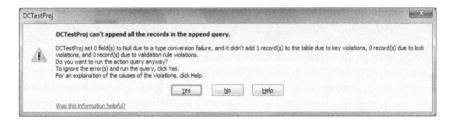

The records not Added should be the same number as the pre-existing records (prior to the Bulk Generator) in your database. Click Yes.

This error message can be avoided by adding the DocType field to the Query shown at Step 6 above and checking off the Show check box (we do not want to merge/append this data)

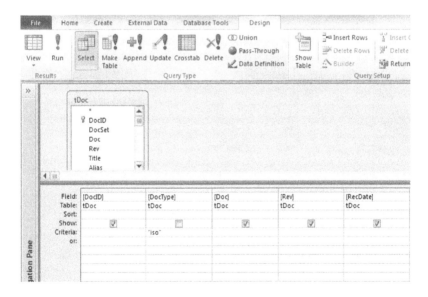

Exit the query and close the query generator form

Return to the Main Menu and Select Document Form

The Revision Subform should now have a line starting with a -

To tidy up the database or if it does go unstable select Database Tools then the button shown below.

Compact and
Repair Database
Tools

Your database will close temporarily and re-open.

You can also use the Create Menu Item and Query Wizard to build Queries.

Later versions of DrawCon will address these issues by making the Rev and DueDate IFR, IFT and IFC fields available in the Block Number Generator.

APPENDIX 10

The Worked Practicals – for download

APPENDIX 11

White Papers and Case Studies

Appendix 11 Part	Description	From	Copyright	Notes
A.	Tech–Clarity_Insight_EDM.pdf	www.Tech–clarity.com	Tech–Clarity	
B.	nuts–bolts–web.pdf	www.synergissoftware.com	Synergis Software	
C.	whitepaper–edm–requirements.pdf	www.firsttrace.com	First Trace	
D.	seven–steps–web.pdf	www.synergissoftware.com	Synergis Software	
E.	leveraging–data–web.pdf	www.synergissoftware.com	Synergis Software	
F.	marketstudy–strategicEDM.pdf	www.firsttrace.com	First Trace	
G.	searching–web.pdf	www.synergissoftware.com	Synergis Software	
H.	whitepaper–engineeringVsOffice.pdf	www.firsttrace.com	First Trace	
J.	whitepaper–fivepillars.pdf	www.firsttrace.com	First Trace	
K.	dms_rfp–template_1.pdf	www.technologyevaluation.com	Technical Evaluation Centers	Not sure the document is on the website any more
K.	dms_rfp–template_2.pdf	www.technologyevaluation.com	Technical Evaluation Centers	Not sure the document is on the website any more
K.	dms_rfp–template_3.pdf	www.technologyevaluation.com	Technical Evaluation Centers	Not sure the document is on the website any more
L.	RFP.pdf	Woodside – where they got it no idea	None shown	
M.	document–management–return–on–investment–analysis.pdf	www.	Andrew Bailey	
N.	Top_10_Reasons_Why_SharePoint_is_NOT_an_EDM_Solution.pdf	www.firsttrace.com	First Trace	
P.	8–Reasons–You–Need–a–Strategy–for–Managing–Information.pdf	www.aiim.org	John Mancini/AIIM	
Q.	8 Reasons Why a Big ECM Solution ISNT Always Better	www.pointdynamics.com / www.aiim.org	Dave Berent/Point Dynamics / AIIM	
R.	Why_do_CRM_Projects_Fail.pdf	www.insightfulcrm.com	InsightfulCRM	
S.	basics–of–electronic–document–management.pdf	www.itaz.com	Itaz Globodox	

APPENDIX 12

Tests

Compulsory Subjects

1. Why is it important to experience Document Control from a number of different perspectives – e.g. Vendor DC, Operations DC?

   _____
   _____
   _____
   _____
   _____

2. DC's should take the time to sit with, ask questions of, and observe who other members of the team as a whole do what they do such as CAD operators and schedulers give two good reasons why.

   i. _____
       _____

   ii. _____
       _____

3. How would you deal with a project team member who does not want to follow the DC procedure and is at your desk in a foul mood?

_____

_____

_____

_____

_____

4. There is no such thing as?

_____

_____

_____

_____

_____

5. If you make a mistake what MUST you do?

_____

_____

_____

_____

_____

6. You should ask your employer for?

_____

_____

_____

_____

7. I just saw something I think is unsafe but it's not my area of expertise what must I do?

   a. Ignore it
   b. Run and hide
   c. Stop it and report it
   d. Go get their boss

8. My safety is (responsibility)

   a. My lawyer
   b. My partner
   c. My employer
   d. Mine

9. My first duty when I see an accident is

   a. Ignore it and keep moving
   b. Call the emergency services
   c. Call a lawyer
   d. Take photo's or video with my mobile

10. A DC is critical to the safe outcome of any project – why?

   _____

   _____

   _____

   _____

   _____

11. Describe at least three hazards in a DC work area and what can be done to prevent them

   _____

   _____

   _____

   _____

   _____

12. I should attempt to assist the injured or those affected by an accident

   a. Never
   b. By taking pics/vids for their lawyer
   c. When it is safe to do so
   d. By calling an ambulance, doctor or tow truck

13. I'm bored or frustrated, I think I will

    a. Ask to be moved to a different function/role within the group or outside it
    b. Take a sick day
    c. Take a step back, identify the root cause, take appropriate action
    d. Find another job

14. I am stressed to the max I will

    a. Shout and Yell at co-workers, the PC/IT, or at home and blow it off
    b. Tell someone I am leaving the area and take a break
    c. Play footy on the weekend and try to take it out on the opposition
    d. Just live with it

Unit 1 and 2

_____

Name (PRINT)

1. Submit your Classification Spread-sheet)

   The file name is _____

2. What is a Squad Check and it is also sometimes known as?

   _____

   _____

   _____

   _____

   _____

3. Three "Incoming Status" Codes are?

    i. _____

    ii. _____

    iii. _____

4. Define Discipline in an Engineering sense and name two (one Engineering and one Function/Admin Discipline)?

    Definition:

    _____

    _____

    _____

    _____

    i.   Eng (1) _____
    ii. Eng (2)_____
    iii. Function/Admin _____

5. What does WBS stand for?

    _____

    _____

    _____

    _____

6. What does FEED stand for?

    _____

    _____

    _____

    _____

7. What is a VDDRL?

_____

_____

_____

_____

_____

8. What does IFC mean?

_____

_____

_____

_____

_____

9. What is Review Status?

_____

_____

_____

_____

10. What is an Asset?

_____

_____

_____

_____

11. Two types of contractors are?

1. _____
2. _____

12. What is a rendition?

_____

_____

_____

_____

Unit 3

Name (PRINT)

Test

1. Submit your spread-sheet or database Correspondence Registers

   The File Name is _____

2. Name two types of Document Register (not old projects)

   1. _____
   2. _____

3. Why is it important to have a correspondence register

   _____

   _____

   _____

   _____

   _____

4. Give two reasons why it is not wise to use Spread-sheets as registers

   1. _____

   _____

   _____

   2. _____

   _____

   _____

   _____

5. Name the two types of Hard Copy files correspondence may appear in

1. _____
   _____
   _____
   _____

2. _____
   _____
   _____
   _____

3. _____
   _____
   _____
   _____

6. What is a folio in a file

   _____
   _____
   _____
   _____
   _____

Unit 4

_____

Name (PRINT)

TEST

1. Submit your Matrix Spread-sheet both Internal and External must be completed for the practical set.

   The File Name is _____

2. The two types of Distribution Matrix are

   1. _____
   2. _____

3. Transmittals MUST be used when

_____

_____

_____

_____

_____

4. We must know external recipients received our transmittals and the documents attached to them if sent in printed form or via email/other electronic means for others to print – why

_____

_____

_____

_____

_____

5. The two types of Transmittals are

1. _____
2. _____

6. Two methods of ensuring acknowledgement of receipt of correspondence are

1. _____
2. _____

Name (PRINT)

TEST

1. What is the only kind of correspondence that need not have some form of control

    _____

    _____

    _____

    _____

    _____

2. Engineering documents do not become records until

    _____

    _____

    _____

    _____

    _____

3. Until then they have a _____

    and are_____

4. Name the first two dimensions of the DC big picture

    a. _____

    b. _____

5. Another important dimension (the 4th) is

    _____

    _____

    _____

    _____

    _____

6. Engineering DC is about managing

_____

_____

_____

_____

_____

7. Safe Design, Construction and Operations is a massively important goal that DC's contribute to

True or False

8. Name the two most important laws we must comply with

_____

_____

_____

_____

_____

9. We should also talk to any appointed Regulator – why

_____

_____

_____

_____

_____

10. There are six questions that must be answered/addressed in any DC procedure they are

a. _____
b. _____
c. _____
d. _____
e. _____
f. _____

11. Quite often people do not comply with DC procedures and processes – one good reason why is

_____

_____

_____

_____

_____

12. If something goes wrong, such as an out of date document being used by a constructor it can create delay and/or re-work which

_____

_____

_____

_____

_____

13. The only stupid question is

_____

_____

_____

_____

_____

14. If in Doubt I will ....

_____

_____

_____

_____

15. As a DC it is a good idea for me to spend a little time on a construction site – why

_____

_____

_____

_____

_____

16. My colleague, a lady of small stature, is trying to get a full box of copy paper off the top shelf of a bookcase I will:

    a. Stop her
    b. Take the box down myself (if I can safely – if not ask someone who can to do so)
    c. Relocate all the heavy material above waist height to lower shelves (if I can safely – if not ask someone who can to do so)
    d. All of the above

17. My friend just got hurt I'll take what action(s)

    _____

    _____

    _____

    _____

    _____

    _____

18. The cables under my desk are getting in the way of my feet I will

    _____

    _____

    _____

    _____

    _____

    _____

19. Some of my files are on a shelf out of my reach sitting or standing I will

    a. Stand on my office chair and get them down
    b. Get a step stool/ladder and get them down
    c. Relocate them (safely) to within easy reach
    d. A combination of the above (which)

20. I like to listen to music with my ear buds / headphones on and/or talk on my mobile phone on the way to or from work even crossing roads this is _____ practice and why

_____

_____

_____

_____

_____

_____

21. I have a light weight archive box of material to take up or downstairs I will use:

   a.   the stairs or
   b.   elevator

Unit 6

Name (PRINT)

TEST

1. What is Reactive Document Control and why is it NOT recommended practice

_____

_____

_____

_____

_____

2. What is Proactive Document Control

_____

_____

_____

_____

_____

3. What is the most common form of Document Control

    1. Reactive
    2. Proactive
    3. Hybridised

4. What is meant by Manual Document Control

_____

_____

_____

_____

_____

5. What is meant by Electronic Document Control

_____

_____

_____

_____

_____

6. What is the most common form –

    1. Manual
    2. Electronic
    3. Hybridised

7. Other than meeting the Law/Quality requirements whose requirements are the most important

_____

_____

_____

_____

_____

8. Within some companies (Operating Co.'s in Particular) there could be two types of Document Control – name them

1. _____

2. _____

9. Engineering documents have a life-cycle and do not become records until handed over

True/False

10. A technical Document Controller may have to manage one of three categories of documents name the three

i. _____

ii. _____

iii. _____

11. Not all documents managed at project level are required for operations

True or False

12. The client should provide some form of what

_____

_____

_____

_____

_____

13. We must comply also with the _____

14. Regulator requirements must also be met

    True or False

15. A corporate DC may also be required to manage what

    _____
    _____
    _____
    _____
    _____

Unit 7

Name (PRINT)

TEST

1. Name five controlled document types that are in your classification
    spread-sheet that are NOT in section 7.01 of your course notes.

    a. _____

    b. _____

    c. _____

    d. _____

    e. _____

2. What would be the simplest way of managing a set of drawings that needs to go in to five different controlled hard copy sets

_____

_____

_____

_____

_____

3. Read through the material about document numbering carefully and explain why, without plagiarising, having a simple and logical document numbering method is important

_____

_____

_____

_____

_____

4. Separate numbering methods for different "disciplines" and types of documents :

Design and Vendor (Must Be) _____

_____

Why _____

_____

HSE and QA (Must Be) _____

_____

Why _____

_____

5. Name an exception to the common controlled document numbering method and why the exception applies

_____

_____

_____

_____

_____

6. What is the filing order in an A3 document wallet – provide an example no plagiarising

_____

_____

_____

_____

_____

7. You work for an EPC – your client, Iron Monarchy, has provided you with a Hand Over Guide:

You are responsible for setting up the electronic file system for files on the Asset FEK (Iron King)

The Codes to be used are:

001	Mine
099	Mine Site Wide
100	Administration Area
120	Construction Camp
130	Permanent Camp
170	Airport
200	Workshops and Warehousing
300	Run of Mine Pad
301	Grizzly
302	Chute
400	Plate Feeder
500	Crushing and Screening
600	Stockpile Conveyors and Stackers
700	Load-out
701	Load-Out System - Chute 01
702	Load-Out System - Chute 02
703	Load-Out System - Chute 03
704	Load-Out System - Chute 04
750	Load-out Tunnel

775	Load–Out Clam Shell Gate - 01
776	Load–Out Clam Shell Gate - 02
777	Load–Out Clam Shell Gate - 03
778	Load–Out Clam Shell Gate - 04
800	Port Rail System
900	Reclaim and Ship Loading

And

AA	Architectural
CI	Civil
CO	Communications
EL	Electrical
FS	Fire Safety
GE	Geology/Geotechnical
GN	General
HS	Health, Safety & Environment
HV	High Volume Air-conditioning
HY	Hydraulic
IN	Instrumentation
ME	Mechanical
MI	Mining
PI	Piping
PR	Process
QA	Quality
ST	Structural

Documents and Drawings must be split. So must Images and Natives, Superseded and Current.

7a. Create a "windows explorer" file structure (directories and sub-directories).

_____

_____

The Document Type Codes will be:

ACC	Drawing - Accommodation
AUD	Audit
BLD	Drawing – Building
BLK	Drawing - Block Diagram
BOM	Drawing - Bill of Materials
CAL	Calculation / Analysis
CAR	Corrective Action Request
CEF	Cause and Effect
D3D	3D Model(s)
DAS	Data Sheet
DTL	Drawing – Detail
ELV	Drawing - Elevation
ESH	Drawing - Emergency Shutdown
EST	Estimate
EVA	Evaluation / Review / Assessment
FOR	Forecast
FRM	Form Template
GAR	Drawing - General Arrangement
GND	Drawing - Grounding
HAZ	Drawing - Hazardous Area Classification
HVC	Drawing - Heating Ventilating Air Conditioning
IAF	Interface Agreement
INT	Drawing - Interconnection
ISO	Drawing - Isometric
LAY	Drawing – Layout
LET	Letter
LGN	Drawing – Legend
LOG	Drawing - Logic Diagram
LOP	Drawing - Loop Diagram
LST	List / Register / Index
LVL	Drawing - Level Diagram
MAN	Manual

MAP	Map
MEM	Memorandum
MOC	Management of Change Request
MOM	Minutes of Meeting
MTS	Drawing - Material Selection
PDG	Drawing - Protection Diagram
PFD	Drawing - Process Flow Diagram
PHC	Drawing - Pneumatic / Hydraulic Connection
PHL	Philosophy / Basis
PHO	Photograph
PID	Drawing - Piping and Instrument Diagram
PLN	Plan
PLT	Drawing - Location Plot Plan
PND	Drawing - Panel Junction Box Diagram
POL	Policy
PRO	Procedure
PRS	Presentation
PSC	Drawing - Panel Schedule
PSU	Drawing - Piping Support
REC	Record
REG	Regulation
RFI	Request for Information
RPT	Report
SAF	Drawing - SAFE Chart
SCH	Schedule
SCM	Drawing - Schematic Diagram
SFD	Drawing - Safety Analysis Flow Diagram
SFM	Safety Moments
SHF	Drawing - Shop Fabrication
SKT	Sketch
SLN	Drawing - Single Line Diagram
SOW	Scope of Work
SPC	Specification
STD	Standard / Codes

SUR	Survey
TPD	Drawing - Topology Diagram
TRM	Drawing - Termination Diagram
TRN	Transmittal Sheet
UFD	Drawing - Utility Flow Diagram
VDL	Vendor Document/Data List/Schedule
WRD	Drawing - Wiring Diagram

7b. Provide one document number each for 5 different document types above including DRG – a 5 sheet drawing (individually numbered) for both your company and for an external consultant doing Fire Systems design and also for a vendor.

_____

_____

_____

_____

_____

_____

_____

_____

_____

_____

_____

_____

_____

_____

_____

_____

_____

_____

_____

_____

_____

_____

_____

_____

_____

_____

_____

7c. Then show the file naming convention for the file type .PDF with all the documents at Revision A and Status IFR

8. Give an acceptable drawing title for drawings to be submitted by the shop detailer for Area 701 with the 3rd line being Reserved for Jones's Shoppies and what would the first drawing number be (hint Structural)

L1 _____

L2 _____

L3 _____

L4 _____

Drg No _____

9. The word _____(begins with an O) is NOT used in Engineering we use _____

10. Give one example of where a Revision and Version number may appear on an Engineering Document in the Document Profile

_____

_____

_____

_____

_____

11. I have some filing to do, manually, these are all new revision drawings I must stamp the new revisions _____ and the old _____

12. Give a good subject line/title for a letter of intent to award the Clam Shell gates on asset/project FEK.

_____

_____

_____

_____

13. Name a document that may not be handed directly to operations as an individual document but where it might actually be found if needed

Document _____
Found Where _____

Units 8 and 9

_____

Name (PRINT)

TEST

1. A vendor submits a VDDRL/VDS with the title of a drawing shown as GA Drawing:–

   acceptable or not acceptable

2. A DC of some level must be at PO/Contract Kick-off meetings –

   True/False

3. Some form of VDDRL must go out with every tender package –

   True/False

4. Having engineers expedite vendors is problematic – why

   _____
   _____
   _____
   _____
   _____

5. Vendors provide native drawings

    a. Sometimes
    b. Never
    c. All The Time
    d. Only when threatened with money

6. I should keep a file called

    _____
    _____
    _____
    _____
    _____

7. We should have a form 3rd parties submit with documents for review/approval – Yes/No

8. There should be three transmittal files – name them

    1. _____
    2. _____
    3. _____

9. We MUST have a Work Request/Instruction form either printed or electronic – why

    _____
    _____
    _____
    _____
    _____

10. Transmittals from external sources must be checked for what information

_____

_____

_____

_____

_____

11. Some documents are missing from what I was sent based on what the transmittal says I will

    a. Plow on regardless
    b. Tell the sender and not process anything until they fix it
    c. Send the whole lot back and tell them to do it again
    d. Tell the sender and process what I can

12. An outside party sent us some stuff on a transmittal as IFI and all the docs have IFI stamped all over them – I'll add them to the DC database, file them and do nothing more – what is wrong with this statement

_____

_____

_____

_____

_____

13. Why must we spend time to expedite overdue transmittal acknowledgements

_____

_____

_____

_____

_____

14. After I check the documents against the transmittal I must?

_____

_____

_____

_____

_____

15. Incorrect what are never to be tolerated

_____

_____

_____

_____

_____

16. I've marked up a drawing with some comments especially the title and number and the Package Engineer ticked 1. Reviewed – Proceed – Submit IFC/Certified final my next action will be

_____

_____

_____

_____

_____

17. My DC tool has an excel upload tool and I just got 100 drawings from a vendor, who has submitted a .csv file of the transmittal, I will

_____

_____

_____

_____

_____

Name (PRINT)

TEST

1. A vendor who listed on their SDS a GA Drawing (singular) has sent in the drawing in one file but it is 5 sheets all of whioch have the same drawing number on them, without having the sequence numbers 0002 to 0005 available to give them I must now? (include how the drawings are to be processed too)

    _____

    _____

    _____

    _____

    _____

2. Our specification says that all drawings must be in both English and Mongolian – we just received drawings in Chinese only I will?

    _____

    _____

    _____

    _____

    _____

3. An EPC has just sent in some drawings for approval – they appear to be A1 drawings reduced to A3 and then scanned they are almost completely illegible – I will?

    _____

    _____

    _____

    _____

    _____

4. A drawing we just received from a vendor which appears to be for pipe parts has a title that is entirely gobbley-gook to me I will?

_____

_____

_____

_____

_____

5. An EPC has just sent in from a Vendor an electrical drawing – when opened it is 5 sheets (all of which have the same drawing number on them) in one file and each is a different drawing type, the last is a parts list, I will (include the process)

_____

_____

_____

_____

_____

6. We just got from an EPC via a Vendor a group of drawings for a conveyor all numbered and coded Mechanical – they are:

   a. A GA of the foundations
   b. A box section drawing
   c. An electric motor drawing
   d. A P&ID for the lubrication circuit
   e. Some Idler, Pulley and Roller GA/Sections
   f. A connection diagram for the power
   g. A hydraulic/piping GA for the lubrication circuit.

The Correct Discipline and Document Numbers for them are (in the order above):

	Correct Discipline	Correct Document Number*
A		
B		
C		
D		
E		
F		
G		

*FEK-600-__-____-Vnnnn where 0001 is the first available sequence number for each provide a new drawing number for each and enter them in to your DCTrain DrawCon database (submit the DCTrain.mdb file). What will you also do with the drawings?

Units 11 and 12

Name (PRINT)

NO TEST – SUBMIT PRACTICAL

Open a new DrawCon Database and Complete the following:

Document Profiles are Per Chapter 11 (11.04.0x)

Transmittals as Per Chapter 12 (List of Engineers) – Add to "Recipient Names" – Make up the Names – in your Database and Chapter 12 (12.06)

**The File Name is: DC_____
.MDB / ACCDB**

Name (PRINT)

TEST

1. Submit the reports from Section 14

    The File Names are _____
    And _____

2. As a DC I should ask to be involved in the Tender Evaluation
    process – why

    _____
    _____
    _____
    _____
    _____
    _____
    _____

3. One of our Tenderers, when I checked against the VDDRL they
    were sent, has not submitted all the material with the tender the
    VDDRL required and the RFI records do not have any record
    of the vendor having asked for an exemption, I will....

    _____
    _____
    _____
    _____
    _____
    _____
    _____

4. DC has been excluded from the tender evaluation team but I know, from experience, that one of the Tenderers submits very good material on time every time and one has to be regularly expedited I will

_____

_____

_____

_____

_____

_____

_____

5. An ECR system should be used to permit changes to IFC/IFU signed off documents – why

_____

_____

_____

_____

_____

_____

_____

6. We have received an ECR for a P&ID what must we check

_____

_____

_____

_____

_____

_____

_____

Unit 16

Name (PRINT)

TEST

1. Submit your Document Classification spread-sheet with the AB-HO worksheet completed

   The File Name is: _____

2. Open your DrawCon DCTrain Project

   a. Select from the Main Menu – C Projects
      1. T1 is Greyed Out – Accept it as being To Be As Built
      2. Add/change T2 to To Be H/O
      3. Return to main menu
      4. Open the Document Form and check/tick T1 and T2 the drawings and documents you believe would be As Built and/or Handed-over
      5. zip the file DCTrain and submit
         The File Name Is:_____
         _____.MDB / ACCDB

3. We are working for a Vendor what we call As Built someone else might call

   _____
   _____
   _____
   _____
   _____
   _____
   _____

4. We as an EPC are actually doing commissioning and a limited plant run. Most of the IFC documents to be As Built are at Rev 0. There will be a pre-commissioning phase for all our own deliverables. All drawings that require As ...... at each phase will be marked up by hand only and an alpha "version" will appear on each drawing what will they be and what revision with the actual CAD As Built be.

Rev _____ (As _____)
Rev _____ (As _____)
Rev _____ (As _____)
Rev _____ (As _____)
Rev_____ (As Built)

Unit 17

Name (PRINT)

TEST

1. Submit your Document Classification Spread-sheet and your DCTrain database for assessment.

   The Spread-sheet file name is:_____
   The Database file name is:_____ .MDB / ACCDB

2. Our law(s) allow for electronic signatures on ALL our design deliverables. Any printed/marked-up material is scanned we must check for?

   _____
   _____
   _____
   _____
   _____

3. Everything is to be kept electronically. We have to check that they systems in place are ISO _____ compliant.

4. We have an old asset and are about to sell it. The new owner wants everything electronically but when we tried to open some old Data-sheets that were exported to Excel (pre 95) they would not open with our current tools, nor would they open in the current version of the CAD tool that they were exported from, the new owner has the same tool-set and will NOT accept documents that do not open. What do we have to do?

_____

_____

_____

_____

_____

5. What is the Catch-22 of paper archiving

_____

_____

_____

_____

_____

6. Paper archive stores must have

_____

_____

_____

_____

_____

7. Archive Store for electronic records must have

_____

_____

_____

_____

_____

8. Microfiche also have a limited life – True/False

9. One of our remote sites has limited bandwidth and is using excel registers and windows explorer to store files how do we address sending them files

   _____

   _____

   _____

   _____

   _____

10. What is a differential back-up

    _____

    _____

    _____

    _____

    _____

Units 18, 19, 20 & 21

Name (PRINT)

TEST

1. An LDC is_____

2. An SDC is_____

3. An IMC is_____

4. A PCM is_____

5. An IMC is_____

6. The documents that form a Quality Management System are driven from _____

7. We believe we have a problem with one of our DC processes the best way to attempt to identify and resolve the problem is to

_____

_____

_____

_____

_____

8. Why are flowcharts important

_____

_____

_____

_____

9. Submit your flowchart and Work Instruction from the practical in 20.03

   The File Name(s) are:

   _____

   _____

   _____

   _____

10. Submit your Procedure from the practical in 21.01

    The File Name is: _____

11. The aim of Work Instructions is/are to........... and they must be (acronym)

    _____

    _____

    _____

    _____

    _____

    Acronym_____

Unit 23

Name (PRINT)

TEST

1. What does MoC stand for: _____

2. Why is having an MoC process important

   _____
   _____
   _____
   _____
   _____

3. What is a Planned Technical MoC – do not copy the example given – give another

   _____
   _____
   _____
   _____
   _____

4. The organisational structure is to be changed and new Org Charts issued this is what Type/Form of MoC

5. _____

   _____
   _____
   _____
   _____
   _____

6. Go back to your DCTrain Database. Update the P&ID's to Rev 0 IFC then Rev 1 As Built. Assume they have been handed over and an MoC has been raised for one only P&ID to take it to Rev 2. What other drawings and documents might also change – list them.

_____

_____

_____

_____

_____

7. A pump in the system has broken down before its expected life. It's been replaced but the new one is smaller (does the same job etc.) this is an _____ MoC.

Unit 24

Name (PRINT)

TEST

We have been tasked with developing a floor plan for a new Document Control Centre and have also been asked what furniture, fittings and electronic equipment we need. The company insists on keeping all paper Revisions, the entire history including squad check mark-ups, of all documents – we intend to scan everything to PDF and the CAD team hand over either a native file or zip file with every revision with all Xrefs bound on and a rendition file too. We will use a compactus for A4/Foolscap paper files and plan tanks/cabinets for A2/A1 and A0 drawings. A3 drawings will be kept in Landscape files in document wallets. We have a DC database tool but it does not have a viewer/mark-up function but does map to files stored in Sharepoint.

Including yourself you will have a large core group of 5 DC's, not including yourself, some of whom might be delegated to specific projects at specific times.

1. Describe the equipment you will need, hardware/software and furniture etc., including the number of workstations.

   _____

   _____

   _____

   _____

   _____

2. What must be done before the compactus is installed?

   _____

   _____

   _____

   _____

Unit 25

_____

Name (PRINT)

TEST

1. We are considering a new DC Tool. The database only has a one to one relationship between the document number and equipment/tag numbers in the profile – this is limiting, why

   _____

   _____

   _____

   _____

   _____

   _____

2. Genuine one to one relationships between Document Numbers and other fields do exist name 3

   i. _____

   ii. _____

   iii. _____

3. Name a One to Many relationship that can exist between a Document Number and another field in a document profile (do not name Equipment/Tag numbers)

   _____

   _____

   _____

   _____

   _____

4. Some SaaS applications are excellent collaboration tools but are NOT intended as DC Tools – True/False

5. Some ECM/EDMS applications do not work for Engineering – True/False

6. An advantage of having a DC Tool that the provider uses a Type 1 software development model for is_____

   _____

   _____

   _____

   _____

7. A disadvantage to Type 1 software development models is

   _____

   _____

   _____

   _____

   _____

8. An advantage of Type 2 software development models is

_____

_____

_____

_____

_____

9. A disadvantage of Type 2 software development models is

_____

_____

_____

_____

_____

10. We use the entire Bentley suite of CAD tools but do not have an integrated DC tool – google Bentley – what application do they have that will do both DC and integrate to the rest of their tool-set.

_____

_____

_____

_____

_____

Unit 26

_____

Name (PRINT)

TEST

For the following questions imagine that you are a Lead DC that the IT people have approached about acquiring a new DC Tool. The company's IT policy does not support going to the cloud or OpenSource applications and initial feedback from IT/

Others is that this is unlikely to change but they will consider an application that provides access for third parties via a web based tool.

The organisation is an EPC who employs 10,000 people globally and has some people in very remote, low bandwidth areas. We use the full AutoDesk suite of design tools and will want to integrate to it and develop and set-up templates against Document Types in the system. We also use MS Office 2010 Pro Version patched to SP2. We want to integrate to Word and Excel and develop and set-up templates against Document Types in the system. The system must support integration to Outlook or replace it and email form (for example RFI's) development.

> Do some preliminary research and download/read some white papers etc. (do this) submit a link to at least two good white papers you have found not all from the same vendor

> _____
> _____
> _____
> _____
> _____

> Also do this http://www.technologyevaluation.com/register. aspx?redirectURL=http://itadvisor.technologyevaluation.com/ SurveyStart.aspx?AreaModelId%3d464%26SessionLanguageId %3d0%26StartQuestion%3d2734932 (NOTE not everyone submits their applications to this site for assessment)

Take a screen shot, Alt and PrtSc together then open Word or OpenOffice Text format the page to A4 Landscape and narrow margins then press CTRL and V together, submit the screen shots for each question and the final resolution.

The File Name Is:_____

We now have some good ideas about which systems should be considered based on our knowledge of DC

1. Why is not being able to go to the cloud limiting?

   _____
   _____
   _____
   _____
   _____

2. We spotted at least one very good option that is OpenSource will the current IT policy be a limiting factor and why?

   _____
   _____
   _____
   _____
   _____

3. List some of the questions we need to ask of the other ourselves before we develop a Request for Proposal document for the market place.

   _____
   _____
   _____
   _____
   _____
   _____
   _____
   _____
   _____

4. How might we best address the low bandwidth issue?

   _____
   _____
   _____
   _____

5. Based on your own research name 5 vendors you might send an RFP document to and for which, some sell more than one, product(s)

_____

_____

_____

_____

_____

Full Practical

<u>NO TEST – SUBMIT PRACTICAL</u>

<u>Open a new DrawCon Database and Complete the following:</u>

Chapter 22 (Select one of A, B or C) and Appendices 3, 8 (Select one of A, B or C – corresponds to Chapter 22) and 9.

The File Name is: DC_____.MDB / ACCDB

www.ingramcontent.com/pod-product-compliance
Lightning Source LLC
Chambersburg PA
CBHW051043050326
40690CB00006B/583